A Song is Born

Robert J. Taylor

A Song Is Born

Robert J. Taylor, Jr.

Proofreading
Gloria Nicole
Cyndie Lowry
Barbara Taylor

Typesetting / Music Typography
Taylor Publications
R. J. Taylor, Jr.

Cover Design
Digial Designs

ISBN: 1-932711-00-7
Book #B801

A Song Is Born
© Copyright 2004 by Taylor Publications
20171 Hilltop Ranch Dr.
Montgomery, TX 77316
www.taylorpublications.com

Unless otherwise indicated, Scripture taken from the
HOLY BIBLE: NEW INTERNATIONAL VERSION
Copyright © 1973, 1978, 1984 by the International Bible Society.
Used by permission of Zondervan Bibles Publishers

Preface

I feel a little bit like the song, "Where do I begin, to tell the story of how great a love can be." It is no secret that I love music, but I have a passion for 'one another' or as we call it, 'congregational' singing. Music is such an intricate part of everyones life. Its influence is felt in everything we do. Alan Bloom once said, *"The most powerful influence in the lives of young people is their music –."* Many years ago, Andrew Fletcher said, *"I care not who makes your laws, give me the one who makes the songs."* Given this importance of music, I felt we should pay closer attention to the songs we sing.

I call this effort, "Grass Roots Hymnology." I have traveled extensively to the places where the authors lived, worked, worshipped and where they wrote the song. Every song has a story. It may have been a unique circumstance under which the song was written; it might have been influenced by events occurring when it was written, or, it might just be in the life of the author, their trials and triumphs. I tried to walk in the steps of those who have provided us so much comfort through their hymns.

Hymn writers come from all walks of life and from various religious beliefs. Some wrote their best songs in the twilight of their lives, while others were very young. Most were just ordinary people, each struggling to live a good life as best they could, but sometimes stumbling. Yet, God used them to provide comfort to His people through their hymns, just like he will use us if we let Him. Thank you, Lord, for hymns.

A Song Is Born is unique in that it contains hymn stories never before known or printed, along with some older, familiar stories, all with a personal touch of having been there. Many of the stories reveal how the Lord opened the doors for me to locate the information. Additionally, each song contains comments regarding the application of this song in today's world, along with scripture references.

I hope you enjoy the journey!

R. J. Taylor, Jr.

A Song Is Born

Precious Memories
Psalm 145:7

J. B. F. Wright, 1925   J. B. F. Wright, 1925

1. Pre-cious mem-'ries, un-seen an-gels, Sent from some-where to my soul;
2. Pre-cious fa-ther, lov-ing moth-er, Fly a-cross the lone-ly years,
3. In the still-ness of the mid-night, Ech-oes from the past I hear;
4. As I tra-vel on life's path-way, Know not what the years may hold;

Fine

How they lin-ger, ev-er near me, And the sa-cred past un-fold.
And old home scenes of my child-hood, In fond mem-o-ry ap-pears.
Old time sing-ing, glad-ness bring-ing, From that love-ly land some-where.
As I pon-der, hope grows fond-er, Pre-cious mem-'ries flood my soul.

D.S. In the still-ness of the mid-night, Pre-cious, sa-cred scenes un-fold.

Chorus   D.S.

Pre-cious mem-'ries, how they lin-ger, How they ev-er flood my soul;

First appeared in *Harbor Bells*, 1925 by Stamps-Baxter Music Co.

Remember your Creator in the days of your youth.
[Ecclesiastes 12:1]

PRECIOUS MEMORIES

*O*ne crisp, autumn night in 1923, at his home near Hamlin, Texas, the thoughts of a gentle, unassuming farmhand turned to the days of his youth - days before the family circle was broken. Days when cares of the world were unknown. J. B. F. Wright was not yet an old man, but several events had occurred which caused him to reflect back upon happier days. He was born in Tennessee, February 21, 1877, the fifth of twelve children. His parents, George Washington and Casandra (Coley) Wright III, moved to Limestone County, Texas, when he was only two years old. It was there in a community called Box Church, located just four miles southeast of Groesbeck, Texas, that he spent the happy days of his youth. He attended the community school, fell in love, and married a local girl named Fannie Jackson. To this union were born eight children.

Box Church is a unique name for a town. Some local folks speculate the community received its name from a circuit preacher named "Box," who often came to the area to preach, thus "Box's" church. Others feel that the name came when one of the first church buildings constructed in the area was square, like a box, thus "The Box Church". However the settlement developed its name, Box Church became a thriving community of 300-400 people, complete with several stores, churches, and even a sawmill. In 1902, Mr. Wright took his young bride, left the old homestead and, as he puts it, "rambled over Texas for many years." He was a farmer by trade, but later he became the custodian and nurseryman for Cisco Junior College, Cisco, Texas, from which he retired in the early 1950s.

John Wright's mother was one of "the sweetest singers of her generation," as he told Clint Bonner, a hymnologist. The songwriter's earliest memories were of his father and mother singing together the songs of their youth. It was this early environment which inspired Mr. Wright to write more than 500 songs. He falls into a category with a fortunate few who spend a lifetime writing songs, and for some unexplainable reason, comes up with THE SONG which eclipses all the others, and lifts one to an imperishable place in the hearts of the people. This happened to John Braselton Fillmore Wright when he wrote *Precious Memories*.

In 1909, word came to John Wright that his mother had "gone home to glory." Five years later his father died. The now middle-aged songwriter recounts that the loss of his parents had a "tremendous effect on my life" and their memory "has lingered through all these changing years." Once before, Mr. Wright returned to the scenes of his childhood and wrote a few sentimental songs, but these songs have long since been forgotten. But it was on the still, autumn night of October 23,

A Song Is Born

1923, while he lived in Hamlin, Texas, that scenes of the home he had left 20 years before unfolded in his mind, and he was inspired to write his famous song.

Perhaps the event, which weighed most heavily on his heart that autumn night, was the recent death of their youngest son, Everett Jackson Wright. "We lived by the railroad, below Hamlin, Texas" Mr. Wright wrote some years later. "Little three-year-old Everett would watch for the 'chwains,' as he called them, and he would stand at the frontyard gate and wave his little hands to the trainmen as they passed our house. They would always wave back to him. On Sunday evening, January 22, 1922, he (Everett) was stricken with "Membrane's Croup" (now known as Diphtheria) and the next day, just as the sun went down, our little boy was dead. For many days after this, when the trains would pass the trainmen would be watching for little Everett to wave, but he was not there. Many times I watched them looking for him, and I wept and cried." Some time later as he reflected back on that autumn night in 1923 when he wrote his famous hymn, Mr. Wright said, *"when my thoughts turned to my own little son whom we had buried the year before, I bathed my pillow in tears."* Thus, true to the line of the poem, it was actually in the stillness of midnight that he wrote:

> *Precious mem'ries, how they linger,*
> *How they ever flood my soul;*
> *In the stillness of the midnight,*
> *Precious, sacred scenes unfold.*

Recently, Barbara and I had the opportunity to visit Hamlin and to locate the old J. L. Keen farm just east of town where the Wright family lived and worked. Only a few remnants of sheds still exist where once vibrant families worked and played. The railroad no longer exists even though the built-up roadbed remains. Standing there along a modern highway which now cuts through the front yard of the old homestead, you can still capture a mental picture of times gone by, a time when Mr. Wright was inspired to write *Precious Memories*. It's easy to visualize the trains coming by so near to the house. If you looked about a mile west, you could see the cemetery where Everett Wright was buried and

A Song Is Born

imagined what Mr. Wright must have felt when he was inspired to write his famous hymn. The song first appeared in "Harbor Bells," published by V. O. Stamps in 1925. It listed J. B. F. Wright as the owner, but with no copyright. According to Nellie Wright, a distant cousin, "a verbal agreement (was made) with Mr. Stamps that every time the song was recorded, he'd get a certain percentage royalty. He only got royalty from the first recording that amounted to $36.00. Then Mr. Stamps died and his heirs would not honor the agreement."

We often talk about one's education and what academic level of higher learning we have achieved. There is no doubt that formal education is essential in today's world. However, some good, sacred memory preserved from childhood is perhaps the best education one could obtain. There is nothing higher, nothing stronger, nothing more wholesome, and nothing better for life in the future than some good memory, especially a memory of childhood, of church, or of home. One of the most critical factors in making right decisions is precious memories.

Fond memories can bring comfort and peace and even help us make it through the day. But negative memories can drain us and keep us from enjoying life. The uniqueness of memories is that we have control. You chose what to remember. It is not a single, negative experience that causes one to be so depressed that they cannot function. It is the accumulation of negative thoughts in one's memory that can render us helpless. How can we control our thoughts so that our positive memories are the ones that influence us? Remember all our experiences, good or bad, but do not dwell on either. Rather, heed the words of Paul in his letter to the Philippians.

> *Whatever is true, whatever is noble, whatever is right, whatever is pure, whatever is lovely, whatever is admirable, if anything is excellent or praiseworthy, think about such things.* [Philippians 4:8]

—— *RJT* ——

A Song Is Born

All People That On Earth Do Dwell

Psalm 100

William Kethe (1535-1594)   Bourgeois's Genevan Psalter

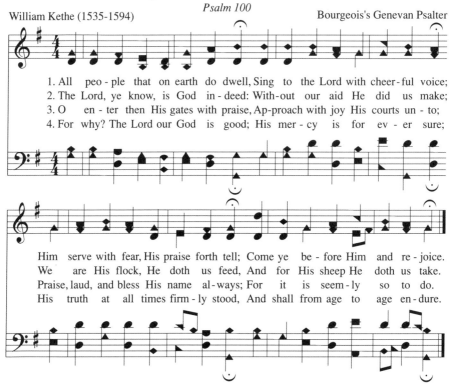

1. All people that on earth do dwell, Sing to the Lord with cheerful voice; Him serve with fear, His praise forth tell; Come ye before Him and rejoice.
2. The Lord, ye know, is God indeed: Without our aid He did us make; We are His flock, He doth us feed, And for His sheep He doth us take.
3. O enter then His gates with praise, Approach with joy His courts unto; Praise, laud, and bless His name always; For it is seemly so to do.
4. For why? The Lord our God is good; His mercy is for ever sure; His truth at all times firmly stood, And shall from age to age endure.

Words first appeared in *Fourscore and Seven Psalms of David*, 1561; Music first appeared in 1551, Genevan Psalter to other words: Appeared 1561 in *Fourscore and Seven Psalms of David* with W. Kethe's words

All people that on earth do dwell,
Sing to the Lord with cheerful voice;
Him serve with fear, His praise forth tell;
Come ye before Him and rejoice.

ALL PEOPLE THAT ON EARTH DO DWELL

*V*ery little is known about William Kethe, the author of this hymn. It is believed that he was one of the scholars who worked on the English-translated Geneva Bible in 1560, and that at one time he served as a Chaplin to the British troops, but not much else is known about him. What we do know is that his poem, *All People that on Earth do Dwell* written in 1561, has served to inspire Christians ever since. Psalm 100, often called the psalm of

A Song Is Born

thanksgiving, inspired this enduring hymn written over 400 years ago, and has served to inspire each generation since.

Located high above tree-line in the Colorado Rockies near our home in Silverton, stands an old boarding house for miners - built nearly 100 years ago. I marvel each time I look through my field glasses at this remarkable structure. I marvel at its size. It is a huge, three-story building capable of housing fifty miners complete with dining facilities! I marvel at its location – protruding dangerously out of the mountain  at 12,000 feet above sea level, accessible only by the serious mountain climber. I also marvel at its name! **Old Hundred!** The mine and boarding house were given this name on February 20, 1898, by Reinheart Niegold. The Niegold's were avid singers and named it for the Protestant hymn we know and love as *All People that on Earth do Dwell*.

In one of the harshest, year-round living environments in America, almost completely removed from the outside world in 1904, these hard working, hard living miners still remembered their God. The Old Hundred Mine and Boarding House remains as a tribute to the power of this resilient hymn, and to the need for men and women to praise and give thanks to their God.

Rowland E. Prothero in his book *The Psalms in Human Life* says that this hymn and tune *"survives all the changes of thought and fashion that the progress of four centuries has witnessed."* You may live in the busiest metropolitan area in America, surrounded by millions of people seemingly too busy to acknowledge God, or you may travel to the most isolated location in the world; however, God is still there! Praise God!

Make a joyful noise unto the Lord, all ye lands. Serve the Lord with gladness: come before his presence with singing. Know ye that the Lord he is God: it is he that hath made us, - we are his people, - Enter into his gates with thanksgiving, and into his courts with praise. [Psalm 100:1-4]

God saw all that he had made, and it was very good. [Genesis 1:31]

ALL THINGS BRIGHT AND BEAUTIFUL

Cecil Francis Alexander, born in Ireland, began writing poems at the age of nine. Shy and uncertain of her efforts, she hides them under the carpet in her room. One day her father discovered a bulge in the floor and found them. As he read the poems, he realized the talent of his young daughter. The following Saturday evening, he gathered the family together and began what became a weekly tradition in their home, to read together the poems Cecil had written that week. With this kind of encouragement, she went on to write more that 400 poems and hymn text, mostly intended for children.

Cecil was a shy, humble person who did not like to be praised for her accomplishments. She just quietly went about serving her Master. William Alexander, her husband once said *"From one poor home to another she went. Christ was ever with her, in her and all felt her influence."* Cecil Alexander never lost her love for the children and the desire to teach them spiritual truths, which she found was easier to teach through poems and hymns, great hymns like *There is a Green Hill Far Away, Jesus Calls Us* and *All Things Bright and Beautiful*.

How can we look at God's creation and not know that there is a Supreme Being. Mrs. Alexander's hymn, *All Things Bright and Beautiful*, emphasizes the eternal truth that God is the author of all beauty, all wisdom, and all creation. Each little flower that opens, each bird that sings, each mountain we climb, all are products of His everlasting Majesty. This poem is a declaration of our belief in God, the Father, the Almighty, maker of Heaven and earth.

Let me sing the praises of Jehovah's goodness, and of His marvelous deeds, in return for all that He has done for us. [Isaiah 63:7]

═══ RJT ═══

A Song Is Born

. . . Our citizenship is in heaven. And we eagerly await a Savior from there, the Lord Jesus Christ, who by the power that enables him to bring everything under his control, will transform our lowly bodies, - [Philippians 3:20-21]

WALKING ALONE AT EVE

William Washington Slater, better known as Will W. Slater, was born February 2, 1885, in Arkansas but moved with the family to Oklahoma Territory near Sallisaw about 1890. He was the oldest of fourteen children, three of which died in infancy. Around the turn of the 20th Century, times were tough in the Indian Territory of Oklahoma and, at times, the people were even tougher. It was within this often hostile environment that Will W. Slater was converted, and where he developed his first aspirations to become a preacher and singer.

William David Slater, Will's dad, made an agreement with some Territory residences in Sequoyah County, Oklahoma Territory, to clear the land in return for being able to keep the harvest of any crops. The men were rough characters, known for not living up to their word. Sure enough, as the crops were ready for harvest, attempts were made to frighten off the hired hands and to order the Slater family to leave. One evening, four or five men rode up to the Slater home and demanded *"leave, or be dragged out with a rope, we're going to burn your home."* Mr. Slater had slipped out the back and stood in the shadows with his shotgun. "Boys," he begins, "You can't see me but I can see you good in this moonlight. I've got this double-barrel shotgun aimed at you, and I'll get two of you before you turn around. Now get out and never come back." They left, never again to threaten the Slater family.

All was quiet until some three or four years later, around 1901, when efforts to bring a gospel preacher into the community rekindled new strife. No established churches were located in the area. An itinerant preacher remembered only as Brother Cecil from Arkansas wanted to come and conduct a series of meetings. When he arrived, he stayed with David and Melvina Slater while neighbors hurried to build a brush arbor for the meeting. Some of these rough and lawless men rode by and threatened to *"Drag anyone out of the county with a rope, if they stood up to preach."* David asked the preacher what he wanted to do?

"They crucified my Lord, killed many Apostles, put to death a lot of early Christians, and these men can't do any worse to me. If you want me to, I'd like to preach," he replied. With this, David buckled on his pistol, picked up a rifle and they all went off to the meeting. When everyone had gathered, David stood up and announced: *"If any one drags him out of here, it will be over my dead body. Preacher, it's all yours."* Each night of the meeting, Mr. Slater sat in his chair with the rifle across his lap. No one interfered. William Washington Slater and his mother were converted and baptized during that meeting. Will W. Slater became a powerful influence for the cause of Christ both in his preaching and his singing. He wrote more than 80 hymns and published 54 songbooks.

Thomas R. Sweatman, the author of the works, was inspired to write *Walking Alone at Eve* after a visit to an elderly lady in his congregation. She had recently lost her husband and was lonely. *"How are you doing?"* Mr. Sweatman inquired. *"Well, I'm walking alone in the evening shades of my life,"* she responded. The conversation continued and it seemed to her as if she were walking the last steps of her life alone, but with great anticipation, longing for the promised home of the soul.

This song, *Alone at Eve,* pictures one who is in the last days (eve) of their life, when their loved ones have already gone home and they long to join them in Heaven. Often the elderly sit around watching as the shadows of life gather around them, spending countless hours waiting for the end to come. It could become unbearable if the picture of heaven were not firmly planted in their mind. Too often we focus our thoughts and energy on the negatives of life, on the sorrow, pain and hurt. How much better is it to focus our attention on heaven? A Christian should never live as one filled with despair or as one without hope, but as one with an earnest longing for *"a home with God"* and *"a rest for the weary soul."* Oh, how beautiful heaven must be.

And I heard a loud voice from the throne saying, Now the dwelling of God is with men, and he will live with them, They will be his people and God himself will be with them and be their God. He will wipe every tear from their eyes. There will be no more death or mourning or crying or pain, for the old order of things has passed away. [Revelation 21:3-4]

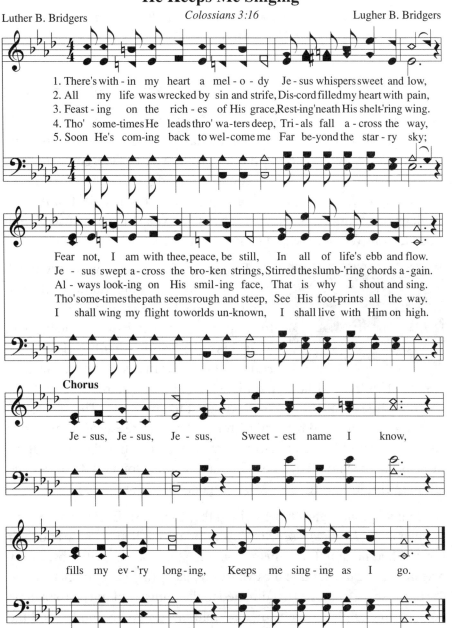

A Song Is Born

> *I have told you these things, so that in me you may have peace. In this world you will have trouble. But take heart! I have overcome the world.* [John 16:33]

HE KEEPS ME SINGING

*L*uther B. Bridgers was born in Margaretsville, North Carolina, in 1884. He spent most of his boyhood days in and around Norfolk and Portsmouth, Virginia, before the family moved to Georgia. The year 1901 was a banner year for the young Mr. Bridgers. At the age of 17, he began a long career of preaching, even while still a student of Asbury College, in Wilmore, Kentucky. That same year Luther married Sarah Veatch from Wilmore whom he met at college.

By 1909, Mr. Bridgers was very much in demand as an evangelistic Methodist minister. One day he received an invitation to help conduct a two-week meeting in Middlesboro, about 100 miles from Harrodsburg, Kentucky, where Sarah's parents then lived. Luther left his wife and three young boys with her parents while he continued on to conduct the meeting. The successful meeting was just ending when Luther Bridgers received a telephone call telling him about a disastrous fire. He learned that the home of his in-laws had been destroyed by fire, and that his young wife Sarah and all three children were lost. Mr. Bridgers fell unconscious!

Many hymnologists have written that Luther B. Bridgers wrote his popular song, *He Keeps Me Singing*, after a fire killed his wife and their boys. I had no doubt that this was a true story, but as with most of my research, I like to examine the event and places first hand. So, I traveled to Harrodsburg and was first directed to the minister of music for a large downtown church. It seems he had told the story one Sunday and the locals thought he might help, but it turns out his only source was a hymn storybook. He had never verified the story. In fact, he seemed surprised to learn that the tragedy happened in Harrodsburg.

After unsuccessful efforts to locate more information in the local library, I then went to the historical society. At first, they could not remember anything, but as I sat down and just talked about the possibilities, one elderly lady begins to remember. She disappeared briefly and brought back a torn newspaper clipping of the event. Oddly enough, the tragedy occurred March 26, 1911, not 1910 as most hymnologists had indicated. Here in part is the newspaper article from the Harrodsburg Herald:

> "One of the greatest shocks ever given this community was the burning of Mrs. Luther Bridgers and her three little children, when the home of her father, Mr. John T. Veatch, was consumed by fire last Sunday night. Nothing in years has roused the whole population to such deep sorrow as the tragic death of this lovely young woman, and to her stricken family the heartfelt sympathy of everyone is extended. The fire which took such terrible toll occurred Sunday night between ten and eleven o'clock. The Veatch home is about four miles from town on the Frankfort pike, and stands within a few hundred yards of the Louisville Southern railroad. As the train which reaches here at 10:45 passed along Sunday night the crew saw the Veatch home in flames and no one about. The engineer slowed his train and shrieked the whistle repeatedly, and this awakened Mrs. Veatch, who in turn roused her husband."

> "The house was then a mass of flames, and Mr. Veatch hurriedly called his sleeping family who fled from the flame-swept building without clothing or the chance to save a single article. As the three unmarried daughters, Misses Belle, Mary, and Lucile, ran through the hall, Miss Belle saw Mrs. Bridgers come to her door, but a burst of smoke puffed in and she quickly shut it. A moment later one of the unfortunate woman's brothers saw her at a window of her room with the two eldest children in her arms, and he called to her to remain there until he could get a ladder. The only window that could be reached by the ladder had the shutters closed, and while the rescuers were trying frantically to unfasten these, the terrible flames drove them back and the building crashed in. The children were Hughes, age 5, Veatch, age 3, and a baby of seven months. All were unusually bright and attractive, and greatly loved."

Sarah and her three precious boys were buried in Wilmore, but a family member moved their remains to Harrodsburg in 1958. Luther

A Song Is Born

Bridgers, grief stricken beyond words, continued to preach and slowly put his life back together. In 1914, he married Miss Aline Winburn of Gainesville, Georgia. They had one child, Luther Bridgers, Jr. At the age of 64, this life-long Methodist evangelist, song leader, and songwriter passed away in Atlanta, May 27, 1948.

Whether Mr. Bridgers wrote the words and music of his song we know today as *He Keeps Me Singing* before or after this horrific tragedy, I can't be certain. In either case, the song contains his unique spiritual autobiography. We can see the faith and presence of mind that Mr. Bridgers must have had as he wrote:

"There's within my heart a melody,
Jesus whispers sweet and low,
Fear not, I am with thee, peace, be still,
In all of life's ebb and flow."

In one verse, which many of our hymnbooks have left out, we can clearly see a troubled Mr. Bridgers. It could be an indication that the poem was written after the death of his entire family.

"Tho sometimes He leads through waters deep,
Trials fall across the way.
Tho sometimes the path seems rough and steep,
See His footprints all the way."

What would you do if tragedy struck you or your family today? What would your response be? If you were required to write down your feelings and thoughts after losing one of your children, what would you say? This song, *He Keeps Me Singing,* provides the perfect formula for Christians to follow, remembering that Christ promised to always be with us even during the storms of life.

He put a new song in my mouth, a hymn of praise to our God. [Psalm 40:3]

——— RJT ———

A Song Is Born

> *As the deer pants for streams of water, so my soul pants for you, O God. My soul thirsts for God, for the living God.* [Psalm 42:1-2]

As The Deer

He was born Martin J. Nystrom October 17, 1956 in Seattle, Washington. After graduating from Oral Roberts University in 1980, Marty Nystrom said he found himself struggling with his spirituality. In the fall of 1981, he enrolled in a six-week class at Christ for the Nations in Dallas. While this may seem like a noble effort to improve his spirituality, in fact, it was to pursue the attention of a young lady, a relationship that did not work out. Now with a bruised heart, in strange surroundings, on a less than inspiring campus and experiencing the Dallas heat in July, his spirits were definitely down. Additionally, he had come to CFN with emotional baggage he said. *"I'd traded my initial desire to serve God – for the need to win man's approval."* One day a somewhat radical classmate challenged him to a fast, which he did with some reluctance. On the nineteenth day of the fast, and responding to what he had been reading in Psalm 42, Mr. Nystrom began to renew his faith and strengthen his relationship with Christ. *"It was just water, Dallas water at that,"* he remembers thinking, but his body longed for that cool stream. "Something about the fast immediately broke me," said Mr. Nystrom. One day he set down to the "very out-of-tune piano in the men's dorm of CFN, and begin to offer up praise to God. "The first verse and music seem to come straight through," he said.

> *As the deer pants for the water*
> *So my soul longs after You!*
> *You alone are my heart's desire*
> *And I long to worship You.*

From this experience, Marty Nystrom developed a deeper longing to worship the Savior. He expressed this renewed commitment through his beautiful song. Marty went on to teach at CFN, the New York campus, for five years before joining the staff of Hosanna! Integrity as Song

Development Manager. Since then he has toured extensively and has worked with several churches in his home state.

Do you have a yearning to be near God? Do you thirst for His teachings? As our bodies depend upon water, so our spiritual lives depend upon God. Sometimes we need to challenge our complacent attitudes toward God, and develop a sincere desire to worship the Lord.

Jesus answered, "Everyone who drinks this water will be thirsty again, but whoever drinks the water I give him will never thirst. Indeed the water I give him will become in him a spring of water welling up to eternal life." [John 4:13-14]

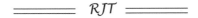

RJT

A Song Is Born

> *For it is by grace you have been saved, through faith – and this not from yourselves, it is the gift of God – not by works, so that no one can boast.* [Ephesians 2:8]

AMAZING GRACE

John Newton was born in London, England, 1725, the son of a sea Captain. His mother died when he was six and by age eleven he had joined his father at sea. John's early life was one of immorality, sensuous pleasure, deceit, and failure. He was rejected by his father, in trouble with all his employers, and finally jailed after being publicly degraded. At one point, he joined the British navy, deserted, was caught, put in irons, and whipped in public. He signed on to a slave ship and later became a Captain, and all this occurred before he was 23 years old.

At one point, John Newton had sunk so low that even the ship crew despised him. On one occasion, it is reported that the drunken captain fell overboard, but the men did not so much as make an effort to drop a boat over the side to rescue him. They simply took sport in using a whaling harpoon and threw it at him. It caught John Newton in his hip and the crew hauled him aboard. From this injury John limped the rest of his life.

By the age of 23, John Newton was sick with fever and sick of the slave traffic. At the depth of his despair, he became a believer in Christ and eventually a minister for the Lord the rest of his days. He knew that only by the grace of God did he have a hope of salvation. Mr. Newton worked by day as a clerk and educated himself by night until he was ordained as a minister. He preached in Olney, England, for some 17 years before moving to London. *Amazing Grace*, originally titled *"Faith's Review and Expectation,"* was written during the early years of Newton's ministry at Olney and first appeared in 1779.

For all the beauty of this poem, it remained mostly unnoticed for over 100 years, until an American songbook editor married Newton's poem with an American folk melody of uncertain origin. The tune, which is now instantly recognizable by millions, was first published in

A Song Is Born

1831. Around 1900, E. O. Excell arranged this tune to fit Newton's poem and added the verse that begins *"When we've been there ten thousand years—"*. This combination proved successful, and the hymn was on its way to the top of American Hymnody.

John Newton never lost his love for the sea. Once he entered the pulpit dressed in His sailor uniform, with the Bible in one hand and a songbook in the other. Shortly before his death at the age of 82, a spokesman for the church suggested that he consider retirement because of his failing health, poor eyesight, and memory loss. To this complaint he proclaimed loudly from the pulpit: *"my memory is nearly gone, but I remember two things, that I am a great sinner and that Christ is a great Savior."*

How lost do we feel? Many today do not feel lost even without God's grace. We like to *"pay our own way,"* *"stand on our own two feet,"* or *"do our own thing."* This often leads us to feel that we deserve or that we can earn a just reward. John Newton understood how hopeless he was without God's grace. Without surrendering everything to Christ and coming in contact with God's saving Grace, we have no hope of salvation, no matter how good we think we are.

First, there is grace. God has provided salvation by His grace. Ephesians 2:8 *"For by grace are ye are saved (how) through faith and that not of your selves: it is the gift of God."* Next, there is faith. God's salvation can only be reached if we have faith. And last, there is obedience. This is a faith which works by love. Galatians 5:6 *"For in Jesus Christ neither circumcision availeth anything, nor uncircumcision; but faith which worketh by love"* James. 2:17 *"Even so, Faith if it hath not works, is dead."*

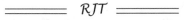

RJT

A Song Is Born

As The Life Of A Flower

But the one who is rich should take pride in his low position, because he will pass away like a wild flower. [James 1:10]

As the Life Of A Flower

Upon arriving in the rural communities of Wabaunsee and Zeandale, just east of Manhattan, Kansas, three things immediately caught my attention, neither of which had anything to do with the research for this song. Kansas, known as the "Heartland of America," is filled with miles of cultivated fields of corn and grain, but I did not expect to see so many beautiful fields of native prairie grass and gentle rolling hills that help to create a spectacular beauty along this particular section of the Kansas River. One could easily understand why so many early settlers from New England were eager to settle in this area when it first opened in 1854.

The second thing that caught my attention was the name Tabor. There was Tabor Lane, Tabor Creek, Tabor Hill, and Tabor Valley. Having spent many summers vacationing in Colorado, I knew that the name "Tabor" was indelibly etched into that state's history. Could this be the same "Tabor" whose story of going from rags to riches, to political power, even to becoming a U.S. Senator, and then back to an rags again? Could this be the same Haroce Tabor who divorced his wife Augusta and married the infamous "Baby Doe" Tabor? It turns out it is the same person, who along with his first wife Augusta, settled in this part of Kansas in 1856, and gave the valley its name before moving on to Colorado for fame and fortune. A plaque in honor of Augusta Tabor was erected on the schoolyard grounds where Laura Newell went to school and where she later taught.

The third thing that caught my attention was the mentioning of a unique church located in Wabaunsee, Kansas, called "Beecher's Bible and Rifle Church". For a church to have within its name "Rifle" was enough to stir considerable interest, but the name "Beecher" really caught my attention. I remembered this name being associated with several great preachers in the New England area in years past. And who could forget the name Harriet Beecher Stowe, author of the hymn *Still, Still with Thee*, but, probably more famous for her timely novel, *"Uncle Tom's Cabin."* True enough, the Beecher in this church's name referred to Henry Ward Beecher, famed preacher for the Congregational Church of Brooklyn, NY, and a brother to Harriet Beecher Stowe. Before I get into the story of Laura Newell, the author of our hymn *As the Life of a Flower*, I should explain how the "Beecher's Bible and Rifle Church" got its name.

After the Kansas-Nebraska territory bill passed in the U.S. Congress in May 1854, it opened up the areas for settlement. Many well-known and respected citizens of New England expressed considerable interest in settling this new territory called Kansas, especially to try and make it a "Free State." In 1856, a Connecticut Colony was formed to move westward. Before leaving New Haven, Connecticut, Henry Ward Beecher of Brooklyn was invited to give an address on the "Kansas Question." The objective was to help raise money to pay the considerable expenses for the 60-70 men expedition. At the close of Mr. Beecher's speech, a gentleman rose, and without prior arrangements, proposed to raise the money there and then to furnish 50 Sharpe rifles for the Colony. He pledged one rifle, at a cost of $25 each, and soon a few others did the same. Mr. Beecher became caught up in the excitement and pledged his New York congregation to give enough funds to purchase 25 rifles if the residents could match this with 25 more. They did and he did! When the money arrived for the rifles, someone in his congregation had also donated 25 bibles. These bibles were packed on top of the rifles to provide cover as they traveled through areas that favored slavery. It turns out the rifles were never needed. By 1862, enough funds had been raised to complete the erection of a beautiful stone church building in

A Song Is Born

Wabaunsee, and it became known as *"The First Church of Christ in Wabaunsee."* Yet, everyone continued to refer to it as the "Beecher's Bible and Rifle Church," a name it could not escape. The original church building still stands today.

Mrs. Newell, the author of our hymn, spent all but four years of her life in Kansas. Like the story of the church, our story really begins in New England. She was born Laura Emeline Pixley on February 5, 1854, at New Marlborough, MA. Her mother died soon after her birth and her mother's sister, Mrs. Hiram Mabie, adopted Laura. Shortly after the adoption, Hiram Mabie, her stepfather, went to Kansas as part of that original Colony and was joined a few months later by his wife and Laura. On May 5, 1859, Hiram died thrusting Mrs. Mabie into the role of family provider. She once again took up teaching school. She taught first in Topeka and Wabaunsee before starting a school in her home near Zeandale. In 1864, Mrs. Mabie married J. W. Emerson and in 1867 they, along with Laura, took up residence on 80 acres of land granted to them by Ulysses S. Grant. One acre was set aside for a school that still stands.

Mrs. Laura E. Newell received much of her education at home from her very talented mother. She was a prolific writer who began writing poetry at an early age. Her first works were published when she was only 14, but it was some five years later before she began writing sacred hymn text and went on to have more than 2000 hymn poems published. In 1871, Laura married Lauren Newell. To this union were born four sons, two daughters, and several grandchildren. Mr. Newell was an architect and builder of considerable skill. For 45 years, Laura E. Newell lived in Tabor Valley where her influence was deeply felt through her activity in church, school, and community. She was a member of the Congregational Church of Wabaunsee, now known as "Beecher's Bible and Rifle Church" which we discussed earlier.

I was privileged to visit the original acreage and homesite currently owned by Eleanor Vilander. She graciously allowed me to walk the grounds and even go into her home. The original home of Mrs. Newell was torn down in the early 1920s, but the current home was built on the same foundation. Standing on her back porch, I could see the oak tree-lined ravine running behind the Newell home, and imagine the beautiful native lilacs that line the banks each spring which I'm sure became the inspiration for her song, *As the Life of a Flower*.

Laura Newell was surely no stranger to the brevity of life. She lost both of her parents before the age of two, and then lost her first adoptive father before she was six. Now, as she approached the 20th century, both adoptive parents were gone, and one of her six children had accidentally died from a fall. *As the Life of a Flower* was written not long after her adoptive mother had passed away. This song has seemingly lost favor with the current generation. Perhaps it's because of the message of impending death that no one wants to be reminded about. But Mrs. Newell's song is as much about living as it is about dying. When I stood on the porch of the Newell home near Wabaunsee, Kansas, and saw the wild flowers in bloom, my first thoughts were not of death, but of life. Her second verse immediately came to me.

> *"As the life of a flower be our lives pure and sweet,*
> *May we brighten the way for the friends that we greet;*
> *As sweet incense arise, from our hearts as we live*
> *Close to Him who doth teach us to love and forgive."*

A sea of flowers that bloom for a season, then fade, surrounded Mrs. Newell. What a beautiful comparison to our life as we grow and blossom into servants for the Lord.

Do you brighten the life of those you meet like the flowers we adore or has your beauty already faded before its time? Do you let the beauty of Christ shine through your actions and words, or is the beauty hidden among the weeds of life? Mrs. Laura E. Newell died October 13, 1916, and is buried in Wabaunsee, Kansas. Her funeral was held at the Tabor Valley Schoolhouse on property donated by her parents and where she taught school. The stone building still stands today though not in use since 1973. Ironically, this year the schoolhouse and property revert back to the original or current owners of the 80-acre Newell homestead.

> *For you have been born again, not of perishable seed, but of imperishable, through the living and enduring word of God. For, all men are like grass, and all their glory is like the flowers of the field; The grass withers and the flowers fall, but the word of the Lord stands forever.* [1 Peter 1:23-24]

A Song Is Born

> *My steps have held to your paths; my feet have not slipped.*
> [Psalm 17:5]

STEP BY STEP

*T*he author of *Step by Step, Awesome God, Sing your praise to the Lord*, (made popular by Amy Grant), plus many, many more great contemporary songs, was killed September 19, 1997, in a single-car accident. Richard Wayne Mullins, born in Richmond, Indiana, October 21, 1955, embarked upon a Christian music career a little more than a decade ago, just as he was emerging from several years of spiritual darkness. "I came to Nashville with a chip on my shoulder," Rich Mullins once said. "I was going to be Nashville's bad boy. I was not going to be your typical, run-of-the-mill, Pollyanna, goody-two shoes Christian musician. I became so bored trying to be bad that I gave up the pursuit."

Cynicism had clouded and limited his perception. "From my junior year of high school until age 30," Rich said, "I felt tormented all the time. I didn't like myself, and I didn't like anybody who was around me. Part of the reason was, it (life) was so dark, it was so dull." During this time, Rich's faith also seemed empty. "I never tried to be an atheist," he said. "That never made much sense to me. But I remember thinking I just wouldn't have anything to do with God. Yet, even then, I felt driven back to God. I remember thinking, "God please save me from this cynical spirit, because I'm going to become such a nasty old man."

For years, Rich told us of his secret struggles through his songs, fighting with God and friends and the devil right out loud as we looked on, safe, but captivated. "I think sometimes I have a tendency to be a little overly idealistic and I want to see the world the way that I think it ought to be." Mr. Mullins once said. "I didn't sit down and write 20 songs about the way the world really is, but it's kind of been the thing that I've been working on personally, which finds its way into my songs."

"With *Step by Step*," he tells us, "if I had to make an overall statement, it's that faith is walking with God. The biggest problem with life is that it's just daily. You can never get so healthy that you don't have to continue to eat right. Every day I have to make the right choices about

A Song Is Born

what I eat and how much exercise I need. Spiritually we're in much the same place. I go on these binges where it's like 'I'm going to memorize the five books of Moses.' I expect to be able to live off the momentum. So, it's not what you did, and not what you say you're going to do, it's what you do today."

Like most of us who find our way to God, it was a series of many small steps, scarcely remembered later, that brought Rich Mullins back into a closer relationship with the Savior. How fitting that his song, *Step by Step* details our walk through life. Many today are searching for an active church, a more meaningful worship, a "good feeling" experience each Sunday hoping it will sustain them through the week. Remember this "One Day" of feasting on God's goodness will not sustain us for a week of service. We need to feast upon his greatness each day. Also, ask yourself the question, has the "Sunday" experience really affected my daily living?

And, in likeness, one day of extraordinary service will not provide adequate exercise for our beliefs. Mr. Mullins put it this way, "Start realizing that your ministry is how much of a tip you leave when you eat in a restaurant. Take care how you leave the hotel room, whether you leave it all messed up or not. Your ministry is the way that you love people, and you love people when you write something that is encouraging to them, something challenging. You love people when you call your wife and say, "I'm going to be late for dinner," instead of letting her burn the meal. Loving people - being respectful toward them - is much more important than writing or doing music. Sometimes we think that our writing and our music is so important that we have the right to run over people. We don't. Remember what St. Francis said: "Preach always, If necessary, use words.""

Gloria Gaither, another talented songwriter, had some interesting thoughts about realism in our daily lives in her book *"Because He Lives."*

> "What we do when the stage is dark and bare is so much more important than what we do when it's bright and full. When our traveling groups meet for a time of prayer before concerts, we have often prayed that we would be as real at McDonald's after the concert as we seem during the concert. That our lives with the stagehands and the auditorium's staff would be as con-

vincing as our lives in front of the spotlight."

Many of us showcase our Christianity on Sunday as if we were performers in a play, but you could never identify the cast of players on Monday at the workplace. To win souls for Christ, it's important to reflect Christ in our daily lives.

If you are to be led by the Lord one step at a time, you must take that first step - committing your life to Christ - Do it Now! Then, let your daily life reflect the beliefs you talk about each Sunday.

To this you were called, because Christ suffered for you leaving you an example, that you should follow in His steps. He committed no sin - no deceit was found in His mouth. When they hurled insults - He did not retaliate - made no threats. [1 Peter 2:21]

Rich wrote a song titled *If I Stand*. One line of this song seems fitting to repeat now:

> "So if I stand, let me stand on the promise
> That you will pull me through,
> And if I can't, let me fall on the grace
> That first brought me to you.
>
> If I sing let me sing for the joy
> That has been born in me, these songs,
> But if I weep, let it be as a man
> Who is longing for his home."

Rich Mullins is now home.

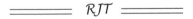

RJT

A Song Is Born

For there will be no night there. [Revelation 21:25]

No Night There

John R. Clements was born in County Armagh, Ireland, in 1868 and immigrated to the United States with his parents just two years later. They settled in the New York - Pennsylvania area where John began work as a grocery clerk at age 13 and continued in that business most of his life. It was in 1898 when John Clements made a trip by train from New York to California. As the train traveled west, the wonders of this great land were revealed to him. The spacious skies, the amber waves of grain, the mountains' majesties made a lasting impression on Mr. Clements.

Barbara and I have been privileged to travel extensively and view first-hand this great country we call America. We are constantly amazed at its beauty and diversity. From the gentle rolling hillsides of New England, filled with maple trees, picturesque farms, and so much history to the towering Rockies of Colorado, Wyoming and Montana. From the mile after mile of plains in Texas, Oklahoma, and Kansas to the cool, inviting shores of California, Oregon, and Washington. And don't forget those painted deserts, where "earth tones" become a reality to the great canyons of Arizona and Utah. Images of these places are firmly etched in our minds, and we could probably drive to each one without a roadmap. However, there is another natural wonder that constantly takes our breath away. It occurs frequently and in all locations, but you can not find it on a roadmap. This beautiful phenomenon that happens when the sun sets in the West and the skies are filled with color. We call this unique event a sunset.

Of all the wonders of this great land John Clements had seen on this trip, one stands out above them all. It was a sunset witnessed as they arrived at California's Golden Gate Bridge, a scene he will never forget. The sky was filled with every hue in the spectrum of color. As John viewed the sunset, he was afraid to move or turn away, afraid that the beauty would disappear, and then a thought came to him. "Darkness will soon follow and this great spectacle will disappear," said John. "But someday I'll be in the land where there is no night, only eternal day, with no pain, no death, and no fears. Just one great glorious day that

A Song Is Born

will never end. In a place that our Lord Jesus has gone to prepare for us. I was so overwhelmed that I could not dismiss the glory from my mind and that evening, I wrote (the poem) *No Night There*."

And he carried me away in the Spirit to a mountain great and high, and showed me the Holy City – the City does not need the sun or the moon to shine on it, for the glory of God gives it light – On no day will its gates ever be shut, for there will be no night there. [Revelation 21:10; 25]

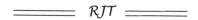

RJT

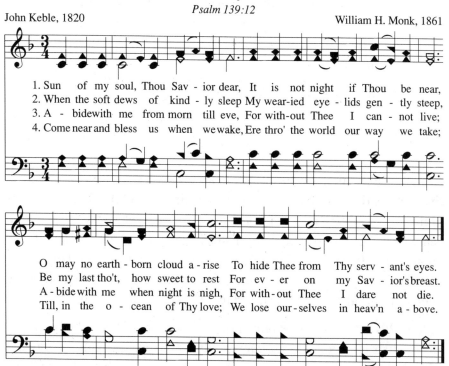

Text first appeared in America in the Collection of Songs and Hymns, 1835

A Song Is Born

> *But they urged him strongly, "Stay with us, for it is nearly evening; the day is almost over."* [Luke 24:29]

SUN OF MY SOUL

Sun Of My Soul was written in by John Keble in 1820. The years between 1820 and 1840 were stirring years in England. New intellectual forces were being felt all around. English poetry was flourishing. It was a period when great hymns like *Lead Kindly Light* by John H. Newton, *In the Hour Of Trial* by James Montgomery, and *Holy, Holy, Holy* by Reginald Heber, were born. The Great Spiritual Awakening, lead by John and Charles Wesley and George Whitefield, aroused the common people: and at Oxford, John Henry Newman, John Keble, and others were writing tracts and preaching spiritual revival. On Sunday, July 14, 1833, John Keble preached a sermon titled *"National Apostasy,"* condemning the spiritual state of the official Church. Mr. Keble was trying to raise the standards of the spiritual condition of the Church of England. John Henry Newton credits this sermon as the beginning of the Oxford Movement, and that it was the inspiration for him and others to leave the Church of England establishing independent beliefs. However, John Keble, the author of the sermon and of our hymn, never left the Church of England.

Long after the tracts of doctrine have disappeared, long after the intellectual or political freedom speeches are long forgotten, Keble's beautiful hymn is as fresh and inspiring today as when it was written in 1820.

John Keble, the son of an Anglican country preacher, was born in England April 25, 1792. Following his training at Oxford, he served as professor of poetry and other positions for several years. The last 30 years of his life he served as minister for a small church in Hursley, a village of 1500 people. In 1835 John's father died. It was then, at the age of 43, he married a lady whom he loved very much, but she only lived two months after their marriage. He was heartbroken!

Sun Of My Soul is a true prayer of the believer. Most of the beauty of this hymn is lost today because few study its words. It begins by drawing a parallel between nature, that is, day and night, and the light of Christ in our lives. Next is an acknowledgment of what God means to us; *"It is not night if Thou be near."* Then follows this thought with an earnest request that any disheartening thought may be driven out of our minds; *"no earthborn cloud arise."* Indeed, the first three verses are devoted to an earnest plea for a right relationship with God. Verse four seeks divine guidance throughout our lives; *"Come near and bless. . ."*

When earth's sun slips down the western sky and twilight deepens into darkness; when troubles and trials darken our spirits and we feel alone in the dark; when fear and uncertainty settle over us like a great cloud; remember, *"It is not night"* if our Savior is near. When Jesus is on our minds and in our hearts, we are covered in light. When Christ is master of our lives and His light is shining through us, there is no darkness. Constantly pray that Jesus will *"come near and bless us"* each day.

If I say, "Surely the darkness will hide me and the light become night around me," even the darkness will not be dark to you; the night will shine like day, for darkness is as light to you. [Psalm 139:11-12]

RJT

I will tell of the kindnesses of the Lord, the deeds for which he is to be praised, according to all the Lord has done for us. [Isaiah 63:7]

NO ONE EVER CARED FOR ME LIKE JESUS

I firmly believe that most truly great hymns are born from some personal experience, often from some deep suffering, sorrow, or tragedy. *No One Ever Cared For Me Like Jesus* was written after the author's wife left him, declaring her love for him had ended and their marriage was over.

Charles F. Weigle was born in Lafayette, Indiana, in 1871. He studied music at the Cincinnati Conservatory of Music and traveled extensively as an evangelistic singer and itinerant preacher. One day after returning home from one of his crusades, he discovered that his wife had left him, taking with her their only son. "I'm leaving Charlie," the note read. "I want to go the other way - to the bright lights." She did not share his commitment to the gospel of Christ and was not content to be a preacher's wife. For several years, Mr. Weigle suffered through periods of deep depression, wondering if anyone cared for him.

Warren Roberts, a gospel music disc jockey and author of the beautiful song *God Bless You, Go With God,* recalled the day when Mr. Weigle visited his studio in Atlanta, Georgia. Warren was the producer and narrator for a weekly TV program that featured Gospel singing groups. The program contained one segment where Mr. Roberts would sit in his big easy chair, tell the story about a particular song, and then some featured group would perform the number. But on this day in 1963, Charles Weigle himself sat in the big chair and told his own story of how *No One Ever Cared For Me, Like Jesus* came about. "Even now, at the age of 92, you could still feel the pain and hurt as he told how his wife left, taking with her his hopes for a happy family life," Warren said.

"I became so despondent during the next several years that there were even times I contemplated suicide," Mr. Weigle said. "One day, I walked down to the dock near the Gulf of Mexico and briefly felt like jumping in, but somehow the Lord told me not to. Later, as I sat down at the piano, I kept thinking how Jesus knows all about us and he truly cares for us more than any other. As my hands felt the (piano) keys, I began to play and sing, and in less than thirty minutes, this hymn was written."

After Charles Weigle told his story that day, he sang his own song with such feeling and emotion that everyone in the studio wept openly. Mr. Weigle eventually overcame his despair, renewed his commitment to the Lord, and devoted his life to the service of a loving God. He went on to write nearly 400 songs.

To love and to be loved is the most important thing in our life. It is the glue that binds us together in our marriages, our families, and in all our human relationships. Human love is not simply a feeling of romantic excitement or sexual attraction. Love is having an intense awareness of someone's needs and unselfishly giving of oneself to help them. Love is fragile and requires constant nurturing. We don't "fall in love," but we develop love through caring, sharing, and hard work. When human love fails, the world around us seems to crumble. In these moments of sorrow, trouble, and disappointment, our hearts cry out for sympathy and understanding. Remember that Christ is always there for us.

Christ loves you and me. He gave his life willingly to cleanse us and to show us a perfect love. When our world falls apart, he is still there. He will never leave you or forsake you. His love is everlasting.

No one ever cared for me like Jesus,
There's no other friend so kind as He.
No one else could take the sin and darkness from me,
O how much He cared for me.

In all their distress he too was distressed, and the angel of his presence saved them. In his love and mercy he redeemed them; he lifted them up and carried them all the days of old. [Isaiah 63:9]

A Song Is Born

> *And God will wipe away every tear from their eyes.* [Revelation 7:17]

NO TEARS IN HEAVEN

What will Heaven be like? Many songs have been written about Heaven. Ira Stanphill wrote about our *Mansion over the Hilltop*. Mrs. Bridgewater wrote *How Beautiful Heaven Must Be*. Albert E. Brumley wrote many songs about heaven such as: *If We Never Meet Again This Side of Heaven*, or his most popular song *I'll Fly Away*. Perhaps for you, Heaven will be a time to have your questions answered or a time to just feel the Peace of God and share the presence of our Lord and Savior. Happiness and gladness will surely reign. Sorrow, sadness, or tears will not be allowed. In 1982, Robert S. Arnold related to me the following story about the background of *No Tears in Heaven*.

"In 1934, I was teaching a singing school at night at Iliex, Texas, near Albany. A Gospel meeting was in progress at Morgan, Texas. I could only attend in the mornings and I can not even remember the preachers' name, but he made a statement that there would not be any tears in Heaven. The music and part of the words flashed through my mind. I returned to the place where I was staying and, within 30 minutes, I had the music including all four parts and part of the words to *No Tears in Heaven*."

Robert S. Arnold was born January 26, 1905, in Coleman, Texas, to Millard F. and Victoria Arnold. He developed a love for singing at an early age. By the time he was 18, Mr. Arnold was well on his way to a lifelong career in quartet singing, song writing, piano tuning, songbook publishing, teaching singing schools, and raising cattle. Robert S. Arnold has published or edited more than 60 songbooks, most of these have been through the National Music Company, which he now owns. The National Music Company was organized in Fort Worth, Texas, in 1937 and their first songbook produced was "Echoes of Heaven". The company at one time had two full-time quartets that attended singings in the South. They also had a weekly radio program and, even for a while, a daily program over station KFJZ in Fort Worth. Mr. Arnold

A Song Is Born

conducted singing schools each summer and published the National Music News each month. During the 1940's, World War II came, causing members to leave for other work. In 1945, Robert and Cora purchased the National Music Company, only to have to sell 49% of the company later that year. But in 1946, they were able, once again, to become sole owners and have remained so to this day. In addition to his work with the National Music Company, Brother Arnold has written over 400 songs.

In 1928, Robert Arnold married Mildred Cora. They moved to Fort Worth, Texas, for some 28 years and then lived in Jefferson, Texas, for 20 years before moving back to the farm in Coleman. In 1988, Cora died, but Mr. Arnold continued to live on a farm just 300 yards from where he grew up, writing songs, producing songbooks and raising cattle.

I asked him how he got into the cattle business. *"When I was nine, living just across the street there,"* he said, *"our family cow was about to give birth. I ask mother if I could have the calf. She said no because they needed it for family income. Repeatedly I kept asking for that calf until one day she said if I could come up with $35, I could have the calf. I worked hard, saved, and paid her $35. The calf was a heifer, and I've been in the cattle business ever since."*

Robert S. Arnold continued to write songs and publish songbooks until his death February 8, 2003, at the age of 98. He had a beautiful, clear first tenor voice that could be heard at the many singings he attended.

Never again will they hunger; never again will they thirst. The sun will not beat upon them, nor any scorching heat. For the Lamb at the center of the throne will be their shepherd; he will lead them to springs of living water. And God will wipe away every tear from their eyes. [Revelation 7:16-17]

As Christians, our journey on earth is made easier because of the beautiful images of heaven we have been given. The road may be rough and the trials many, but we have hope. A hope of a better world! A hope of seeing our sweet Savior face to face!

RJT

A Song Is Born

Surely Goodness And Mercy

Words & Music by
John W. Peterson/ Alfred B. Smith, 1958

Psalm 23:6

1. A pilgrim was I and a-wand'ring, In the cold night of sin I did roam; When Jesus the kind Shepherd found me, And now I am on my way home.
2. He restoreth my soul when I'm weary, He giveth me strength day by day; He leads me beside the still waters, He guards me each step of the way.
3. When I walk thro' that dark lonesome valley, My Savior will walk with me there; And safely His great hand will lead me To the mansions He's gone to prepare.

Chorus

Surely goodness and mercy shall follow me All the days, all the days of my life. Surely goodness and mercy shall follow me All the

© Copyright 1958 by Singspiration Music. All Rights Reserved. Used by Permission.

A Song Is Born

Surely goodness and mercy will follow me all the days of my life. [Psalm 23:6]

Surely Goodness and Mercy

Many hymns are born out of life's tragedies and misfortunes. Others come because of a chance remark or sermon. Some hymns just seem to come from nowhere – almost by accident or by God's providence. Of all the songs inspired by the 23rd Psalm, perhaps none have had a more interesting beginning than *Surely Goodness and Mercy*. A six-year-old barefoot boy and his first teacher became the inspiration for this great song.

It all started near the small town of Rome, Pennsylvania, located about 25 miles west of Montrose where hymnologist Alfred Smith lived at the time this hymn was born. More than 100 years ago, Rome was home for Daniel Towner, James McGranahan, and Philip Bliss, three of the great songwriters of that day. Even today, some of the descendants of Philip Bliss still live in the area. Alfred Smith was a frequent visitor to Rome and often helped to document the life of Philip Bliss. It was in Rome where Philip Bliss met and later married Lucy Young, and where he purchased a home for his aging parents. This home is now a museum.

A Song Is Born

Mr. Smith tells the story in his book "Hymn Histories" of how he received a note from one of these descendants, and related the following story about the young Philip Bliss.

"Uncle Phil, when he was a barefoot boy about 6 years old, went to school for the first time. As he entered the one room schoolhouse, his heart skipped a beat when he saw the teacher. She was very petite, with red hair and blue-green eyes, whose name was Miss Murphy. To little Bliss, he had never seen anything so beautiful. He fell in love. She taught the class to memorize the 23rd Psalm. As she came to "surely goodness and mercy shall follow me all the days," little Bliss, who couldn't read yet, thought for sure that it said, "Surely good Miss Murphy shall follow me—". He soon found out differently."

One day in 1958, Alfred Smith and John Peterson were working on some new songs. After reading this note again, it gave them an idea for a new song. Before the day was out, the hymn was born.

The comparison between sheep and people is a common parallel found in the scriptures. The picture is seen in Isaiah 53:6, *"All we like sheep have gone astray."* Jesus relates how the sheep know the shepherd's voice, and follow him, and how the "Good Shepherd" is willing to give His life to save the flock. [John 10:11] Peter continues the comparison in his epistle, with sheep as representative of a people confused, bewildered, and lost if they are without a leader. If we, like sheep, follow the *"Good Shepherd,"* surely goodness and mercy will be with us all our days.

For you were like sheep going astray, but now you have returned to the Shepherd and Overseer of your souls. [1 Peter 2:25]

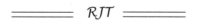

A Song Is Born

> *The steps of a good man are ordered by the Lord: and He delights in his way, though he stumble, he will not fall.* [Psalm 37:23-24]

MY GOD AND I

$\mathcal{M}$any attempts had been made by several hymnologists to locate the author of *My God and I*, each without success. We were reasonably sure that the name "I. B. Sergei" was a pseudonym and that the author's real name was Austris Wihtol, and that he lived in Glendale, California, in the 1970s.

In April 1995, I traveled to California for a little research in the Glendale library. There, in the old city directories, I located Austris Wihtol living in Glendale in 1972. The next and only directory they had was 1974, and he was not listed. However, Elly Wihtol was listed as a widow. *"Mr. Wihtol must have died somewhere between 1972 and 1974,"* I thought. The question now was when and where was he was buried? As I walked out of the library, pondering which cemetery to try first in this satellite city to Los Angeles, I noticed the street sign on the corner. It was the same street listed in 1972 as being the address of Mr. Wihtol. I wondered what the area might look like where they had lived. In among the rows of commercial buildings and condominiums was one little house, and it had the same address that I had jotted down. Wow! Who

lived there now? I knocked on the door. After a few minutes of moving around inside, an elderly lady opened the door. "I'm looking for the person who wrote a song called *My God and I*," I told her not expecting her to understand, but just tying to establish a dialogue.

"That was my husband," she replied in broken English. Somewhat taken back that I had so easily found the widow of Austris Wihtol, I asked if I could sit down for a few minutes and collect some facts about her and her husband. *"I don't have time"* she replied rather quickly. Wow, I had come 2000 miles, and come this close to uncovering some information on Mr. Wihtol. "So when would you have the time" I

A Song Is Born

pleaded. *"In about two or three hours"* she answered, "after I finish cooking for a special occasion at the church." We set a time and I came back. We had a delightful two-hour visit remembering many happy events of the past and also a few sad memories for Elly. She allowed me to climb up to the top of her closet where she had stored many files from their publishing company, material she had not been able to look at for years. In this material I found what to me was a buried treasure, a little booklet titled *"The Writing of My God and I."* Mr. Wihtol wrote the book in which he explained the birth of his famous song, which spanned more than 30 years and several countries.

Elly was born in Holland and came to the U. S. in 1930. She was trained in the Royal Conservatory and sang with the Holland Metropolitan Opera. One time she was highly complimented by Queen Wilhelmina. On another occasion she was the skating partner to Princess Juliana who later became the Queen. She came to the U.S. with an invitation to sing in the New York Metropolitan Opera, but moved to California because her brother moved there, and her parents would not let her stay in New York alone. She met Austris Wihtol in 1932 at the Wilshire Christian Church where she attended. He was practicing with his Latvia chorus for a performance. Austris was 18 years her senior. Their common love of music became the bond that tied them together in marriage.

Born January 24, 1889, one of six children in Riga, Latvia, Austris August Wihtol received most of his education in Russia. He performed in concert extensively with the Latvian Singers, which he founded upon arriving in the U.S. In his youth he wrote operas, symphonies, and other major works, but in his later years he devoted most of his time to the writing of practical choral music. The Latvia Choir sang in concerts around the country for many years. Elly estimates more than 1000 performances. They lived in Chicago from 1933 to 1944, which became the center for their tours during that time. She indicates that all of the singing was acappella, even though Austris was an accomplished pianist and composer of operas, etc. Austris worked in a conservatory in Los Angeles for some years before he began his own conservatory in

A Song Is Born

Glendale in 1953, called Kama.

Austris Wihtol wrote the song *My God and I* over a 30-year period, completing the current version February 22, 1932, in Glendale. He was not sure this was the masterpiece he wanted so he signed it with the pen name of I. B. Sergei. In fact, Mr. Wihtol composed hundreds of versions of *My God and I* but was never happy with them. Once he made the song into an opera. After its performance, he discarded it, continuing to try for the "Perfect" arrangement.

About 10 years later, after completing the version we now use written in 1932, he was browsing through a bookstore in Chicago and noticed a hymn book with his song *My God and I* included. He also noticed that a popular publishing company was listed as owning the copyrights. Austris had never released the song to anyone! Not able to find a lawyer willing or competent in copyright law to defend his rights, he purchased a 30-volume set of copyright law books and proceeded to file suit against the publisher and won. Elly still had the set of law books. The loss hurt the company and many other publishers who unknowingly published his material. Fresh with his victory, Austris was almost ruthless in his pursuit of any unauthorized publisher.

Things seemed to go well for the Wihtol's and their publishing business, until the mid 1960s when Mr. Wihtol developed Alzheimer's. Elly learned of his illness by chance one day while dining at a restaurant. He turned to her and said, *"You are a lovely lady, but who is your husband."* At first, she thought he was kidding, but soon learned he did not recognize her. This was the first indication of his Alzheimer's. After much discussion and persuasion, she managed to get him to let her take him home. (He first refused to ride in a car with a strange woman.) On the way home, he returned to himself. She never told him of the incident. Elly continued to take care of him and manage the business.

The publishing company that had lost the lawsuit continued to pursue the Wihtol's for the copyrights to *My God and I,* but Elly would not sell. This had become their principle source of income. One day, during the time of Mr. Wihtol's illness, someone from the company caught Elly away from the house and Austris home alone. According to Elly, they convinced Mr. Wihtol to sell the copyrights to *My God and I,* along with all his songs. Elly said she received very little money (never would tell

A Song Is Born

me how much). This left Elly without a source of income. She managed to continue caring for him until he died of a heart attack April 3, 1974. Elly told of many events that occurred during his illness. At one time, he withdrew about $30,000 from their joint account without her knowledge. She has never found the money or any indication as to where the money went.

Elly learned many years after their marriage that Austris had been married before and that his first wife had died in childbirth. She had vowed never to marry someone who had been married before. Austris knew this and did not tell her for many years. Elly still does not know anything about the other wife and very little about his family in Latvia. In 1988, fourteen years after Austris had died, their only child, Charlotte, was killed by a burglar in her home in Upland, California. Elly has five grandchildren, but according to her, none seem to visit or take care of her needs. Elly is left alone in the same home they purchased in 1947, surrounded by townhouses and businesses with only a small Social Security check for support. Elly Wihtol died the next year (1996) after I visited her, at age 90. Her remains were cremated by prior arrangement. The funeral home indicated no funeral or memorial services were conducted. How sad to die alone!

The inspirations for *My God and I* began in his youth, back in his homeland of Latvia . "The concept of *'go in the field together..."* 'began when I was a boy about seven years old" he said. "In our family there were two places of environment, the home and the field. Home was the place of all kinds of troubles. On the other hand, the fields were a place of beauty and happiness. *'He tells me of the years that went before me...'* To me, in my walks, it was wonderful to note that everything in nature was made ready for me to enjoy. *'My God And I Will Go For Aye Together...'* That to me is the best thought of all."

Additional inspiration came a few years later when he met an orphan girl named "Happy Anna." She help to inspired the phrase "*My God and I, go in the fields together.*" She was a girl about sixteen years of age when Austris met her, singing every day to the Riga harbor workers at noon, and developed quite a following among the stevedores and convicts. Committed to a *"gruesome, cruel, dirty"* orphanage early in life, Anna kept up her spirits with constant prayer to God for deliverance, promising that if God would deliver her from that terrible place, she

A Song Is Born

would devote her life to Him. At age 12, she escaped. With no one to care for her, she traveled from place to place much like a gypsy, receiving charity at times, and often singing to earn her meals. She obtained the title "Happy" because of her constant smile and cheerful attitude. The full story of "Happy Anna" is much too long to tell in this article.

The uncertainty of daily life faced by Happy Anna, and the peace and comfort Austris felt when he walked in the fields became the early inspiration for this song. "In my boyhood days, in our Lutheran churches," Mr. Wihtol said, "God was presented as a stern, even a heartless judge. He had written His law in tablets of stone and we lived in constant fear of the punishment that was due to us for having failed to obey this law of the stone tablets. Happy Anna brought to me a new conception of God. My conception of God is described in the words of my poem. A God that walks with me in the fields. A God that is with me when I do the best acts of my life."

With God's hand firmly clasp in ours, we can face each day. In later years, Austris would have to defend his song from many who felt is was too *"Personal,"* and that one should not be talking about God in such personal terms. Perhaps this song was an early indicator of the contemporary Christian music soon to become very popular!

Though I walk in the midst of trouble, you preserve my life; you stretch our your hand against the anger of my foes, with your right hand you save me. [Psalm 138:7]

RJT

A Song Is Born

Then Agrippa said to Paul, Do you think that in such a short time you can persuade me to be a Christian? Paul replied, "Short time or long – I pray God that not only you but all who are listening to me today may become what I am, except for these chains." [Acts 26:28-29]

ALMOST PERSUADED

Philip Bliss was born July 9, 1838, in a rural area of Pennsylvania. He grew up in dismal poverty and developed a strong work ethic at an early age. By the age of 11, he had left home to work during the summers

A Song Is Born

on farms or in sawmills and attend various schools during the winters. He continued this practice all through his teenage years. In 1850, at the age of 12, he confessed Christ and was baptized by a Christian Church minister. Philip Bliss was very religious from boyhood and continued this commitment of hard work and service to the Savior throughout his short lifetime!

Blessed with a beautiful voice and outstanding musical skills, P. P. Bliss was constantly in demand to sing or lead the singing for evangelistic meetings. This required constant travel, but he never missed an opportunity to attend church even while traveling. One Sunday night in 1870, while waiting for a train to take him from Ohio to Chicago, he slipped into a church and took a back seat. The preacher, Mr. Brundage, was reading from Acts 26:28, *"Almost thou persuadest me to be a Christian."* Then Mr. Brundage added, *"he who is almost persuaded is almost saved, but to be almost saved is to be entirely lost."*

Bliss was impressed with the thought and immediately set about to write the song we have used so often as an invitation hymn. *Almost Persuaded* was written just five years before his untimely death in a tragic train wreck on December 29, 1876.

"Almost" is incomplete, never quite obtaining the goal. It's like being close to achieving the reward, but as they say, "close only counts in horseshoes." Almost is but to fail. Our victory is in Christ, but to receive this victory we must believe, change the way we live, acknowledge Him as our Savior, and be buried with Him in baptism. Anything short of this is just almost becoming a Christian.

However, if you suffer as a Christian, do not be ashamed, but praise God that you bear that name. [1 Peter 4:16]

======= *RJT* =======

A Song Is Born

Blessed is the nation whose God is the Lord. [Psalm 33:12]

AMERICA, THE BEAUTIFUL

Four hundred years after Columbus discovered America, a great nation-wide celebration took place in this country. In 1892, Chicago sponsored an Exposition that ran for more than a year. Attending this event were a group of schoolteachers from Wellesley, a famous girls college in Massachusetts. They were thoroughly impressed with the "Windy City" and its wide array of structures built for this Exposition often referred to as "the White City" because of the gleaming buildings, but continued westward on their journey to Colorado Springs, Colorado. The teachers took a mule-drawn wagon trip up Pike's Peak and viewed the great expanse of mountains and endless fields on the plains. Later that evening, the teachers spent hours talking about the events of the day.

They compared the Chicago Exposition, a man-made spectacle, to the Rocky Mountains fashioned by the hand of God. Soon the teachers were comparing the America of their day with the America of the Pilgrim settlers in 1607. They spoke of the two stones that played an important part in this nation's history – The Ten Commandments (Freedom of Religion) and Plymouth Rock. Each agreed that if we could couple the daring of the early pilgrims with the moral teachings of Moses, they would really have something.

In this discussion group was Miss Katharine Lee Bates, a professor of English at Wellesley College. In her pursuit of an education, she had traveled abroad extensively, to England, France, Spain, Switzerland, Egypt, Syria, Italy, etc. But it was America, its beauty and its purpose that impressed Miss Bates. After the discussions of the evening and with her mind still filled with visions of splendor both man-made and those created by God, she retired to her room and started writing. What flowed from her pen that night became the enduring poem we sing today. It's called *America the Beautiful*.

Miss Bates filed the poem away not giving it much thought until two years later when it was published in a church paper on July 4, 1895. The poem was an immediate success and many began to propose melodies for the poem. The problem that bothered Miss Bates was that

A Song Is Born

often the words were altered. In 1904, she made a couple of revisions to her poem and offered it free to anyone providing the text remained unchanged.

Sam Ward, an organist from Newark, New Jersey, provided a tune that some thought inferior to the noble text, but it soon won the hearts of all Americans, and continues to be a worthy carrier for this patriotic legend.

This song is not just about the beauty of this land, but about its purposes. A land where freedom reigns! A land where a belief in God is celebrated! Where we actively seek God's guidance and His infinite Grace. God Bless America!

Blessed is the nation whose God is the Lord, - From heaven the Lord looks down and sees all mankind; - We wait in hope for the Lord; he is our help and our shield. In him our hearts rejoice, for we trust in his holy name. May your unfailing love rest upon us, O Lord, even as we put our hope in you. [Psalm 33:12; 20-22]

RJT

A Charge To Keep I Have

Ephesians 4:1-3

Charles Wesley (1707-1788) Lowell Mason (1792-1872)

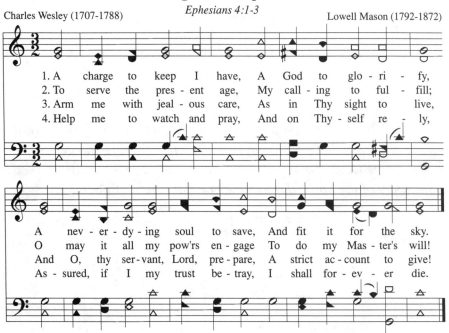

1. A charge to keep I have, A God to glo-ri-fy, A nev-er-dy-ing soul to save, And fit it for the sky.
2. To serve the pres-ent age, My call-ing to ful-fill; O may it all my pow'rs en-gage To do my Mas-ter's will!
3. Arm me with jeal-ous care, As in Thy sight to live, And O, thy ser-vant, Lord, pre-pare, A strict ac-count to give!
4. Help me to watch and pray, And on Thy-self re-ly, As-sured, if I my trust be-tray, I shall for-ev-er die.

Words first appeared in *Short Hymns on Select Passages of Holy Scriptures, Volume I*, 1782:
Music appeared in *The Choir, or Union Collection of Chruch Music*, 1832

A Song Is Born

A charge to keep I have,
A God to glorify,
A never dying soul to save,
And fit it for the sky.

A Charge To Keep I Have

"We have a charge to keep, an eternal God to glorify, an immortal soul to provide for, one generation to serve." These were the words in Matthew Henry's commentary that inspired Charles Wesley to write this hymn. It is important for us to hold firmly to the trust that has been given us as Christians: to present the Gospel of Christ in our teachings and in our daily living, even if it cost us time or humiliation! I am confidant that this was the intent of Charles Wesley when he wrote the verses, and it should be our goal today. As Christians, we must seek out opportunities to serve all people, and especially see to the needs of those who belong to the family of believers. *Therefore, as we have opportunity, let us do good to all people, especially to those who belong to the family of believers.* [Galatians 6:10]

To serve the present age,
My calling to fulfill;
O may it all my powers engage
To do my Master's will!

As a prisoner for the Lord, then, I urge you to live a life worthy of the calling you have received. Be completely humble and gentle: be patient, bearing with one another in love. Make every effort to keep the unity of the Spirit through the bond of peace. [Ephesians 4:1-3]

RJT

A Song Is Born

Text given as 1858 with the first appearance in England in *The London Hymn Book*, 1864.
The tune was composed for text in 1876 and first appeared in *The Service of Song for Baptist*.

We love because he first loved us. [1 John 4:19]

My Jesus, I Love Thee

As I study the background of hymns, I am constantly amazed how God works to inspire and preserve songs for all generations to use. We know very little about the circumstances that inspired the enduring hymn *My Jesus I Love Thee*. Yet there is a fascinating story about the various events which came together to make this hymn a classic.

A Song Is Born

One day in 1864, A. J. Gordon, a Baptist minister, was causally leafing through the London Hymnal when a hymn caught his eye. He thought to himself, "how superbly written are the verses of this hymn." The authorship for the poem was listed as anonymous, but whomever the poet, he felt the lines were well written. "It could have easily been penned by such renown poets as Isaac Watts or Charles Wesley," he thought to himself. "These words deserve a better tune." In a moment of inspiration, a beautiful new tune was born in the mind of Mr. Gordon. The combination of this anonymous poem set to the newly composed tune by A. J. Gordon became very popular, ranking up there with the renowned hymns of his day, such as *Amazing Grace* or *Rock of Ages.*

Within the last few years, the authorship of this popular hymn has been identified as William Ralph Featherstone, born in Montreal, Canada, in 1846. It is reported that he wrote the poem at the time of his conversion at the age of 16, and he sent it to his aunt, Mrs. E. Featherston Wilson, who then lived in Los Angeles.

How strange for the hymn A. J. Gordon considered a masterpiece to have been written by a 16-year-old Canadian boy. How unlikely that a poem written in Canada and sent to a relative in America could find its way into an English Hymnbook! What are the odds for this poem to be discovered by a songbook editor an be included in his newest hymnbook!

Sometimes it is difficult to realize that a teenage boy wrote this beautiful hymn, which profoundly expresses our love and gratitude to Christ.

Though you have not seen him, you love him; and even though you do not see him now, you believe in him and are filled with an inexpressible and glorious joy, for you are receiving the goal of your faith, the salvation of your souls. [1 Peter 1:8-9]

The following incident relating to the use of this song was given to a large audience in St. Louis, Missouri, many years back, and recorded in Sankey's Story of the Gospel Hymns.

A young, talented actress was passing along the street of a large city many years ago. Through a half-open door she saw a pale, sick girl lying on the couch. She thought to herself, "With a pleasant conversation I might cheer up this invalid." The young, sick girl was a devoted Christian, and her words, patience, submission, and uplifting countenance

A Song Is Born

so exemplified her beliefs that the actress was touched and converted to become a faithful follower of Christ. She told her father, the leader of the theater troupe, of her experience and of her desire to abandon the stage, feeling that she could not live the Christian life and still remain an actress. He was astonished and told his daughter that their living depended on her. If she followed through with this commitment, their business would be ruined. His persistence set her back, and she reluctantly agreed to continue. Every preparation was made for the next play. The evening came and the father rejoiced that he had won his daughter back. The hour arrived, the audience was in place, the curtain rose, and the young actress stepped forward amid the applause. There in the breathless silence she spoke:

> *My Jesus I love the, I know thou art mine;*
> *For Thee all the follies of sin I resign;*
> *My gracious Redeemer, my Savior art thou;*
> *If ever I loved Thee, my Jesus, tis now.*

That was all. Leaving the audience in tears she retired from the stage, never again to appear as an actress. Through her influence her father was converted, and together they led many to Christ. The commitment made from the heart of this young actress may have cost her her livelihood, but she gained eternity. The power of a radiant life, even though an invalid, combined with a hymn poem written by a teenage boy provided the most effective sermon anyone could have ever proclaimed.

So often we wait and search for some "great" thing to do that will help us teach others of the love of Jesus when just a simple, honest declaration of our love and commitment will do.

> *Dear friends, let us love one another, for love comes from God. Everyone who loves has been born of God. Whoever does not love does not know God, because God is love.* [1 John 4:7-8]

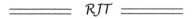

RJT

A Song Is Born

For the message of the cross is foolishness to those who are perishing, but to us who are being saved it is the power of God.
[1 Corinthians 1:18]

AT THE CROSS

Some hymns survive the test of time unchanged from their original form while others go through various modifications. *Alas! And Did My Savior Bleed,* written by Isaac Watts in 1707, has been modified several times. It was written with six stanzas and no chorus. The first stanza has been altered in many hymnbooks. Some use *"Such a one as I,"* while others use *"Sinners such as I,"* feeling that the expression *"Worm"* is inappropriate. For those who object, it might well be remembered that the worm as a caterpillar, is the only thing God created that can change into a beautiful butterfly. The transformation in our hearts brought about by our obedience to Christ where the old person dies and we become new creatures, could be likened to the process of nature as a caterpillar dies and a beautiful butterfly is born.

Ralph Hudson developed the current tune and chorus in 1885. It is generally accepted that the words and music of the chorus emerged from the camp meeting era. You might notice that it actually seems like two different songs.

Of all Christian symbols, the cross is the most widely used. Originally, the cross was a symbol of defeat and of a shameful death, but our Savior changed all that. The cross of Christ is a symbol of Christianity, of God's love for sinful man, and of triumphant hope! May we like the apostle Paul, learn to glory in the cross of Christ.

He was despised and rejected by men, a man of sorrows, and familiar with suffering. –But he was pierced for our transgressions, he was crushed for our iniquities; the punishment that brought us peace was upon him, and by his wounds we are healed.
[Isaiah 53:3; 5]

RJT

A Song Is Born

Awesome God
Psalm 66:5

Rich Mullins, 1988 — Rich Mullins, 1988

1. When He rolls up His sleeves He ain't just puttin' on the Ritz. Our God is an awesome God. There is thunder in His footsteps and lightning in His fists. Our God is an awesome God. And the Lord wasn't jokin' when He kicked 'em out of Eden, it wasn't for no reason that He shed His blood. His return is very close and so you better be believin' that our

2. And when the sky was starless in the void of the night, Our God is an awesome God. He spoke into the darkness and created the light. Our God is an awesome God. The judgement and wrath He poured out on Sodom; the mercy and grace He gave us at the cross; I hope that we have not too quickly forgotten that our

© 1988 by Edward Grant, Inc. All Rights Reserved.

A Song Is Born

The great and awesome God keeps His covenant of love.
[Nehemiah 1:5]

Awesome God

*I*n his career as a contemporary Christian musician, Rich Mullins logged thousands of miles on the road. He often drove in silence, enjoying the opportunity to think and reflect. In 1982, as he made the trip from Nashville, Tennessee, to Bolivar, Missouri, for a *"Christ in Youth"* conference, he began to develop a new song. He imagined what a fiery preacher might say in a sermon to create the verses of his new song, and then he used simple acclamations of God's attributes for the chorus. Mr. Mullins then applied a stirring melody to the whole thing. Because his traveling companion was asleep, he had to compose the song, both words and music, in his head. When they arrived at their destination, he headed straight for a piano to refine what he had in mind. That night, his song, *Awesome God,* was introduced to the conference attendees and it met with immediate acceptance.

Awesome is a word used frequently today, mostly to express anything exciting or different, and I fear sometimes that we might be overusing the word. Awesome is defined as impressive, exalted, grand, frightening, or majestic. Rich Mullins wrote this song thinking about the tremendous power of God, the power to create or destroy, to eliminate mankind, or to forgive. The verses, which we seldom sing, will give you a sense of the fear and respect Mr. Mullins had in mind when he wrote his song, *Awesome God.*

> *When He rolls up His sleeves He ain't just putting on the Ritz,*
> *Our God is an Awesome God.*
> *There is thunder in His footsteps and lightning in His fists,*
> *Our God is an Awesome God.*
> *The Lord wasn't jokin' when He kicked them out of Eden,*
> *It wasn't for no reason that He shed His blood.*
> *His return is very close and so you better be believin' that*
> *Our God is an Awesome God.*

Rich was always very conscious of minimizing his own presence and lifting up God. He once was asked about his reluctance to be

A Song Is Born

introduced at concerts and about his general appearance when performing, which usually consisted of blue jeans and tee shirt. Often he would walk onto the stage before the announcer could introduce him, and he would just begin to play or sing.

> "I find it embarrassing to be introduced," he once said. "When I was in fourth grade, I got asked to play the communion meditation at church. I practiced and my piano teacher worked with me. I went back Tuesday to my lesson after I had played Sunday, and my teacher said, "How did you do?" and I told her, 'Everybody said they loved it, everyone said I did great.' And she said, "Well, then you failed." I was crushed, but she put her hand on my shoulder and said, "Richard, when you play in church, you are to direct people's attention to God, not to your playing." Ever since then there's something about "And now, Ladies and Gentlemen, here's Rich Mullins," and I keep thinking that Mary Kellner is going to come up and say, "Now Richard, when you play in church —"

Rich Mullins once wrote a series of articles for a leading Christian magazine. I really like what he said in the spring 1993 article titled "The Way We Were."

> "Before we had stifled the cross into a symbol, before we had softened grace into a sentiment, before we had systematized the power and mystery of God's greatest revelation of Himself into a set of dogmas, we were the children that we must become again.
>
> When we were kids, we sang for the joy of singing, we colored and cut and pasted for the fun of doing it. We ran for the love of running, and laughed and got scared and saw the world as a real place full of real dangers, and real beauty and real rights and wrongs.
>
> And if the cross is more than a symbol (and it is): and if grace is more than a sentiment (and, thank God, it is): If Jesus Christ is really God's revelation of Himself and not the product of human imagination (and He is): then we will become the children we once were and must become again. We will pray and run and work and give ourselves over to faith. And God

A Song Is Born

will be our Father and His Kingdom will be our home, for we will be those children we once were, and "of such is the Kingdom of Heaven."

Richard Wayne Mullins met an untimely death in a one-car accident while on his way to another youth rally. (See the song Step by Step for more information.) He will be missed, but his talent and teachings live on through his songs.

Great is the Lord and mighty in power; his understanding has no limit. The Lord sustains the humble but casts the wicked to the ground. Sing to the Lord with thanksgiving; [Psalm 147:5-7]

RJT

God Is The Fountain Whence
Psalm 36:9

Benjamin Beddome (1717-1795)   Lowell Mason (1792-1872)

1. God is the foun-tain whence Ten thou-sand bless-ings flow; To Him my life, my health, and friends, And ev-'ry good I owe.
2. The com-forts He af-fords Are nei-ther few nor small; He is the source of fresh de-lights, My por-tion and my all.
3. He fills my heart with joy, My lips at-tunes for praise; And to His glo-ry I'll de-vote The rem-nant of my days.

Written sometime before 1795. First appeared in Beddome's Hymns adapted to Public Worship or Family Devotion, 1817
The tune GERAR is attributed to Lowell Mason first appeared 1839

For with you is the fountain of life; in your light we see light.
[Psalm 36:9]

God Is the Fountain Whence

*B*enjamin Beddome was born in the year 1717, in Warwickshire, England. His early training was to be a surgeon, but deep religious convictions at the age of twenty changed his life. After studying for the ministry and a short internship, he spent the remaining fifty-five years of his life preaching for one Baptist congregation in Bourton-on-the-water, in England.

Nearly all of his hymns were written to be sung after his sermons, to provide an emphasis upon the lesson for that day. He never intended them for public use, and most were published twenty years after he died in 1795.

Mr. Beddome experienced many sorrows late in his personal life. In 1778, one of his sons, an accomplished medical doctor, died suddenly. Shortly afterwards, a second son died when he accidentally drowned. If this were not enough, in 1784 his wife of thirty-six years died. Yet through all this he could still write *"God is the fountain whence ten thousand blessings flow."* God is our strength, our source of comfort and joy.

This hymn was originally titled *Love Is The Fountain Whence*. God is the epitome of love, and we are taught to pattern our love after His. Everyone believes that love is important, but we usually think of love as just a feeling or emotional experience. In reality, love is a choice! Love is an action! How well do you display your love in the choices you make; in the actions you take each day?

God is love. Whoever lives in love lives in God, and God in him. In this way love is made complete among us so that we will have confidence on the day of judgment. [1 John 4:16-17]

RJT

A Song Is Born

The Lord is my helper; I will not be afraid. What can man do to me? [Hebrews 13:6]

BE WITH ME LORD

On a rural farm in northeast Arkansas near Union Grove, Lloyd Otis Sanderson was born. He weighed in at 13 pounds, 8 ounces, indicative of his six-foot two statue he would become.

From the beginning, religious loyalties were divided in the Sanderson household. His young mother, Lucy Ann Hunt, twenty-five years younger than his father, was a fervent believer of the Restoration Movement. His father, James Porter Sanderson, was a Methodist by inheritance and a Mason by conviction. Open discussion of religion was never allowed in the home. L. O. Sanderson grew up attending the Methodist church and became a member at the age of 10. He quickly became active in their music programs, singing in the choirs, leading singing, and teaching music. Even as a teen, he had developed a respectable income.

Music occupied a central part of the Sanderson's evening entertainment. His father taught music and frequently led singing at the local Methodist church. His mother taught L. O. to sight-read music by the Shape Note method as early as age four. All of his nine brothers and sisters shared in the music tradition and each had the ability to play a variety of instruments, but L. O. excelled in song writing and the teaching of singing schools. He wrote his first of 400 songs at the age of 14 and began teaching singing schools the next year.

Following his father's death in 1920, the Bible was openly and freely discussed in the home. *"I finally read myself into believing that I should be buried with my Lord in baptism,"* Sanderson remembers saying. The decision was difficult for him. He had to change his religious convictions of the past 11 years and possibly lose many friends. Plus, he thought his music career and his source of income would come to an end. In 1922 at the age of 21, he was baptized and the following Sunday was employed by the Bono Church of Christ to lead the singing. Thus began a long, successful ministry of music in the churches of Christ.

Sanderson polished his musical skills by studying at several Universities and the Little Rock Conservatory of Music. He served as Music Editor for the Gospel Advocate of Nashville, Tennessee, for more than forty years, and in that position edited three hymnbooks, **"Christian Hymns I, Christian Hymns II, and Christian Hymns III."** Additionally, Sanderson wrote several music textbooks, such as *"Theory of Music," "First Lessons In Singing, Song Leaders Manual,"* and *"Harmony and Theory of Music."* L.O. Sanderson was a strong advocate of quality songs. He believed that a song must *"appeal to the soul, not to the flesh and to the heart, not to the feet. The words of a song must present a worthy idea, and the form must be as good as the idea. Poems* *should stand the test of English as well as truth."* His talent in hymn writing and song leader training continues to be felt today.

Earlier in his songwriting career, he would often use the pseudonym, "Vana R. Raye," taken partly from his wife's maiden name. Back then, it was believed that for a song to be successful, the words and music could not be written by the same person.

Prior to his conversion most of his time and career choices involved music, but now his interest in preaching grew. *"It seemed everyone in the church wanted me to preach. I enjoyed the simple truth so much that I continued both singing and preaching,"* Sanderson said. Over the next sixty years, he would preach the Gospel for congregations in Arkansas, Missouri, Oklahoma, Tennessee, Kansas, and Texas. It was while preaching for the South National Church of Christ, a newly established congregation in Springfield, Missouri, that he was inspired to write his most popular hymn. He relates the following story.

"In the fall of 1934, on a Monday night past midnight, I was working in my church office, editing and re-arranging materials for Christian Hymns I. It was so late that the police, seeing a light in my office and my car still out, stopped and came in to check on me. A melody kept running through my mind. I finally stopped what I was doing, and wrote out the melody and then returned to my work, but the harmony kept place in my mind. Again, I stopped and wrote the harmony to complete the music."

I have often wondered why the police had taken such personal interest in the safety of L. O. Sanderson. Back then preaching the gospel could be hazardous to your health. A few years earlier, Marshall Spencer Mason, a member at South National and a well-known evangelist, was murdered October 1, 1930, while conducting a meeting in Arkansas. The man was upset over his preaching. Two years later, an individual was offended by a message that Sanderson had given on his weekly radio program in Springfield and threatened to kill him. The threat was taken seriously. An armed policeman was hired to attend worship for a time. Safety for L. O. Sanderson and many other Gospel preachers was a real issue.

He continues: "Some eight days later, a letter came from Thomas O. Chisholm. I had never met him personally, but have purchased many of his poems, and we have corresponded. In his letter was a poem. Mr. Chisholm said he retired one evening but couldn't sleep *"because a theme kept coming to my mind. After midnight, I finally got up, went to my desk, and completed the poem."* Brother Sanderson continued, "This turned out to be on the very same night I had trouble working until I wrote the music. Well, to my surprise, it was a perfect fit for my music."

Thomas O. Chisholm was born in a log cabin near Franklin, Kentucky, in 1866. His writing skills were recognized at an early age when he became the Associate Editor for the local newspaper by the age of 21. Mr. Chisholm became a Methodist Minister but failing health caused him to quit after only one year. He spent most of his life as an insurance salesman and a writer.

Thus, the words and music for *Be With Me Lord* were <u>created separately from a distance</u> of some 1000 miles, but under the same circumstances, on the same night, and at about the same hour. A perfect wedding of words and music!

Whether written by coincidence or by the providence of God, *Be With Me Lord* has been one of Lloyd Otis Sanderson's finest hymns. It brings to mind the comfort that is ours. First to know that we are not in this world alone, and second, to know that the Lord will never leave our side no matter how dark and dreary life seems. I am reminded of the poem *Footprints in the Sand*;

> *"When the last scenes of my life flashed before me, I looked back at the footprints in the sand. I noticed many times there was only one set of prints, and I noticed it happened at the lowest and saddest point in my life. It bothered me, so I questioned the Lord. "My Precious child!" He said. "During your times of trial and suffering, when you saw only one set of footprints in the sand, it was then that I was carrying you."*

We beseech the Lord to abide in us, to carry us through life. *Be With Us Lord!*

A Song Is Born

In later years, L. O. Sanderson would need all the comfort his hymn could give. Their daughter, Lloydene, developed cancer and died August 2, 1984. Just two weeks later on August 15 while walking home from church, which was directly across the street from their home, a teenage driver hit them. Rena Raye Sanderson, his wife of 57 years, was killed. Mr. Sanderson survived, though crippled, and lived another eight years. He went home peacefully January 17, 1992, at the age of ninety.

There hath no temptation taken you but such as is common to man: But God is faithful, who will not suffer you to be tempted above that ye are able; but will with the temptation also make a way to escape, that ye may be able to bear it. [1 Corinthians 10:13]

RJT

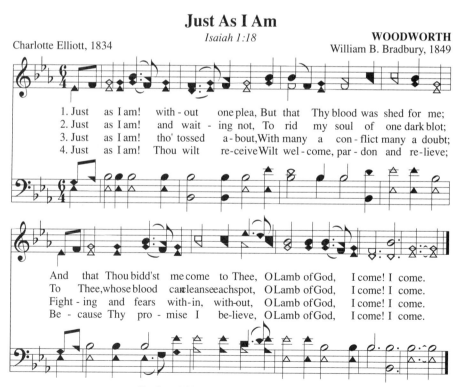

Text first published in the *Invalid's Hymn Book*, 1836
Tune first appeared in Bradbury and Hastings's *Mendelssohn Collection or Third Book of Psalmody*, 1849

A Song Is Born

Come unto me all you who are weary and burdened, and I will give you rest. [Matthew 11:28]

JUST AS I AM

Charlotte Elliott came from a cultured, Christian family, and was well educated. In her youth she lived a carefree life, showing a lot of promise as a portrait artist and as a writer of humorous verse. By the time she was thirty-two years old, a serious illness had left her an invalid. Despite her religious background, she never accepted the peace and happiness known only to those who have put on Christ, no doubt feeling some resentment about her debilitating illness.

The following year, in 1822, a young evangelist named Cesar Malan came to stay with the family for a time. He sensed her restlessness and asked her right out, "Are you a Christian?" Miss Elliott deeply resented this personal question, and more or less told him to mind his own business. A few days later she apologized to Mr. Malan for her rudeness, and indicates, "I've wanted to come to Christ but I don't know how." His reply to her was simple and quick, "Come to Him just as you are." This she did!

Herein lies the real meaning and beauty of this hymn. No doubt Miss Elliott's heart was filled with bitterness and even hatred because of her illness. Like so many of us, Charlotte experienced fears, doubts, and even jealousies. She often exhibited a quick temper and was full of pride and shame. She thought, "how could I ever become a Christian with all of these wrong feelings?" Waiting until her life changed and her emotions improved did not seem to be the answer. You come to Christ just as you are, with all of your fears, doubts, and imperfections, because outside of Christ we have no hope of ever improving.

It is easy for us to recognize how the simple reply by Dr. Malan inspired the song *Just As I Am,* but it was not written until some fourteen years later. H. V. Elliott, Charlotte's brother and himself a minister, had undertaken to build a school for the children of poor clergymen. Amidst all the fundraising activities, Charlotte felt helpless because of her physical impairment. What could she do as an invalid? One day, as she

A Song Is Born

sat in the house all alone and feeling somewhat depressed, she received her yearly letter from Dr. Malan. While the rest of the family and friends were busy raising funds in the community for the school, she reflected back upon the time of her conversion, and remembered those simple words her friend had given, "Come to Him just as you are." At that moment, this beautiful hymn was born. Miss Elliott donated the proceeds from this poem to the school project. It is interesting to note that more funds were raised from this poem than all the other fundraising projects combined.

We should always feel free to come to Christ at any time and from any point in our life, no matter how low or degrading we feel. He has invited us to come! He died on the cross for the sinner! Not one of us is perfect! If we wait until we make all the wrongs in our life right, it will never happen! No improvements, either large or small, will make us more acceptable to Christ. God loves us just as we are and we should come that way.

It is in Christ where we obtain the power to change our life. He alone can solve our problems. He can free us from our feelings of guilt and shame. He can pardon and cleanse us, to make us presentable to God. Without Him, we can do nothing!

We usually consider this song an invitation hymn, used only as a means of encouraging others to "Put on Christ" for the first time. I fear we often consider the coming to Christ a once-in-a-lifetime event. We need to renew our coming daily. Refresh our hearts with the sweet remembrance of His love and care.

"Come now, let us reason together," says the Lord. "Though your sins are like scarlet, they shall be as white as snow; though they are red as crimson, they shall be like wool." [Isaiah 1:18]

RJT

Do not let your hearts be troubled. Trust in God; trust also in me. In my Father's house are many rooms; If it were not so, I would have told you. I am going to prepare a place for you. [John 14:1-2]

I'LL FLY AWAY

Albert E. Brumley was born October 29, 1905, in a small village called "Rock Island," near Spiro, Oklahoma, a short distance from Fort Smith, Arkansas. It was here that he grew up on a cotton farm, went to public school, and attended his first singing school. He was a pretty good cotton picker and loved the farm life. In those days, social activities consisted mostly of sand lot baseball, community singings, and watching the local trains arrive and depart. It is from this difficult, but mostly happy farm background, that he drew many of the ideas for his songs. Some of these were: *There's a little Pine Log Cabin, Cabin in the Valley of the Pines, God's Pretty Bouquet,* and *I'll Fly Away.* Brumley used to say "You have to have faith to be a good farmer - - when you work with the earth, you see God's hand in everything you do."

In the early 1920s and 1930s, singing schools, singing conventions, etc. were very popular within rural America. Students would come from miles away by foot or horseback to the one-room schools or community centers to learn how to sing and write gospel music. These schools lasted from 10 days to 2 weeks. In 1926, Albert Brumley set out on a circuit of teaching singing schools and tuning pianos for a living. He taught a total of 51 singing schools and music Normals in Arkansas, Oklahoma, and Missouri before his marriage in 1931. It was at one of these singing schools in Powell, Missouri, that he met and later married Goldie Edith Schell. She was the daughter of an Elder of the local Church of Christ. Albert and Goldie remained members of this congregation in Powell all the days of their lives.

Rena Presley told me a humorous story about the first singing school Albert Brumley taught. Albert went to the Hartford Music Company then owned by E. M. Bartlett to study music, but he did not have enough funds. Mr. Bartlett agreed to let him enroll, even stay in his home if, when he completed the course, he would teach a singing school or two

A Song Is Born

to help repay the cost. After graduation, Mr. Bartlett took Albert out into a rural area to teach his first singing school. Since it was to last two weeks, Mr. Bartlett returned to Hartford leaving Albert to teach the school. Two days later, Albert showed up in Hartford, Arkansas. When asked why he returned so soon, he replied, *"I taught them everything I knew in two days, so we closed the school."*

Albert had tried his hand at writing songs for several years, but mostly for his own pleasure. It wasn't until after his marriage to Goldie in 1931 that, in his own words, *"At last, I begin to amount to something."* Goldie encouraged Albert to have his songs published. "They are good, Albert," she would say. So, in July of 1931, he submitted his first song for publication to the Hartford Music Company. They were happy to publish *I'll Fly Away*, and sent him a check for $12.50. A small price to pay for what has probably become the most often-recorded gospel song today. He must have invested that $12.50 well, for some 17 years later Albert Brumley was to purchase the Hartford Music Company. From such simple beginnings that hot summer in 1931, a long 46-year career of songwriting begins totaling more than 800 hymns. In the 1930s and 1940s, he would write some 300 songs for the Stamps-Baxter Music Company. In 1944, Albert formed his own company, the Albert E. Brumley and Sons Music, which is still doing business today in Powell, Missouri, operated mostly by Bob Brumley.

Albert Brumley's creativity began at an early age. The title *I'll fly Away*, came to him as a young boy while working on the family farm picking cotton. He wanted to get away from the hard work of farm life, escaping to a better life. A few years later, he would write the song, recalling his youthful days on the farm. Albert's son, Bob Brumley, recalls the inspiration for his dad's most famous song. Albert was humming an old favorite song called *The Prisoner's Tale*. When he came to the part where the prisoner wished he had the wings of an angel to fly over the prison walls, Albert thought, *"This world is a prison and the only freedom is heaven."*

Man has always been intrigued with flying. The early attempts to fly depict man-made wings attached to humans, trying to experience the majestic feeling of the freedom that flying like a bird would offer. *I'll fly Away* seems to capture some of that feeling. To be able to escape the trials, trouble, worry, and cares of this life and simply, like a bird, spread our wings and fly away, leaving it all behind - -flying toward a glorious life where joys will never end. We feel like saying "Hallelujah, let me fly away, now."

Albert's style of songs was simple, upbeat, and about the times in which he lived. "I write basically simple songs because that has been the earmark of nearly all great songs," he says. "The songs with basic simple melodies and simple messages still stand the best chance to endure." These words of advice surely proved to be true. No other gospel songwriter has ever been as well-known to the music world. His simple style impressed people like Elvis Presley, Ray Charles, Supremes, Boston Pops, the Sy Olliver orchestra, etc. Over 28 top names in the Country Music field and over 100 Gospel groups have recorded his songs. *I'll Fly Away* has been recorded more than 1000 times. *"If that ain't a record, it's a doggoned good average,"* as they would say in his hometown.

Albert E. Brumley has been affectionately called, "One of God's Gentle People." He was a quite man of strong religious convictions, with a big heart, a devoted family man, and a very sentimental and caring servant for the master.

For the Lord himself will come down from heaven, with a loud command, with the voice of the archangel and with the trumpet call of God, and the dead in Christ will rise first. After that, we who are still alive and are left will be caught up with them in the clouds to meet the Lord in the air. And so we will be with the Lord forever. [1 Thessalonians 4:16-17]

RJT

A Song Is Born

And He said unto them, Go you into all the world, and preach the gospel to every creature. [Mark 16:15]

Into Our Hands

Mrs. Roy Carruth was born Ruth Johnson in Vashti, Texas, December 21, 1900. Ruth grew up in Bellevue, Texas, where she graduated from Bellevue High School. Even as a child she loved to write poems. After graduation she taught school in New Mexico. "It was one of those little one-room schools," she laughingly says, "No wonder my teaching career was short." Ruth married Roy Lipscomb Carruth after only one year of teaching. She and her husband made their home just outside Vernon, Texas. Roy was injured in World War I, and was unable to work full time. He preached at small congregations around the Vernon area for more than 40 years, and also served as an elder. He then preached in California for a few years. Their son, Vance, was minister for the Bellflower Church of Christ in California for 35 years before retiring. He is now serving as an elder for the same congregation.

Mrs. Carruth was a long-time friend of Tillit S. Teddlie, a renowned songwriter in the early part of the 20th Century. His songs include *Heaven Holds all to Me, True Worship, Worthy Art Thou,* and hundreds more. Vance Carruth reflects upon Mr. Teddlie's visits. "I can still remember fondly during the time that the beloved songwriter lived in our town of Vernon, that he wanted to write music to some of mother's poems. He would come out to our house and spend hours working with mother as they put together words and music. The most popular song to come out of this collaboration is *Into Our Hands.*

"This song was written in 1939," Mr. Teddlie said. "In 1938 I held a meeting up in the Panhandle. We lived at Bonham at that time (we had moved there in 1926). Mrs. Carruth told me she had some poems I might like to have, so I told her I'd pay her $4 each for them. This was one of those poems and it made a good song. It has been translated into a South American language, as well as French and Italian."

A Song Is Born

"My mother was always very missionary-minded, and this is a missionary-centered song," her son Vance said. "In her later years, when she was living alone as a widow in Vernon, Texas, my wife and I would send her money from time to time, because we knew she was living on very little income, mostly social security. After she died, and my wife and I were going through her papers, we found that she had used the money we sent her to support various missionaries. We even found one letter from a missionary in the Philippines who had spoken of his need for a mule to travel on. Mrs. Carruth and her best friend, Ila Clark, together sent him enough money to buy a mule. So, the missionary named the mule "Ila-Ruth." Not many people have the dubious honor of having a mule named after them!"

Mrs. Carruth sold some of her poems to greeting card companies but soon found this required too much time. She was named Poet Laureate of Texas in 1977-78 soon after publishing her book of poems, "Acorn Cups." She wrote all types of poems, from sacred to country and even humor. I particularly like one humorous poem she titled *Capital Punishment*. In part it goes:

> *Of all the boresome topics*
> *I've heard discussed, to date,*
> *I think a fellow's ailments*
> *Above all others rate.*
> *I'll listen to his hobbies -*
> *From golf to postage stamps;*
> *But how I dread the fellow*
> *Who dwells on aches and cramps!*

But Mrs. Carruth's most popular topic was working for the Master and teaching the world about Christ. In addition to the song *Into our Hands,* I think the following poem sums up the works and feelings of Mrs. Carruth. She truly believed the message given to all of us from Jesus in what we have called the "Great Commission." The poem is titled *You can lead some one to Jesus,*

> *There is a wonderful story to tell,*
> *Wonderful work to be done,*
> *Countless the souls who are eager to hear,*
> *Precious the souls to be won!*

A Song Is Born

You can lead someone to Jesus,
You can win someone for Him,
Some precious soul you can add to that roll,
You can win someone for Him.

You and I have been given the charge to deliver the Gospel to a world living in darkness. How we deliver it is up to us, but we must deliver!

We speak as men approved by God to be entrusted with the gospel. [1 Thessalonians 2:4]

RJT

Text and Tune first appeared in a small collection for the National Baptist Sunday School, 1872

A Song Is Born

> *Let us then approach the throne of grace with confidence, so that we may receive mercy and find grace to help us in our time of need.* [Hebrews 4:16]

I Need Thee Every Hour

Many great hymns were born from some deep moving personal experience. One could easily expect to read such a story about this beautiful hymn, but it was not the case. There was no tragedy as experienced by Thomas Dorsey upon the death of his wife and child during childbirth that inspired the hymn *Take My Hand Precious Lord*. The inspiration did not come from some grief, as that suffered by Elizabeth Prentiss who wrote *More Love To Thee, O Christ* after losing her two young boys in an epidemic in New York.

There was no anxiety, such as that experienced by the newly converted young man who lay dying, never having the opportunity to bring one soul to Christ. His piercing question inspired the song *Must I Go and Empty Handed?*

The truth is, one bright lovely morning in 1872, Annie Sherwood Hawks, a thirty-seven year old housewife without a care in this world, wrote the words to this very touching hymn. She was in good health, adored by her husband and family, and content with her role as wife and mother. Mrs. Hawks spoke later of her feelings on that day when she wrote this song.

> "I was so filled with a sense of nearness to my Master, and I began to wonder how anyone could live without him, either in joy or pain. Then these words were flashed into my mind, *I Need Thee Every Hour.* Seating myself by the open window in the balmy air of the bright June day, I caught up my pencil and the words were soon committed to paper, almost as they are being sung now—."

Much of the success for this hymn can be attributed to her minister, Robert Lowry, who quickly composed the tune and added the chorus. Mr. Lowry, a popular minister and graduate of Bucknell University, never had a day of formal music training, yet in 1868 he became editor of

A Song Is Born

Sunday School songbooks for Biglow and Main Publishing Company of New York. Some other familiar hymns written by Robert Lowry, include *Christ Arose, Nothing But The Blood, We're Marching To Zion, All The Way My Savior Leads*, etc.

It was only when Annie Hawks lost her husband in death a few years later did she fully begin to appreciate the beauty of the words of her song. Mrs. Hawks continues, "It was not until years after, when the shadow fell over my way, the shadow of a great loss, that I understood something of the comforting power in the words which I had been permitted to give out to others in my hours of sweet security and peace."

When tragedy strikes our lives, we often find it easy to draw near to one another and to God. When sorrows come upon us, or when troubles fill our days, we seek and find the comfort and nearness of our Savior. We should also feel the same closeness when we are happy, when everything is going our way. Take time to reflect upon the goodness of God. Count your blessings.

Hear, O Lord, and answer me, for I am poor and needy. Guard my life, for I am devoted to you. You are my God; save your servant who trusts in you. Have mercy on me, O Lord, for I call to you all day long. Bring joy to your servant, for to you, O Lord, I lift up my soul. [Psalm 86:1-4]

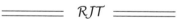

RJT

A Song Is Born

Do not let your hearts be troubled. Trust in God; trust also in me. In my Father's house are many rooms; If it were not so, I would have told you. I am going there to prepare a place for you. And if I go and prepare a place for you, I will come back and take you to be with me. [John 14:1-3]

AN EMPTY MANSION

So often the inspiration for a hymn comes from a single event, a chance remark or some passing conversation. However, this hymn *An Empty Mansion,* was twenty-six years in the making. It was born from the hardships and trials of the Great Depression years.

The story really began in 1911 when two young people met, fell in love, and married. At the age of twenty-two, Beuna Ora Bryant was the oldest single girl in her community and considered by many to be an old maid. The groom, Jess O'Brian Karnes, was also born in 1889. The future looked very promising for this mature newly wed couple.

In 1928, a series of events began to occur which ultimately led to the birth of this song. Jess, a successful homebuilder in Abilene, Texas, lost his lumberyard to a disastrous fire. Like so many others back then, he had no insurance to cover the losses. A few months later the Great Depression set in. Their life's savings and working funds were distributed among three banks, and all three failed before they could remove a penny. By this time Beuna had just given birth to their twelfth child, including two sets of twins. To make matters worse, three of the children were born with a genetic disease know as Frederick's Ataxia, a form of muscular dystrophy. While it did not affect the mind, nor was it considered fatal, one teenage son affected with this disease caught pneumonia and died in 1928.

With the depression in full swing, his business burned to the ground, and no money left to purchase food or shelter, Jess moved his very large family back to the farm. The next few years were filled with the struggle of survival. They worked at sharecropping, picking cotton, or anything just to provide food and a place to sleep. Beuna, a strong well

A Song Is Born

person, never complained about the pain or hardships they suffered. In fact, she also worked to help support the family.

Just when it appeared the worst was over, and the depression would finally end, another series of events began to unfold. In 1937, Beuna's father was hit and killed by a drunk driver as he walked along the sidewalk in Mansfield, Texas. Beuna's mother was so filled with grief and sorrow that she died three months later. With all the events of the past twenty-six years seemingly fresh in her mind, Beuna Ora Karnes sat down one evening and begin to write:

> *Here I labor and toil as I look for a home,*
> *Just an humble abode among men.*
> *While in heaven a mansion is waiting for me*
> *And a gentle voice pleading, "Come In."*

In this beautiful poem, Mrs. Karnes has revealed to us where she obtained her strength. With a strong faith in her Lord, and a confidence that He had a better place prepared for her in heaven, the *"Labor and toiling"* here on earth would end, and there would be a great reunion of family and friends *"near the door of that mansion some day."*

You and I are pressed on every side with the cares and troubles of every day living. It's easy to become burdened down with our daily problems. Our life should have a purpose, a goal, and a reason for living beyond a mere existence in this troubled world. We should be filled with anticipation of the glory of heaven. Keep your eyes and thoughts focused on God. The Psalmist David, whose life also was filled with trials and troubles, wrote: *And I — in righteousness I will see Your face; when I awake, I will be satisfied with seeing your likeness.* [Psalm 17:15]

> *To see His face, this is my goal,*
> *The deepest longing of my soul;*
> *Through storm and stress my path I'll trace*
> *Till satisfied, I see His face!*
>
> Chisholm

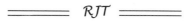

A Song Is Born

It Is No Secret

oth - ers, He'll do for you. With arms wide o - pen, He'll par - don you. It is no se - cret what God can do.

He saved us, not because of righteous things we had done, but because of his mercy. [Titus 3:5]

IT IS NO SECRET

A famous actor, a well-known evangelist, and an old hall clock combined to inspire the writing of this song that has touch the lives of millions throughout the world, and it took only 17 minutes to write. When *It Is No Secret* was introduced in 1949, it set sales records for sheet music in America. The song has been translated into 50 different languages. "It is without a doubt the simplest song I have ever written," said Mr. Hamblen.

Stuart Hamblen came from a very religious family. He was born October 20, 1908, in Kellyville, Texas. His dad was a respected Methodist preacher in and around the west Texas town of Abilene. However, in 1929 Stuart put aside his religious training and struck out for Hollywood to become an actor and singer. As an actor, he appeared in movies with John Wayne, Gene Autry, Roy Rodgers, and others. As a songwriter, he wrote

A Song Is Born

several popular western songs like *Texas Plains* and *Ridin' Old Paint*. For more than 20 years, Stuart Hamblen stayed on top of the popularity charts as a DJ for radio programs such as, "King Cowboy and His Wooly West Review," "Stuart Hamblen and His Lucky Stars," and "Covered Wagon Jubilee."

Through all this popularity, Stuart Hamblen's religious teaching was mostly forgotten, until one day in 1949 when Billy Graham and his evangelistic team came to Los Angeles for a big tent crusade. Stuart met Mr. Graham at a friend's home one evening and later attended some nights of the meeting, not because he wanted to, but because he was trying to appease his wife. "There is somebody in this tent living a double life," Mr. Graham said pointing his finger in Stuart's general direction. This really struck a nerve with Mr. Hamblen and made him very uncomfortable, so  much so that he had to get away. "I stayed away on a hunting trip until I was sure Mr. Graham had left town," he said. "But, when I returned, my Suzy was so excited." "The meeting has been extended for another week." She gleefully exclaimed. The very first night Mr. Hamblen attended the meeting again, he heard Mr. Graham say, "Someone here is a phony." Now Mr. Hamblen was really upset! He argued with his wife and himself all the way home and well into the night. Finally, at about 2:00 a.m., he decided to dedicate his life to Christ. "I'm going to wake up Mr. Graham since he caused all this trouble," Stuart said. They drove downtown to the hotel. "I want you to pray for me," Stuart said as he met Billy Graham at the door. "No," said Mr. Graham. Stuart was shocked, but Mr. Graham continues, "If you mean business with the Lord, there are a number of things in your life you are going to have to give up." Three hours later they finally knelt in prayer.

The conversion was real for Stuart Hamblen. He set about to change his life, to let the Lord be the Master of all things. He lost the radio DJ show because he wouldn't sell beer on his programs. The finance company was about to foreclose on their home. The Hamblens were in a tight spot because of his decision to serve the Lord.

One evening he was visiting his friend and neighbor, John Wayne. Somehow the discussion got around to how people could solve problems with the help of God. "I've heard you've gone 30 days without a drink," John Wayne inquired of Mr. Hamblen. "That's true," he said, making

A Song Is Born

some off-the-cuff statement that it's no secret what God can do in a man's life. Two hours later as the Hamblen's were leaving the party, Mr. Wayne said, "Stuart, that comment you made earlier about it is no secret what God can do, you ought to write a song about that. That's a beautiful thought." As Stuart walked across the lawn to his home that evening, it was nearly midnight. He kept thinking about this challenge his friend John Wayne had given him. "I sat down at the little organ just strumming the keys, waiting for my Suzy to roll her hair. About this time our big old hall clock begins striking the hour of midnight. I got an idea, grabbed a pencil, and started to write:"

> *The chimes of times ring out the news*
> *Another day is through*
> *Someone slipped and fell, was that someone you?*
> *You may have longed for added strength*
> *Your courage to renew*
> *Do not be disheartened for I have news for you.*
> *It is no secret what God can do*
> *What He's done for others, He'll do for you*
> *With arms wide open, He'll pardon you.*
> *It is no secret what God can do.*

"As I finished the song, both words and music, I remember sitting there thinking, without a doubt, it's the simplest song I'd ever written." He could not believe his eyes as he looked at the old clock. It was just 17 minutes past midnight. The Original manuscript of this song is buried in a time capsule in a corner of the Library of Congress, Washington, DC.

God created this world we live in. He delivered the Children of Israel out of bondage. God sent his Son to die and then He raised Him up from the dead to live again. God is all-powerful! It is no secret what God has done throughout history, and it is no secret what He can do in your life! God can help us through any situation, if He is the Master of our lives.

> *I know what it is to be in need, and I know what it is to have plenty. I have learned the secret of being content in any and every situation. I can do everything through Him who gives me strength.* [Philippians 4:12-13]

===== *RJT* =====

A Song Is Born

Because He Lives

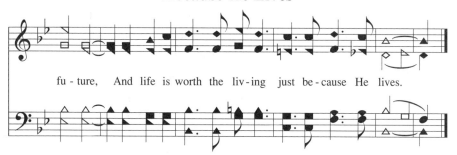

fu - ture, And life is worth the liv-ing just be-cause He lives.

I will not leave you as orphans; I will come to you. Before long, the world will not see me anymore, but you will see me. Because I live, you also will live. [John 14:18-19]

BECAUSE HE LIVES

*T*he very talented husband-wife team of William J. and Gloria Gaither have written more than 500 gospel songs and produced more than 50 recorded albums. Some of their very popular hymns include *He Touched Me, A Hill Called Mount Calvary, The Old Rugged Cross Made the Difference,* and many more. Bill and Gloria were both trained, educated, and eventually became English teachers, but traded their high school classrooms for a full time career in gospel music. They were married in 1962 and have three lovely children.

Bill's interest in gospel music began as a young farm boy from Indiana. Even while earning his degrees in English and music, he continued to have a strong interest in singing. *"We didn't start out to write songs or to make records or to win awards,"* Bill recalls. *"We just had a story to tell."* Gloria adds, *"Our ideas for songs always come from our lives - something we were learning, some new insight, maybe an incident involving our kids."* The song *Because He Lives* was born out of a series of events that occurred just before the birth of their son, Benjy. Bill was recovering from a serious bout of mononucleosis. Both were going through some external family problems, a time when untrue accusations were being hurled at them. *"It was not the best of times,"* Bill recalls.

A Song Is Born

"We wrote *Because He Lives* after a period of time when we had a kind of dry spell and hadn't written any songs for a while," said Bill Gaither. "It was at the end of the 1960s, a time when our country was going through some great turmoil. When the height of the drug culture and the whole 'God is Dead' theory was running wild in our country and also at the peak of the Vietnam War. Gloria was expecting our little son Benjy. I remember at the time we thought, 'brother, this is really a poor time to bring a child into the world.' At times we were even quite discouraged by the whole thing."

In her book *Fully Alive*, Gloria vividly recalls the inspiration for this great song. "It was on New Year's Eve that I sat alone in the darkness and quiet of our living room thinking about the world and our country and Bill's discouragement, and about our baby, yet unborn. Who in their right mind would bring a child into a world like this? And then Benjy came, and so did the lyrics to this song.

> *How sweet to hold our new-born baby*
> *And feel the pride and joy he gives,*
> *But better still the calm assurance*
> *That this child can face uncertain days*
> *Because Christ lives.*

And it gave us courage to say 'Because Christ lives we can face tomorrow' and keep our heads high, and hopefully that could be of some meaning to other people."

Christ came from heaven to walk and talk on this troubled earth. He lived and died for us on the cruel Cross of Calvary, yet I'm thankful that the story of our Savior does not end upon that old rugged cross. I will never forget the feeling I experienced while watching a reenactment of the crucifixion in the Passion Play at Eureka Springs, Arkansas. Death seemed so final until we saw the Empty Tomb and Christ reappearing to his followers.

As Christians, we serve a risen Savior. We can face each new day knowing that Christ conquered sin, death, and the grave. He lives! He's alive and well in heaven and alive in our hearts here on earth. The sweetest words to me are:

A Song Is Born

The angel said to the women, do not be afraid, for I know that you are looking for Jesus who was crucified. He is not here; he has risen, just as he said. Come and see the place where he lay. [Matthew 28:5-6]

═══ RJT ═══

© Copyright 1936, Renewal 1964 by The Rodeheaver Co. (Div. of Word) All Rights Reserved. Used by Permission.

A Song Is Born

> *For now is our salvation nearer than when we believed. The night is far spent, the day is at hand.* [Romans 13:11-12]

BEYOND THE SUNSET

On the beautiful shores of Lake Winona, in Indiana, the Brocks, along with their guests Horace and Grace Burr, watched a very unusual sunset. The sky had been filled with storm clouds that evening in 1936, and the water seemed to be ablaze with the evening sun.

As the foursome gathered around the dinner table, they were still talking about the beauty of the sunset. *"I have never seen a more beautiful sunset,"* said Horace, a remarkable statement since he was totally blind. *"People are always amazed when you talk about seeing,"* commented Virgil. Mr. Burr replied, *"I can see, I see through the eyes of others and I think I often see beyond the sunset."*

The phrase caught Virgil's attention, and he begin to form a few measures while humming a tune. Blanche, his wife, was also caught up in the enthusiasm. She excused herself from the dinner table and began to pick out the melody on the piano. Their guests suggested that they include a verse about the storm clouds, thus verse two: *"No clouds will gather, no storms will threaten, —."* Recalling how Grace had guided Horace during the years of his blindness by the touch of her hand, they wrote verse three; *"A hand will guide me to God the Father, -"* Before the evening meal was complete, the tune and all four verses had been written. Together they sang the new song.

In the fall of 1988, Barbara and I drove through Winona, Indiana, and visited the Winona Lake Cemetery. A very large stone monument has been erected for Virgil and Blanche, with the complete words and music to their popular hymn *Beyond the Sunset* inscribed on the marker. While we sat looking out over Lake Winona, we were blessed with a beautiful sunset on the same lake that inspired this fine gospel hymn, and we were reminded of the words of Paul. *"For now we see through a glass darkly, but then face to face: now I know in part; but then shall I know, even as also I am known."*

A Song Is Born

We have never seen what is beyond this life, but God has drawn us a picture in His word. While we behold the wonders of God's creation, let's learn to look beyond the present, toward a new and wonderful life with Him.

And do this, understanding the present time. The hour has come for you to wake up from your slumber, because our salvation is nearer now than when we first believed. The night is nearly over; the day is almost here. So let us put aside the deeds of darkness and put on the armor of light. [Romans 13:11-12]

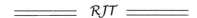

RJT

© Copyright 1911

A Song Is Born

> *Let us draw nearer to God with a sincere heart in full assurance,* — [Hebrews 10:22]

Closer To Thee

Singing songs of rich, spiritual meaning gives encouragement, joy, peace, and happiness to the Christian. Let us continue to press forward, to love life and see good days, love God and sing his praise." These excellent words of exhortation came from Austin Taylor, a tireless servant of God.

Brother Taylor was born 1881 in Kentucky of German immigrants, but began his long distinguished career in Sherman, Texas, in 1899. There, at the age of eighteen, he taught his first singing school. Seventy-three years later, in 1972 in Sabinal, Texas, at the age of ninety-one, he taught his last. Teaching singing schools, writing songs, editing songbooks, and leading singing for gospel meetings became his life's work and love. At one time, he could remember the names of 175 preachers for whom he led the singing in revivals throughout eleven states. Included among that number were some of the giants of God's servants, such as, Foy E. Wallace, Jr., Horace Busby, and General R. M. Gano just to name a few. Brother Gano was a General during the Civil War. He baptized about 1500 people mostly from meetings conducted in North Texas.

Austin Taylor recalls: *"The largest crowd I ever led in singing was in Oklahoma, City. There were more than 5000 people present every night. I nearly cracked my voice leading them."* His love and enthusiasm for the singing of God's praises was always present. Listen to some of his remarks about songs. *"In going about over the country associated with strong, able evangelists, I have witnessed thousands of people surrender to Christ and make the start to heaven while I sang of God, Christ, and his love. This experience has been worth more to me than heaps of gold."*

In 1911, Austin Taylor was appointed Music Editor for the Firm Foundation Publishing Company, a position he maintained for forty-five years. In his lifetime, he was responsible for the publication of at least fifty hymnbooks. The most popular hymnal, Gospel Songs Number

Two, was published in 1914. It sold one million copies over a fifteen-year period. All together, songbooks edited or published by Brother Taylor sold more than three million copies. At the age of 65 when most would think of retirement, Brother Taylor embarked on a new adventure. He, along with Edgar Furr and Holland Boring Sr., agreed to help establish the Texas Normal Singing School in Sabinal, Texas. He taught music and songwriting at the school for 27 years, influencing the lives of more than 1200 song leaders.

"There is no legal excuse for any of us to be idle," **Mr. Taylor once said**, and he sure practiced what he preached. Along with a full time career of song leading, editing, and music teaching, he was a servant of the people. Austin Taylor and his wife, Augusta, moved to Uvalde, Texas, in 1919 and remained there until his death in 1973. He served as an Elder of the Church of Christ in Uvalde for twenty-five years. He also served that city as Judge and did some work for the Federal Government as a land adjuster.

Through his songs and from his effective song leading, Brother Taylor has inspired many to obey the Master's call. Songs like *Closer To Thee, Jesus Keep Me Pure And Holy* and *Do All In The Name Of The Lord* are just a few of the more than two hundred songs written by Austin Taylor. Thousands have been taught how to sing, to write songs, and how to lead singing through his tireless efforts. He had a great love for young people. As a judge he once remarked, *"I never saw one (young person) I did not regard as being better than the Judge. We old heads are the ones that need bumping. Young people need help, kindness, teaching, protection, and a good example. —"*

One day Austin Taylor was having trouble completing one of his songs. It seems he had this melody and words that he liked, but just could not settle on the harmony. The wastebasket was literally filled with discarded arrangements. Nothing seemed to satisfy him. A friend came by and inquired what he might be working on. After explaining his dilemma, the visitor reached into the wastebasket, pulled out a copy, and asked *"what's wrong with this one? I like it!"* The arrangement retrieved from the wastebasket that day in 1911, is the same we use today in the hymn *Closer To Thee*.

How do we draw closer to Christ? We draw closer to Christ through the reading of God's Word, and through prayer. In His Word we learn

A Song Is Born

how Christ lived, how he reacted to adversity, how he cared for you and me so much that he died on Calvary. What do we gain from this nearness? The closer we live to Christ, the happier we are. In His great teachings, we learn how to love and care for one another and how to live in harmony with each other. The Hebrew writer put it this way, *Let us draw nearer to God with a sincere heart in full assurance,* — [Hebrews 10:22]

The righteous cry out, and the Lord hears them; He delivers them from all their troubles. The Lord is close to the broken hearted and saves those who are crushed in spirit. A righteous man may have many troubles, but the Lord delivers him from them all. [Psalm 34:17-19

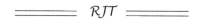

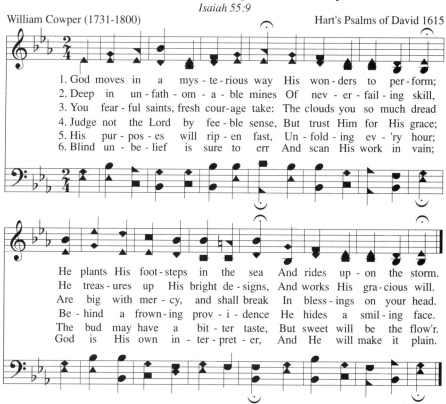

Words first appeared in John Newton's Twenty-Six Letters on Religious Subjects, 1774;
Tune first appeared anonymously in the Supplement to the New Version of the Psalms, 6th edition 1708

As the heavens are higher than the earth, so are my ways higher than your ways... [Isaiah 55:9]

GOD MOVES IN A MYSTERIOUS WAY

William Cowper (pronounced Kooper) was born in England in 1731. The death of his mother when he was only six years old had a profound effect upon his life. Cowper suffered from fear and rejection most all of his life. Each personal setback seem to deepen his periods of despondency, sometimes lasting up to a year and one-half. As a boy, William spent many years in boarding schools, at times with much older boys who severely ridiculed and criticized this emotionally unstable youth. He fell in love with his cousin, Theodra Cowper, only to have his father forbid the marriage. About the same time, Cowper completed his studies to become a lawyer, but the fear of standing before the bar for examination added to his despair. He never completed the examination!

William's emotional behavior became a life of mental illness. He had deep inclinations to commit suicide. Four times Mr. Cowper was committed to an insane asylum. He spent the last twenty-five years convinced that God *"had it in for him."* Yet, remarkably his great hymn poems show little trace of this emotional unstable side of William Cowper.

It is believed that the hymn, *God Moves in a Mysterious Way,* was written after one of these periods of deep depression. In October 1773, William Cowper had determined to end his life by throwing himself into a river. He ordered the carriage driver to take him to the riverbank. Because of a dense fog, the driver could not find the river. Some have suggested that the driver purposely wandered around, knowing the intentions of Mr. Cowper. While riding William went to sleep, and the driver returned him to his home.

Realizing his close brush with death, he remarked to the carriage driver, *"God be thanked for having overruled my foolish designs."* With this experience still fresh in his mind, William Cowper wrote, *God Moves in a Mysterious Way.*

A Song Is Born

The workings of God remain a mystery to us. We do not know how he works, we just know he does work in and for us.

Jesus replied, "You do not realize now what I am doing, but later you will understand." [John 13:7]

— RJT —

Words First appeared in *Songs of Devotion*, Biglow and Main, 1870
Tune in pamphlet *Forest Songs for Chatauqua Assemblies*, Biglow and Main, 1888

A Song Is Born

He said to them, "Go into all the world and preach the good news to all creation. Whoever believes and is baptized will be saved, but whoever does not believe will be condemned." [Mark 16:15-16]

CHRIST FOR THE WORLD WE SING

*T*he theme for the YMCA convention in Cleveland, Ohio, in 1869 was *"Christ for the world and the world for Christ,"* "Who makes up slogans?" the young man insisted. "Where do they come from? I still want to know who thought up this slogan." Someone replied with some lightheartedness, *"The committee, I think."* Another chimed in "Maybe the grandson of the man who invented the slogan *'Remember the Alamo'* or a cousin to the politician who went to the White House on the slogan *'Tippecanoe and Tyler too'*."

As several sat around outside the convention hall, pondering the slogan, someone ask Samuel Wolcott, *"Do you think the people of the world want Christ as much as we think they ought to?"* Wolcott thought for a moment, then answered: *"God sent Christ because he knew we needed Him, whether we knew it or not. We go into the world to teach them because we know they need Him, whether they realize it or not."*

Someone suggested to Mr. Wolcott that the slogan *"Christ for the world and the world for Christ"* would make a good hymn and that he was the one who could create it. Samuel had written only one other hymn before this night, outlining it much like a sermon. He replied, "I wouldn't know where to start except to say *'Christ for the world we sing'*."

Samuel Wolcott, who had never written so much as a poem prior to his 56th birthday, was now forming lines with a spontaneity that surprised himself and the others. Phrases formed in his mind as friends wrote down all four stanzas. Thus, a hymn was born. Before Samuel's death 17 years later, he was to have written more than 200 hymns.

Christ is *for* this World, and the World *must be for* Christ, whether they realize it or not, and this will only happen through us. We are his eyes, ears, feet, and spokesman as expressed in stanza three *"With us the work to share, — with us the cross to bear, for Christ our Lord."*

A Song Is Born

Through this song we proclaim our fervent prayer to take the world for Christ. If we are to succeed, two things must happen. Christ must be seen in us, both in word and deed, and we must get busy telling the world about Christ. If ever the world needed the God of love and peace, it's now when so many are serving a god of hate and destruction!

We are therefore Christ's ambassadors, as though God were making his appeal through us. We implore you on Christ's behalf: Be reconciled to God. [2 Corinthians 5:20]

═══ RJT ═══

Jesus, Savior, Pilot Me
Luke 8:25

Edward Hopper　　　　　　　　　　　　　　　　　　**PILOT**
　　　　　　　　　　　　　　　　　　　　　　　John E. Gould

1. Je - sus Sav - ior, pi - lot me O - ver life's tem - pest - uous sea;
2. As a moth - er stills her child, Thou canst hush the o - cean wild;
3. When at last I near the shore, And the fear - ful break - ers roar

Un - known waves be - fore me roll, Hid - ing rock and treach - erous shoal;
Bois - t'rous waves o - bey Thy will When Thou say'st to them, "Be still!"
"Twixt me and the peace - ful rest, Then while lean - ing on Thy breast,

Chart and com - pass came from Thee. Je - sus, Sav - ior, pi - lot me.
Won - drous Sov - reign of the sea, Je - sus, Sav - ior pi - lot me.
May I hear Thee say to me, "Fear not, I will pi - lot thee!"

First appeared in The Sailor's Magazine, Vol. 43, March 3, 1871.

A Song Is Born

Thou wilt show me the path of life. In Thy presence is fullness of joy: at Thy right hand there are pleasures for evermore. [Psalm 16:11]

JESUS, SAVIOR, PILOT ME

Our Lord taught many profound spiritual truths with earthly associations. He often spoke of Christians as soldiers, pilgrims, shepherds, sheep, precious jewels, and many other relationships in life that are meaningful to us. Likewise, many of our fine hymns have been written with the same symbolic imagery that makes them more readily understood. To discard all these hymns as old, useless, out-of-date, not relevant in today's hi-tech world, could hurt our chances of understanding Christ' message in the first century. A better solution is to study the old hymns and develop a better understanding of the imagery taught within, better equipping us to understand the biblical message.

Jesus, Savior, Pilot Me was written especially for sailors in a language they knew well -- charts, compasses, and the absolute need for a competent pilot to guide their crafts over the tempestuous seas.

An American Presbyterian minister named Edward Hopper wrote this hymn, and it was first published in the year 1871. Hopper was born in New York City on February 17, 1818. Following his graduation from Union Theological Seminary in 1842, Hopper served two Presbyterian churches in the New York area before he began the most fruitful phase of his ministry in 1870, serving a small church in the New York harbor area known as the **Church of Sea and Land**. For the next 18 years, he ministered effectively to the many sailors who made their way to and from their ships.

It was while ministering at his sailors' mission in New York City that Edward Hopper wrote this hymn text especially for the spiritual needs of these seafaring men. The theme of this hymn text was suggested by the gospel account recorded in Matthew 8:23-27, where Jesus calmed the raging sea of Galilee and, in so doing, quieted the fears of His disciples.

A Song Is Born

> *And when He was entered into a ship, His disciples followed Him. And, behold, there arose a great tempest in the sea, insomuch that the ship was covered with the waves; but He was asleep. And His disciples came to Him, and awoke Him, saying, "Lord, save us; we perish. And He saith unto them, "Why are Ye fearful, O Ye of little faith?" Then He arose and rebuked the winds and the sea; and there was a great calm. But the men marveled saying, "What manner of man is this, that even the winds and the sea obey Him?"*

Mr. Hopper wrote the hymn anonymously as he did all of his works, and for some time no one ever knew that the minister for the sailors was also the author of the sailors' favorite hymn. This was typical of Hopper's humble, gentle spirit in all that he did for God.

In 1880, a special anniversary celebration for the Seamen's Friend Society was held in New York City, and Edward Hopper was asked to write a new hymn for that occasion. Instead, he brought and read *"Jesus, Savior, Pilot Me"* which had already become quite widely known in its inclusion in various hymnal publications. For the first time the secret of Hopper's authorship of this hymn text became known.

Though this is the only hymn text that Edward Hopper has written that is still in common usage, it can be said of him as it can of many other hymn writers: *"Happy is the man who can produce one song which the world will keep on singing after its author shall have passed away."*

Originally Hopper's text included six stanzas, but hymnals today make use of only the first, the fifth, and sixth verses from the poem. The omitted verses are:

> *When the Apostles' fragile bark*
> *struggled with the billows dark,*
> *On the stormy Galilee,*
> *Thou didst walk upon the sea;*
> *And when they beheld Thy form,*
> *Safe they glided through the storm.*

> *Through the sea he smooth and bright,*
> *sparkling with the stars of night,*
> *And my ship's path be ablaze*
> *With the light of halcyon days,*
> *Still I know my need of Thee:*
> *Jesus, Savior, pilot me.*

A Song Is Born

When the darkling heavens frown,
And the wrathful winds come down,
And the fierce waves, tossed on high,
Lash themsleves against the sky,
Jesus, Savior, pilot me
Over life's tempestuous sea.

It was on April 23, 1888, that Edward Hopper settled back in his chair in his study and began outlining a new poem. For many years he had suffered with a weak heart and on this night the struggle would end. When they found him the next morning, the pencil was still in his hand and a piece of paper with the outline of a new poem lay nearby. No author credits were listed, as was his practice, but inscribed on top was the title *"Heaven."* Now, Edward Hopper's prayer expressed in the third stanza of his own hymn had its fulfillment: *"When at last I near the shore, - May I hear Thee say to me, "Fear not, I will pilot Thee."*

Nearly 100 years earlier, another noted poet expressed similar imagery between our life and life the on the high seas.

The billows swell, the winds are high,
Clouds overcast my wintry sky;
Out of the depths to Thee I call,
My fears are great, my strength is small.

O Lord, the pilot's part perform,
And guide and guard me through the storm:
Defend me from each threatening ill.
Control the waves, say, 'Peace, be still'
    William Cowper 1731 - 1800

RJT

A Song Is Born

Beautiful Star of Bethlehem

We saw His star in the east [Matthew 2:2]

BEAUTIFUL STAR OF BETHLEHEM

*I*t was the fall of 1994 – Barbara and I traveled to Diana, Tennessee, to attend a gospel singing. We had heard about the *"Diana Singing"* for several years and I wanted to experience this much talked about event firsthand. Diana, Tennessee, is a small community with 15 or 20 homes, 2 or 3 churches, and not much else. But when this first Friday evening in September came around, a crowd of nearly 3000 singers had assembled. People were seated everywhere. An open-air pavilion accommodated about 2500 and the rest gathered around outside. We began singing at 7 p.m. By midnight I was exhausted and had to call it quits, but they continued until 2 a.m. It's a great singing and one that everyone should experience. When 3000 voices blend together in pure acappella harmony, you can feel the power of music move you closer to God.

We had arrived in Diana a day early, on Thursday, and since the little Church of Christ there was having a meeting, we attended that evening. We met another couple, Lawrence and Dot Taylor, who were also visiting. Since we both had the same last name, it was easy to strike up a conversation. We eventually got around to asking what each did for a living. When I mentioned that I researched hymns and their writers, Lawrence said, *"My Grandfather on my mother's side wrote a song, called Beautiful Star of Bethlehem."* We had a great visit and later he sent me the story about this popular Christmas Carol.

"Robert Fisher Boyce was a farmer from Rutherford County, Tennessee," said Franklin Boyce, the youngest of three Boyce children. "My dad wrote the song in the summer months while seated on a milking stool in the hallway of the barn. Father initially tried to write his song in our farmhouse when we were little children, but the noise of the household filled with little children was distracting. That's when he took his pencil and paper, walked across the road to the barn and sat down on his milking stool, and the song began to flow. It took several days to complete. My father wrote several songs, but this was the only song he ever had published."

Consequently, we have a song whose words and music were born in a barn that houses animals, telling the story about the Christ Child, who also was born in a barn, thus from barn to barn comes this inspiring Christmas Hymn. The Judd's, a Mother-daughter Country singing duet, popularized this song. I remember hearing it for the first time when the Judd's performed it live on one of Bob Hope's TV specials.

In 1994, Naomi Judd had been able to track down Lawrence Taylor, the couple we met in Diana, and wrote him a sweet letter about his grandfather's song.

"Dear Taylor Family: The Christmas of 1977 was the most memorable one my daughters Wynonna and Ashley and I have ever known. Living on a hilltop in rural Kentucky, we had only handmade gifts to give each other, but we had the warmth and security of our love. Our musical friend, Songbird, taught twelve-year-old Wynonna and me *Beautiful Star of Bethlehem*. It's not only our favorite all-time carol, but a reminder of the most magical time in our lives. Music helps us keep memories alive. Love and Blessings, Naomi Judd."

Music does help us keep memories alive! There is tremendous power in music! Whatever the nature of the star, or the identity of the Magi, just remember that they traveled thousands of miles in search of a king, and they found him. You and I must pursue the Savior with the same perseverance.

After Jesus was born in Bethlehem in Judea, during the time of King Herod, Magi from the east came to Jerusalem and asked, "Where is the one who has been born king of the Jews? We saw his star in the east and have come to worship him." [Matthew 2:1-2]

═══ RJT ═══

Son, go work today in my vineyard. [Matthew 21:28]

CALL FOR WORKERS

John Henry Sheppard was inspired by the words of the parable of the two sons in Matthew 21:28 to write his once very popular song, *"Call For Workers."* in 1906. Jesus was a great storyteller! He used each story to teach many lessons. We've understood this parable to teach that one son refused, but repented and did his father's work, while the other kept promising but never obeyed. No doubt this is a parallel between how the Gentiles and the Jews responded to God's call – yet the story also teaches that everyone is expected to work in the Fathers Vineyard. Our religion must be active, not passive. God has always intended for his children to work in his Kingdom. The choice to be a Christian, once made, reflects in every aspect of our lives, including economic, social, moral, and spiritual. John Henry Sheppard's song *Call for Workers,* reminds us of our task here on earth.

> "In my family many individuals have sought the will of their Father, God, and have committed themselves to toiling in this field." said Cheryl Hutson, a great-granddaughter of J. H. Sheppard. "Because of their love and faith in God, my relatives have used their talents in music, speech, and deeds to glorify the Lord. The church has affected my family economically, socially, and religiously for at least three generations; it has and will remain the center of our lives."

Cheryl's father, Cecil Alton Hutson, Sr., is a minister for the Katy Church of Christ. Her grandfather, Joseph Bernard Hutson, served many years as an elder. Her brother, Cecil Hutson, Jr., has served as a youth minister for several congregations. But the one who began this heritage of service was the author of this song, *"Call for Workers,"* her great-grandfather, J. H. Sheppard.

He was born John Henry Sheppard in Monroe, Louisiana, October 19, 1868, just three years after the Civil War ended. Early childhood was difficult for John. His mother died when he was eight, and his father died six years later making it necessary for him to live with an

Aunt near Waco, Texas. With less than five months of formal schooling, Mr. Sheppard taught himself to read and write, and he also learned the art of music. John Henry grew up to be a tall, gruff looking character, with a mustache and only one eye, perhaps mirroring the hard times in which he lived. He lost the eye in an accident before he met and married Fannie Ethel Coyel of Rosenthal, Texas, in 1898. They had five children, Mattie Sue, Frank, Henry Cecil, Evie Leah Engelke, and Francis Lucile Sweeten. *"His rough exterior may have been a reflection of the hard lives in which the people of his era were forced to try and find happiness,"* said one of his daughters. *"He was stern and strict with a personality that seemed to match his appearance."*

John Henry lived in a time and place filled with dynamic singers and music teachers. Men such as F. L. Eiland, J. B. Franklin, J. W. Ferrill, and J. E. Thomas all lived within a forty-mile radius of his modest farm on the Brazos river. Two nearby influential music companies, The Trio Music Company and The Quartet Music Company, had their beginning and flourished during this time period. It's easy to see how Mr. Sheppard was influenced to sing, write, and teach music. As a young man, he traveled a lot, often gone for three or four months at a time teaching singing schools. During these years as a singing instructor, he learned the truth about Jesus and was converted. He never worked full time as a minister, but often preached for small congregations in central Texas cities like Waco, Mart, Marlin, Thorton, Lott, Tyson, and Goldson.

John Henry's income came from various occupations. In addition to teaching singing schools, he farmed. Up until the 1920s, they lived on a farm along the Brazos River, in a community called Chalk Bluff located about eight miles east of Waco. When they moved into town (Waco), he owned and operated a wood yard, collecting and selling firewood. The Sheppard's were active members of the Columbus Avenue Church of Christ in Waco for many years. Mr. Sheppard spent the last few years of his life in or near Houston with his children, and attended the Wayside and Sherman Church of Christ. He died in the summer of 1937, and is buried in Pearland, Texas. I do not remember John Henry Sheppard, but I do remember his sons, Frank and Henry Cecil (known as Bunk). When I was very young, we were members of the Lyons and Majestic Church of Christ where Frank and Bunk Sheppard were also members. Both Frank and Bunk owned separate automotive repair shops in East

A Song Is Born

Houston. I can remember spending summers helping dad, who worked for Bunk Sheppard in his car repair shop on Broadway Avenue, near the Houston Ship Channel.

"In the vineyard of the Lord, There is work for all to do;
Will you go and work today, With a purpose strong and true?"

"This verse from one of great-grandfather's song, *Call for Workers,* has challenged members of my family since 1906 when it was written," said Cheryl Hutson. "As the song suggested, we have tried to lift the banner high so the lost can see the way." For three generations this family has faithfully *"heeded the call"* to serve the Lord. Even though written more than 90 years ago, the challenge of John Henry Sheppard's song remains viable for every Christian today.

If ever there was a time in our history when we need to accept the mission of Matthew 21, it's now. Growing up in the 1950s and 1960s, people spoke freely and often of their belief in God. I never thought I would live to see the day when just saying *"I believe the Bible is the infallible word of God"* would be considered "Politically Incorrect." A current TV program by that name, posed this very question to four panelists. Only one expressed an affirmative answer of their belief in the Bible, and he was severally ridiculed for that belief. There was a time we could assume our friends believed in Jesus, and the only problems were our differing views as to how to serve Him. Today, it takes strong courage just to express our belief in Jesus. *"Let your eyes see the need of workers today."*

Therefore go and make disciples of all nations, baptizing them in the name of the Father and of the Son and of the Holy Spirit, teaching them to obey everything I have commanded you. [Matthew 28:19-20]

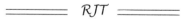

A Song Is Born

> *He who goes out weeping, carrying seed to sow, will return with songs of joy, carrying sheaves with him.* [Psalm 126:6]

BRINGING IN THE SHEAVES

Knowles Shaw wrote *Bringing In The Sheaves*, both words and music in memory of a very close and dear friend, A. D. Fillmore. A touching reference to his death can clearly be seen in the second verse: *"By and by the harvest, and our labor ended, we shall come rejoicing, Bringing in the sheaves."* However, sometimes the real story of a hymn is found in the life of the author. Such is the case with *Bringing in the Sheaves*. Knowles Shaw was born in 1834, in Butler County, Ohio. When he was only weeks old, the family moved to Rush County, Indiana, where he spent most of his life.

One day, when Knowles was nearly 13, his father, Albin Shaw, felt the end of his life was near. He called the young boy to his bedside to give him his parting words, *"My son, be good to your mother and prepare to meet your God."* His last gift to Knowles was a violin, a legacy that soon become a source of income to fulfill his father's first request *"Be good to your mother,"* but would prove to be a hindrance toward the second request, *"prepare to meet your God."* His stepfather, James Whitinger, Sr., trained and encouraged him to play the violin. Knowles talent was soon recognized, and he received many invitations to play at social gatherings.

One of the greatest evils of his time was alcohol. Whiskey seemed a necessity for every function. By the age of 18, this tall, somewhat awkward but kind-hearted, good-tempered, and industrious young man was the life of every social gathering, especially the young people. Hundreds would dance and drink to his music.

Little did Knowles Shaw know or expect the sudden dramatic change that was about to take place in his life. One night, he was playing the violin for a group of about 40 dancers. The last words of his father kept coming to his mind, *"prepare to meet your God."* After a brief intermission, the call came to "strike up the band." To the astonishment of all, Knowles Shaw responded *"I can not play and will never do so for another dance."* It was a turning point in his life.

He began to attend church, and on September 13, 1852, at the age of 18, he was converted, baptized by elder George Thomas in near-by Mud Creek. The next few years passed with little to show the new direction his life would take, but his excellent memory, quick and lively wit, plus his thirst for knowledge all served to prepare Knowles for what was yet to come.

Four years later, he was asked to give a talk at the worship service. This was another great turning point in his life. Now at the age of 24, with less confidence in his own natural abilities than at any other time, there began to awaken within him an unknown power to move and affect people. Though with little formal education, he was now called upon to preach and to teach in public schools. His musical talents once again begin to surface, as he would sing solos and direct the congregation in singing. Knowles quickly became known as *"The Singing Evangelist."*

Knowles was never a conventional preacher, either in dress, mannerism, habits, or conversation. He lived among the people whom he taught. He went to them, where they worked, always in conversation, teaching and exhorting, but never delaying their work. He would chip in and help with the task, no matter what it was. If the clock was broken, he would fix it. If the sewing machine would not work properly, he would repair it. He met the people where they were in life. The preaching style of Knowles did not conform to any standard. He defied all rules. His transitions from logic to rhetoric, serious to humorous, or tragedy to comedy were sudden and frequent. If the audience seemed restless, he would stop preaching and tell a story, or walk out into the crowd, stand upon a bench and sing a song. The chief charm of his singing ability was his distinct enunciation. Every word was distinctly heard, though it be a whisper. He was a singer equal to other notable gospel singers of his day, such as Ira Sankey and Philip Bliss. His custom was to begin singing for about 30 minutes, usually while the people gathered. Then he would read scripture, make comments, have prayer and then preach for an hour or more. He would average two sermons per day, and many times preach three or four each day.

Knowles Shaw was not without his faults, often criticized for being eccentric and peculiar. Others explained that *"He reasons like Paul, was as bold as Peter, and as tender as John."* He never claimed to be a

A Song Is Born

finished orator, but he wielded a strange power over his audiences. They would come from all walks of life to listen. It made no difference about their current religious beliefs, social standing, or that they hadn't been inside a church building since their youth.

After completing a very successful five-week meeting at the Commerce Street Christian Church in Dallas, Texas, on June 6, 1879, Knowles set out to make an unscheduled trip to McKinney, Texas, for a meeting. That night there were tremendous rains, weakening the roadbed. A broken rail near Wilson Creek just south of McKinney, Texas, caused the train to go over the embankment, injuring 28 and killing one. That one casualty was Knowles Shaw, a tragic end to a powerful servant of God. On board was Kirk Baxter, a fellow minister and traveling companion, who recalls what became the last words of Mr. Shaw as he said: *"Oh, it is a grand thing to rally people to the Cross of Christ."*

In his 21 years of service to our Master and at the young age of 45, Knowles Shaw had preached the gospel to hundreds of thousands of people. He converted and baptized 11,400 by his own record, though some give the number as 20,000. Among the other 118 songs he wrote, we still sing *I Am The Vine, Tarry With Me*, and *We Saw Thee Not When Thou Didst Come*. His unwavering faith and strong will power served him well.

Bringing In The Sheaves encourages us to be busy about our Master's work, spreading His goodness in word and deed, preparing for the harvest, that is, the end of time when the Lord shall claim his own. It has been said that, "People don't care how much you know until they know how much you care." The best way to preach the word today is the same way Mr. Shaw did years ago. Show someone you care by helping him or her with their needs, while at the same time teaching them about Christ.

The one who sowed the good seed is the Son of Man. The field is the world, and the good seed stands for the sons of the kingdom. The weeds are the sons of the evil one, and the enemy who sows them is the devil; the harvest is the end of the world; and the reapers are the angels. [Matthew 13:37-39]

═══ *RJT* ═══

A Song Is Born

For here we do not have an enduring city, but we are looking for the city that is to come. [Hebrews 13:14]

Sweet By and By

Sanford Bennett was born June 21, 1836, in Eden New York, but moved at an early age to Elkhorn, Wisconsin, where he became the Associate Editor of the local paper. After returning from the Civil War in 1865, he became the owner of a drugstore, and there began his study of medicine. Joseph Webster was born March 22, 1819, in Manchester, New York. He studied music in New Hampshire and Boston before spending several years teaching in New York and Connecticut. He moved to Elkhorn shortly before the Civil War broke out. These two men developed a friendship and at times a partnership in the writing of songs. Joseph Webster was the musician and Sanford Bennett became the verse writer. They often met in Bennett's drugstore around the old stove for friendly discussions.

Webster, like so many other artists even today, was temperamental and often gloomy, subject to periods of depression. He was often prone to look upon the dark side of everything. He had what we often call "his off days." When Mr. Webster was in one of these periods of melancholy, it was Sanford Bennett's habit to give him a "dose" of new verses, and cure his depression by putting him to work creating the music. Bennett tells this story of one quiet Fall-Winter afternoon in Elkhorn, Wisconsin, 1867:

"He came into my place of business, walked down to the stove, and turned his back on me without speaking. I was at my desk writing. Turning to him I said, *"Webster, what is the matter now?"* Joseph Webster began to pour out all his aches, pains, disappointments, and frustrations. Bennett just listened. "It's no matter," Webster replied after a while, *"It will be all right by and by."* "The idea came to me like a flash of sunlight," said Mr. Bennett. *"The Sweet By and By!* Why would not that make a good hymn? Turning to my desk, I penned the words as fast as I could write. I handed the words to Webster. As he read, his eyes kindled, and stepping to the desk, he began writing the notes. He picked up his violin and began playing the melody, as he continued to write the

A Song Is Born

notes. By that time, two other friends who could sing came into the store. It was not over thirty minutes from the time I took my pen to write the words before the four of us were singing the hymn, *Sweet By and By.*

So it goes that a hymn, born in a drugstore as a prescription for the blues, is still used more than 120 years later. The home where Joseph Webster lived in Elkhorn, Wisconsin, is still standing and available for visits. The violin he used to develop this great gospel hymn is also on display.

Have you ever had the blues? Have you ever felt melancholy, filled with sadness or depression? By looking at how this song was developed, it gives us a clue at how to cure the blues. Stay busy, put a song in your heart as you work for the Lord, and keep your eyes focused on Heaven.

Do not let your hearts be troubled. Trust in God; trust also in me. In my Father's house are many rooms; if it were not so, I would have told you. I am going there to prepare a place for you. And if I go and prepare a place for you, I will come back and take you to be with me that you also may be where I am. You know the way to the place where I am going. [John 14:1-3]

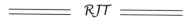

RJT

A Song Is Born

Someone To Care

tears from your eyes, You're His child and He cares for you.

My command is this: Love each other as I have loved you.
[John 15:12]

SOMEONE TO CARE

James (Jimmie) Houston Davis was born in Quitman, Louisiana, in 1899. He grew up on a farm, sharing in the duties of a sharecropper. Through hard work and determination, Mr. Davis graduated from L.S.U., and went on to obtain Masters and Doctorate degrees. In the late 1930s he entered politics, first becoming the Commissioner of Louisiana 1938-42, and later serving two terms as Governor of Louisiana in 1944-48 and again in 1960-64. His first love has been, and still is, the singing of gospel songs. Through the years, Jimmie has written an estimated 800 songs, and recorded many of them on the Decca label. Up until his death November 5, 2000, at the age of 101, he continued to sing and record under his own label, the Jimmie Davis Music Company, of Baton Rouge, Louisiana.

In 1990, Mr. Davis graciously related to me the following events that prompted the writing of his beautiful song, *Someone To Care*.

"At this particular time in life (1938), I was preparing to run for state office. In laying the ground work, I had seen so many people, been so many places day and night, every day for months, and I felt very much what we sometimes call "down in the dumps," whatever that is. I guess perhaps that I was just tired. I said to a couple of friends of mine, Lindsay Coit and Lamar Loe, I would like to get into some place for a week, back in the woods where I wouldn't see anybody or hear an airplane fly over, nor a train whistle. They said to me, 'If that is what you want, we have got the place for you.'

"Well, let's go," I said. I packed my little bag; we got in a pickup truck and rode for quite a few miles, until we couldn't go any further in the truck. So, we saddled three horses and kept going — going, the woods got thicker and thicker and the miles got longer and longer, when we finally came up on an old house, perhaps built 100 years ago, maybe more. This may had been a farm at one time, but it was nothing more than woods when we got there. They used it for a hunting lodge where you had several kinds of game, including deer, bear, wolves, foxes, — and whatever. I took with me some canned goods, crackers and whatnot and stayed there five days and nights by myself. For a light at night, I had an old kerosene lamp.

When you get in a place like that, just you and the Lord and wild game, you have time to think about a lot of things - - where you have been, the things you have done and where you are going when it is all over, and sometimes wondering who cares. And there I came up with the idea of *Someone To Care.* "

Jimmy Davis was a remarkable man! Not only did he serve two terms as Governor, he wrote songs, performed in concerts, preached, and his career even included staring in movies. There was even a movie about his life, *Louisiana: the Jimmie Davis Story* where he played himself. Jimmie's wife Alvern died of cancer during his second term as Governor. Several years later, in 1969, he married Anna "Carter" Gordan of the famous Chuck Wagon Gang. This man, who jokingly said "I am the only Gospel Singer in America that has lived in three centuries: the 18th, 19[th,] and 20th, served his state and his country." He had influence from the White House to the Court House. He has mixed with the rich and famous, having been born poor, having lived in a two-room cabin with 14 family members, and having lived in the Governor's mansion, he experienced life from both sides of the tracks and was loved by all.

An interesting note, one of the most popular jingles we as parents have sung to our children for years was written by Jimmy Davis in 1942;

You are my sunshine, my only sunshine
You make me happy when skies are gray
You'll never know dear how much I love you

Please don't take my sunshine away.

To feel lonely, does not necessarily mean we are alone. It is very easy to be lonely in a crowd. Sometimes loneliness comes from the absence of a meaningful relationship.

"No man is an island to himself." We need to love and to be loved. We must have the love and companionship of others in order to grow and develop. Yet, paradoxically, life is a series of separations. We grow up, leave home, and go off to school, marry, have children, change jobs, move to another town, and experience the death of loved ones. This necessitates the development of new friends; constantly requiring us to seek out those who really care. We need always to build warm and lasting fellowships with those of like faith, thereby averting loneliness. But the real friend is Christ. It makes no difference where we move, how often we change jobs, etc., if Christ is our friend, how can I (we) be lonely?

Above anything else in life or death, develop a relationship with Christ now! Then show kindness and love to the Saints!

Be devoted to one another in brotherly love. Honor one another above yourselves. Never be lacking in zeal, but keep your spiritual fervor, serving the Lord. — Rejoice with those who rejoice; mourn with those who mourn. Live in harmony with one another —. [Romans 12:10-12]

RJT

A Song Is Born

But thanks be to God! He gives us the victory through our Lord Jesus Christ. Therefore, my dear brothers, stand firm. Let nothing move you. Always give yourselves fully to the work of the Lord, because you know that your labor in the Lord is not in vain. [1 Corinthians 15:57-58]

STAND UP, STAND UP FOR JESUS

George Duffield, Jr. wrote the words to this hymn, but the story really develops around another minister, Dudley Atkins Tyng. Mr. Tyng was a spirited, outspoken young preacher whose bold and straightforward condemnation of sin disturbed the conservative members of the congregation in Philadelphia where he preached. He believed that all men and women were sinners who needed to repent and be converted. At this time in our country (1856), the anti-slavery sentiment was growing. He was firmly convinced that slavery was wrong and could not be practiced by Christians, a feeling he expressed many times from the pulpit.

Mr. Dudley would often speak at the noonday YMCA lectures. Back then, the YMCA was more than a health club. It was at one of these noonday lectures in Jaynes' Hall of Philadelphia on Tuesday, March 30, 1858, where he spoke to 5000 men. He used Exodus 10:11 as a text: *"Ye that are men — serve the Lord."* More than 1000 men responded to the stirring message that day. During the sermon, the young preacher made the statement, "I must tell my Master's errand, and I would rather that this right arm be amputated at the trunk, than I should come short of my duty to you in delivering God's message."

His words were strangely prophetic. The next week he returned to his family home in the country. On Tuesday, April 13, 1858, Dudley strolled outside to watch the operation of a mule-drawn corn-thrasher in his barn. As he reached out to stroke the animal, the loose sleeve of his morning gown caught between the cogs, severely mangling his arm. Four days later, mortification set in and his right arm was amputated. Two days later, on Monday, April 19, the shock to his system proved fatal.

The newspapers gave a detailed account of his last moments. They wrote: *"Taking his aged father's hand, he said with much earnestness, 'Stand up for Jesus, father — and tell my brethren of the ministry - to stand up for Jesus.'"*

The following Sunday, Tyng's close friend and fellow worker, George Duffield Jr., preached from a passage in Ephesians 6:14,15. *"Stand firm then, with the belt of truth buckled around your waist, with the breastplate of righteousness in place, and with your feet fitted with the gospel of peace as a firm footing."* At the end of his sermon, he read a poem that he had written, inspired by the dying words of his friend Dudley Atkins Tyng, which began:

> *Stand up, Stand up for Jesus ye soldiers of the cross,*
> *Lift high His royal banner; It must not suffer loss;*
> *From victory unto victory His army shall He lead,*
> *Till every foe is vanquished, and Christ is Lord indeed.*

It was some six years later, in 1864, while Mr. Duffield was visiting the Union Army Camps, when he heard soldiers singing his poem for the first time. Until then, he wasn't aware his poem had been set to music. The tune by George J. Webb had been written some 30 years earlier for a musical show on board a ship crossing the Atlantic, and it fit perfectly this new poem.

There are many issues that confront us each day, and we tend to ignore or overlook most of them, not taking the time to develop an opinion. Yet, when we feel our personal rights are infringed upon, we are quick to take a stand. Young people learn very early in life to stand up for their rights. Most of us will stand up for our children when they have been wronged. As soldiers, we are taught to stand up and fight for our country. The question is how do we as Christians stand up for Jesus?

It takes real men and women to stand up for Jesus in the office or at work. It takes courageous men and women to stand up for Christ in the neighborhood and at the social club. It takes brave boys and girls to stand up for Christ in the classrooms and on the sports fields. Let us take a stand for Christ and His Church, at least as strongly as we do for this country, for our politics, or next week's sporting event.

A Song Is Born

Finally, be strong in the Lord and in his mighty power. Put on the full armor of God so that you can take your stand against the devil's schemes. For our struggle is not against flesh and blood, but against the rulers, against the authorities, against the powers of this dark world and against the spiritual forces of evil in the heavenly realms. Therefore put on the full armor of God, so that when the day of evil comes, you may be able to stand your ground, and after you have done everything to stand. Stand firm then, with the belt of truth buckled around your waist, with the breastplate of righteousness in place. [Ephesians 6:10-14]

RJT

Words 1853, first published in *The Plymouth Collection* of 1855; Music 1873

A Song Is Born

How precious to me are your thoughts, O God! How vast is the sum of them! Were I to count them, they would outnumber the grains of sand. When I awake, I am still with you. [Psalm 139:17-18]

Still, Still With Thee

The author of this well-known hymn was better known for writing a fictional novel about a noble-minded Christian slave who is sold to Simon Legree, a degenerate planter. The work showed a good understanding of both slaves and slaveholders, both from a Yankee or Southern prospective, and revealed the degenerating effects of slavery on both. The novel was instrumental in awakening national resistance to slavery, which was an issue of the forthcoming Civil War. What was the novel? Who was the author? What hymn did she write?

While Harriet Beecher Stowe is best known for her novel, *Uncle Tom's Cabin*, she also wrote a few hymns, and one of them surely deserves a place in our best collections. "For sheer poetic beauty there is probably not a single American Lyric that can excel '*Still, Still with Thee*,'" said Dr. E. E. Ryden in his book, *"The Story of Christian Hymnody."* Mrs. Stowe had an amazing background. She was born June 14, 1811, in Litchfield, CN. Her father was the most powerful Puritan preacher of his generation in the United States. Her mother, a devout Christian, died before Harriet was four years old. When Mrs. Beecher was dying, her last prayer was that her six sons might be called to the ministry. The prayer was answered in years to come when all six became preachers. The youngest son, Henry Ward Beecher, Harriet's brother, became the greatest preacher of his time. Yet, ironically, her daughter may be remembered longer for her literary work and have had more influence upon others through her hymn than any of the six sons.

On a recent trip to Kansas to research the song *"As the Life of a Flower,"* a historical marker near the town of Wabaunsee caught my attention. It read "Beecher's Bible and Rifle Church." For a church to have within its name "Rifle" was enough to stir considerable interest, but the name "Beecher" really caught my attention. I remembered this name being associated with several great preachers in the New England area in years past. And I quickly remembered the name Harriet Beecher Stowe, author of the hymn *"Still, Still with Thee."* True enough, the Beecher in this church's name referred to Henry Ward Beecher, famed preacher for the Congregational Church of Brooklyn, NY, and a brother to Harriet Beecher Stowe. For more information on this unique church and its name, see the story of the song, *"As the Life of a Flower."*

Harriet Beecher Stowe had a bright mind with a remarkable memory. When she was six, she could read very well and had memorized over twenty-five hymns plus two long chapters from the Bible. In 1836 she married Dr. Calvin Stowe, a professor and leading authority on the Bible. He had a fine sense of humor, which matched her own. Unfortunately, his health was fragile and this caused a severe strain on the finances. To help make ends meet, Harriet began to write articles for a magazine called, *The National Era*. Finding the time and solitude to write was not exactly easy. She was a devoted wife caring for an invalid husband, and a devoted mother to their six children. With help from her sister, she began writing her story in serial form in 1851. Scarcely had the last installment been printed when a Boston publisher wanted to print it in book form. With its publication in 1852, Harriet Beecher Stowe became one of the most famous women in the world. *Uncle Tom's Cabin* had a profound influence on the American people and probably affected the course of the Civil War.

Yet, even with all the notoriety, Harriet was struggling with sorrow and grief. Though she had become a Christian as a young girl, she had many conflicts between faith and doubt. Many of her questions arose due to a series of misfortunes and sorrows. Her sixth child, Charles, a particular favorite of hers, died of cholera. At the same time, her husband was in a sanitarium, which often left him depressed. Additionally, all the problems and anxieties of running the home fell upon her shoulders.

Her hymn *"Still, Still with Thee"* was written in 1855, not long after her son Charles died. Soon afterwards, other family tragedies occurred. Their eldest son Henry drowned at the close of his freshman year at

A Song Is Born

Dartmouth. Their third son Fred was wounded at the battle of Gettysburg and that left him mentally impaired. Through all this grief, her basic faith in the Lord was firm even though she had times of bewilderment. Though she was primarily known as a writer of fiction, particularly, *Uncle Tom's Cabin*; America hymnody has been greatly enriched by her hymn. Harriet was a "morning" person - often getting up at 4:30 a.m. to see the sun rise and to hear nature wake up. This is evident in her hymn.

> *Still, Still with Thee, when purple morning breaketh,*
> *When the bird waketh and the shadows flee;*
> *Fairer than morning, lovelier than the daylight*
> *Dawns the sweet consciousness, I am with Thee.*

With each morning brings a new day. The troubles of yesterday are dulled, and the fears of the night are gone. We should begin each day with a new and fresh outlook. Verse two suggests there is a time for quietness, a time to be alone with God. This is a good opportunity to reflect upon God's goodness, remembering just how great God is. Verse three reflects back on life's troubles, which seem to bring darkness. Yet, when we pause to reflect, Christ is still there. Verse four closes by speaking of death, the ultimate darkness for the sinner, but the ultimate New Morning for the believer. What a beautiful "Son" rise when our new day begins in Heaven.

> *But I will sing of your strength, in the morning I will sing of your love; for you are my fortress, my refuge in times of trouble.* [Psalm 59:16]

RJT

A Song Is Born

God will make a way,
Where there seems to be no way.
He works in ways we cannot see,
He will make a way for me.

GOD WILL MAKE A WAY

Don Moen is one of the most creative writers of Contemporary Christian music today. His songs include *Worthy, You are Worthy, Give Thanks, I Want to be Where You Are, Blessed Be the name of the Lord, God Will Make a Way,* and many more. He was born Donald James Moen June 29, 1950, in Duluth, Minnesota. In May 1972, he married Laura and together they have five children.

While attending Oral Roberts University, Don was hired by Terry Law Ministries to play guitar, trombone, and other instruments. He traveled with the Law's evangelistic musical ministry group "Living Sound" for ten years. Mr. Moen has toured extensively in more than 40 countries. In addition to playing various instruments, he was responsible for much of the groups' musical arrangements and productions.

In 1986, he left the Terry Law Ministries to form his own company. Three years later, he was invited to join the staff of the very popular Integrity Music Company where he is Executive Vice-President and Creative Director. Don Moen has written hundreds of songs and produced over 30 albums. In 1992, he received a nomination from the Gospel Music Association for his song, *God will Make A Way.* Mr. Moen explains how this song was born:

"I wrote this song for my wife's sister and brother-in-law, Susan and Craig. They had just lost their son Jeremy when he was killed in an automobile accident. I wanted to say something that would give them hope in a hopeless situation. As I prayed, God gave me the words and music to this song. One line captured what I really wanted to say to them . . . *'He works in ways we can not see.'* I sang this for them privately and put it away, never intending to have it recorded. Three years later as I was leading worship in our staff meeting at Integrity Music, God reminded me of this song. When I sang it that day, it seemed like almost everyone needed to hear God was working in ways they could not see."

It's obvious from the popularity of this song that it was not destined to lie in a file drawer. Millions of people needed to know that God still works, and often in ways we cannot see.

Sometimes there are moments in our lives when all seems hopeless. There are events or tragedies that occur that turn our world upside down, leaving us to feel we just cannot go on. Some vent their hopelessness through anger; angry with God and angry with those who have caused the tragedy. Many seek revenge for the pain and hopelessness. Our court systems are filled with lawsuits from thousands who want vindication for the pain and suffering, somehow thinking that by inflicting a monetary loss to others, their hope will be restored.

There are others whose faith in God has been strengthened through adversity. One great example is Fanny Crosby, the prolific songwriter. Even though blinded for life by an incompetent doctor at the age of six weeks, she never felt the need to be angry or to seek revenge. A more recent example of one who was strengthened by adversity might be Christopher Reeve. During the height of his popularity as an actor, he fell from a horse, seriously injuring his spine. The once robust actor who often played the role of Superman, no longer is able to walk or move any part of his body. Rather than bitterness, he has made it his purpose in life to further the research and recovery of such injuries. His courage and hope is an inspiration for all to follow.

Someone has said, "When the going gets tough, the tough get going." I believe it's also true that when the faithful are hurt, the hurt are faithful, true to God, His will and His ways. We cannot explain why tragedies occur – especially to those who believe in God and are seeking to follow His way. Yet, it is this belief, this faith, and this hope that God is with us and will sustain us through the pain and suffering. Through it all, God's abiding principles of love, care, hope, and forgiveness will guide us back to spiritual and mental health. Somehow, God will make a way.

As for God, His way is perfect; the word of the Lord is proven; He is a shield to all who trust in Him. - - God is my strength and power, and He makes my way perfect. [2 Samuel 22:31, 33]

===== *RJT* =====

Having been justified by his grace, we might become heirs having the hope of eternal life. [Titus 3:7]

HIS GRACE REACHES ME

*I*n my search for the author of *His Grace Reaches Me,* I had combed the hills of Tennessee, the flat lands of Kansas, Missouri, and many other points east for more than two years without success. I had learned that he played the piano for the Blackwood Brothers Quartet during the 1960s, but Mr. James Blackwood did not know what had happened to him. Since Mr. Gleason had seemingly disappeared from sight, I assumed he must have died. Then, one day while reading an article in "The Singing News," Mr. Gleason's name jumped out at me. After several calls, I learned that he was not only alive, but doing very well in Texas. Never thought to look in my home state!

Jewel Monroe (Whitey) Gleason was born in Kingman, Kansas, May 18, 1932, the third of six children. His dad, Clifford, who was a tool and die maker, came from Michigan and his mother Alta came from Oklahoma. They met and married in Kingman and settled down to raise a family. "Whitey" was a nickname given to him in high school because of his light, blond hair. The nickname stuck, and he has been known by it ever since.

Mr. Gleason completed high school in Kingman, and obtained his B.A. degree from Bethany Nazarene College in 1958. The school is now called Southern Nazarene University, located in Bethany, Oklahoma. In 1959, he opened a music store in Bethany with a motto of "Everything in Music." They sold and repaired instruments, taught music (as many as 220 students at one time) and sang in groups. Also, in 1959 he formed the "Jubilee Quartet." In 1963, Whitey left the Jubilee Quartet and joined the Blackwood Quartet as their piano player. Soon afterwards, he sold the music store to Ken and Lucille Driver. The Driver's music store is still doing business in Bethany. In 1966, Mr. Gleason left the Blackwood Quartet and rejoined the Jubilee Quartet to sing full time for the next 22 years.

In 1977, Mr. Gleason married Pamela (Pam) and by 1983, the couple had moved to Kennedy, Texas, to enjoy the warmer weather and to raise their three children. A chance (or providential) meeting with the superintendent of the Pawnee schools (a small town about 15 miles from Kennedy) lead Mr. Gleason to become a schoolteacher. In the summer of 1997, The Gleason's moved to Garland, Texas, to teach third grade in their two magnet schools. Whitey teaches science and math and Pam teaches language and arts. Whitey's special interest and talent, however, is to use music to teach all subjects. He has written hundreds of songs that help teach math, history, the presidents, etc. He is currently teaching the teachers how to utilize music to teach the children.

"The song *His Grace Reaches Me* was born on a bus while traveling with the Blackwood Quartet." Whitey said, "I had been reading the scripture *'For by grace are you saved, through faith - and this not from yourselves, it is the gift of God - not of works, so that no one can boast. For we are God's workmanship, created in Christ Jesus to do good works.'"* [Ephesians 2:8-10] These thoughts kept running through my mind. Sometimes a song will grow over a period of time, but *His Grace Reaches Me* was written in just 30 minutes. I jotted it down on some old scratch paper, and soon afterwards we sang it in a concert. The melody was written with James Blackwood in mind, arguably the finest quartet lead singer of our time." A sad side note, Mr. James Blackwood passed away February 3, 2002.

Mr. Gleason estimates he has traveled over 3 million miles during his career as a singer and piano player. This afforded him a lot of time to think and compose some of his 2000 songs. About 200 of Mr. Gleason's songs have been published and/or recorded by groups such as: Blackwood Quartet, Oak Ridge Boys, Dottie Rambo, The Rebels, and many, many more. Some of his most popular songs include *Let the Church Roll On; Where Will You Be a Million Years from Now; At the Alter; Nobody;* and *Walk, Talk and Sing.*

The grace of God is offered to mankind out of His goodness. He extends to all the free gift of salvation, but His grace must be accepted. This acceptance will leave us indebted to the giver. How difficult is it for you to receive a free gift?

In 1829, George Wilson, convicted of murder in Pennsylvania, was tried and sentenced to die. Andrew Jackson, The President of the United States, granted him a pardon, but Mr. Wilson refused it. Confused and dismayed, a lawsuit was filed to force Mr. Wilson to accept the pardon. The Supreme Court ruled: "A pardon is a paper, the value of which depends upon its acceptance by the parties implicated. It is hardly to be supposed that one under sentence to die would refuse to accept a pardon. But if it is refused, it is no pardon. George Wilson must hang." And so he did!

This true, unusual, and sad story may be emblematic of many today who refuse the pardon offered by Christ through the Cross. How difficult it is for many to accept a free salvation, for when we accept this free gift, we are in debt to the giver. We become recipients of God's grace through faith, an obedient and grateful faith.

> *"—It was offered at Calv'ry for ev'ry one;*
> *Greatest of treasures, and it's mine today,*
> *Tho' my sins were as scarlet,*
> *He has washed them away.*
> *His Grace Reaches Me -"*

For all have sinned and fall short of the glory of God, and are justified freely by his grace through the redemption that came by Christ Jesus. [Romans 3:23-24]

===== *RJT* =====

A Song Is Born

God's Family

We are God's children; heirs of God and co-heirs with Christ.
[Romans 8:17]

GOD'S FAMILY

*O*ne of the most requested songs today is God's Family. Perhaps the popularity of this song comes from a deep-seated need we so often find missing in our lives, the need to be wanted, to be accepted, and to be loved even with our faults. That's what families can provide best.

We live in a highly mobile society that tends to discourage strong community roots or personal family ties. Marriages are breaking up at record levels, seriously hindering our hopes to rebuild close family ties. Nothing can ever replace the home - a place where children can grow up learning about God, love, and life from a mother and father who care about them and each other.

We live in a world where we feel everything must be bought or earned - - where everybody seems to have a personal agenda or ulterior motive for helping others - -where each mistake we make is magnified or criticized at every turn. Isn't it great to be part of the Family of God,

A Song Is Born

with people who care for us without having to earn it? A family who knows our faults, yet loves us anyway. When we do those dumb things that disappoint even ourselves, the family of God is still there with compassion and prayer. It's great to see the church family learning how to care and accept each other rather than criticize or expecting perfection.

Lanny Wolfe, the author of God's Family, experienced many of these emotions as he penned the words to this great hymn during one midweek service. He relates the following experience that inspired his song.

"We had a missionary from Asia conduct a meeting for us that year (1975). I was captivated by his ability to capture our thoughts, attention, and emotions. I can still remember one illustration he gave. It seems they were invited to share a meal with some local residents of a small community in Asia. Near the end of a delicious meal, the missionary notices others frantically searching and inquiring about a missing dog. As he told the story, you begin to realize that the missing dog could well have been part of the meal. He could make you laugh one minute, and then instantly turn it around, and you knew you were to sober up in your thinking. It was a neat feeling to experience laughter and crying just moments apart. This inspired the lines 'Sometimes we laugh together, sometimes we cry.' "

What Mr. Wolfe experienced that night reminded him of all the perimeters of emotions that happen within one's own family, and within the family of God. We need to be less critical and more caring of others. Open your arms of love and compassion to people who are hurting. Learn to forgive others, and to forgive yourself. Give thanks for the warmth, comfort, and love found within the family of God.

All men will know you are my disciples if you love one another. [John 13:35]

———— *RJT* ————

A Song Is Born

Time is filled with swift transition
Naught of earth unmoved can stand
Build your hopes on things eternal
Hold to God's unchanging hands

HOLD TO GOD'S UNCHANGING HAND

These words, which were written nearly 100 years ago, still ring true today. Sometimes in the search for the history of our songs, a unique story will surface about what inspired the words. Occasionally the composer of the music will have an interesting story of inspiration. But rarely do you find a song where both the author and the composer have unique, yet different, inspirational situations that lead to the birth of the same song. *"Hold to God's Unchanging Hand"* was born because of two unique incidents, each with different motivations yet resulting in the same conclusion. I think this shows the power of a hymn to meet the needs of many situations, in all walks of life.

Jennie Wilson was born in 1857, in South Whitley, Indiana. Soon after her birth, her father passed away. At the age of four, Jennie was struck with a spinal disorder that left her an invalid for the rest of her life. Unable to attend public schools, she studied at home with the help of her dedicated mother. A love for music and a talent for poetry soon led her to write verses which first began to appear in the local papers. It wasn't long before hymn writers were requesting her poems for their music. Though confined to a wheelchair, this small, frail, self-educated sweet lady inspired millions through the words of more than 2200 poems.

In 1902, Jennie's devoted mother passed away. Now at the age of 45, the most dramatic change in her life would present new challenges and more uncertainties. Who would help her in-and-out of the wheelchair? Who would help her bathe, dress, and eat every day? All of her life had been fraught with challenges and uncertainties, but it's at this time of deep sorrow and uncertainty that she would write her finest poem, *"Hold to God's Unchanging Hand."*

Like Miss Jennie Wilson, Franklin L. Eiland had little or no formal public schooling. Yet through his self-taught music skills, his teaching and leadership talents, and a winning personality, Mr. Eiland would inspire millions. He was born March 25, 1860, on a Mississippi

A Song Is Born

plantation. At the age of 18, he, along with his mom, dad, and several other families moved to Texas. They first settled into the rural community of Beck's Prairie in Robertson, County, Texas. Later, the Eilands would move a few miles north to Wooten Wells, Texas. This was a bustling resort town of some 2500 residents at one time, but only a state historical plaque marks the spot now.

Unlike Jennie Wilson, Mr. Eiland was not confined to a wheelchair. However, ironically in the same year that Miss Wilson lost her mom, 1902, Mr. Eiland's health began to fail. This caused him to sell his interest in the very successful "Trio Music Company," and also to cut back on his activities. In just seven short years, in 1909, F. L. Eiland went to be with his Maker at the very young age of 49. But it was not Mr. Eiland's failing health which caused him to write the music for this song, it was the personal struggles of a close friend and fellow songwriter, J. W. Gaines.

In 1903, Mr. Gaines, author and composer of many hymns such as: *Take My Hand and Lead Me* and *When He Comes in Glory,* was struggling with his faith. It seems someone within the brotherhood had said some things that upset Mr. Gaines, and he had made comments about *"leaving the faith."* Even though in poor health, Mr. Eiland traveled from his home in Fort Worth to visit Mr. Gaines in Palo Pinto County, near Mineral Wells, trying to encourage him to hold on to his faith. After a lengthy discussion, Mr. Eiland retreated to a quiet place outside the house for thought and prayer. He searched through his collection of songs and poems, hoping to find something that would help his friend during this crisis. It was then that he found Miss Jennie Wilson's poem, and set about to write suitable music. There, under the big oak tree outside the modest log cabin of J. W. Gaines, F. L. Eiland wrote the beautiful music of this enduring hymn *"Hold To God's Unchanging Hand."* He presented it to his friend, encouraging him to hold onto God's hand in spite of what others say or do. "It is joy beyond expressing," Mr. Eiland said of this song, "that we have at our command and thus to know that we can ever hold to God's unchanging hand!"

A Song Is Born

Whether as with Miss Jennie Wilson, your life is filled with trials and uncertainty, or as with F. L. Eiland, a good friend needs to be encouraged to keep on keeping on, this song will serve both needs. Put your trust and faith in God. He will not let you down, for He has said, "I will never, ever, ever forsake you." Build you hopes and dreams on things eternal, not on earthly wealth and relationships.

Let your conduct be without covetousness; be content with such things as you have. For He Himself has said, "I will never leave you nor forsake you." [Hebrews 13:5]

RJT

Take My Hand, Precious Lord

2 Timothy 4:17-18

Thomas A. Dorsey — Thomas A. Dorsey

1. When my way groweth drear, precious Lord linger near, When my life is almost gone; Hear my cry, hear my call, hold my hand lest I fall; Take my hand, precious Lord, lead me home.

2. When the shadows appear, and the night draweth near, And the day is past and gone; At the river I stand, guide my feet, hold my hand; Take my hand, precious Lord, lead me home.

Chorus Precious Lord, take my hand, lead me on, let me stand, I am tired, I am weak, I am worn; Thru the storm, thru the night, lead me on to the light; Take my hand, precious Lord, lead me home.

© Copyright 1939 by Stamps-Baxter Music & Ptg. Co. All Rights Reserved.

A Song Is Born

Show me your ways, O Lord, teach me your paths; guide me in your truth and teach me. [Psalm 25:4-5]

TAKE MY HAND, PRECIOUS LORD

Thomas Dorsey was born just outside Atlanta, Georgia, in 1899. He grew up singing the jazz and the blues. By the 1920s, he was nationally recognized as a leader in writing and performing clever blues songs. His father was a stern Baptist preacher, who provided a solid spiritual upbringing. In the late 1920s, while still keeping up his jazz career, singing in bars and nightclubs, he quietly began to write religious songs. These songs were partly God-fearing and partly good-time jazz. By merging the fervor of the old spirituals, with the swinging rhythm of blues, a new style of religious song was born that we now call "Gospel Music." Dorsey relates the following story about the development of his hymn, *Take My Hand Precious Lord:*

"Back in 1932, I was 32 years old and a fairly new husband. My wife Nettie and I were living in Chicago's south side. One August afternoon I had to go to St. Louis for a revival. Nettie was in the last month of pregnancy with our first child. I didn't want to go, something was strongly telling me to stay, but people were expecting me and I went.

However, outside the city, I discovered that in my anxiety at leaving, I had forgotten my music case. I wheeled around and headed back. I found Nettie sleeping peacefully. I hesitated by her bed; something was strongly telling me to stay. But eager to get on my way, and not wanting to disturb Nettie, I shrugged off the feeling and quietly slipped out of the room with my music.

The next night, the crowd called on me to sing again and again. When I finally sat down, a messenger ran up with a Western Union telegram. I ripped it open and saw the words *"Your wife is dead."* I rushed to a phone and called home. All I could hear is "Nettie is dead." When I got back, I learned that Nettie had given birth to a boy. *Yet that night, the baby also died.* I buried them both in the same casket, then fell apart.

A Song Is Born

For days I closeted myself. I felt that God had done me an injustice. I didn't want to serve Him anymore. I was lost in grief. A friend took me to a neighborhood music school one day, and left me alone in a room with a piano. It was quiet and the late evening sun shone through the window. I sat at the piano and began to browse over the keys. Something happened to me! I felt a peace. I found myself playing a melody, one I've never heard or played before, and words came into my head. As the words and music came to me, it seemed that my heart was also healed. I learned (from this tragic experience) that when we are in our deepest grief, when we feel farthest from God, this is when He is closest."

Just as it was when Christ walked this earth some 2000 years ago, so it is true today, the hands of Jesus provide the assurance, the healing, and saving power we all need. Like the Apostle Peter, as his faith grew weak and he began to sink into the ocean's waters, he cried out to the Lord for help and *"Immediately Jesus reached out his hand and caught him."* (Matt 14:31) We, today, must reach out for the extended hand of Jesus to help us make it through the days of our lives.

But the Lord stood at my side and gave strength, so that through me the message might be fully proclaimed and all the Gentiles might hear it. – the Lord will rescue me from every evil attack and will bring me safely to his heavenly kingdom. To him be glory for ever and ever. [2 Timothy 4:17-18]

RJT

A Song Is Born

> *For to us a child is born, to us a son is given, and the government will be on his shoulders. And he will be called Wonderful Counselor, Mighty God, Everlasting Father, Prince of Peace.* [Isaiah 9:6]

HIS NAME IS WONDERFUL

"Christmas came on Sunday that year" (1958) said Audrey Mieir, "and for once Jesus' birth seemed more important to everyone than toys and presents. A kind of hushed expectancy filled the place as *Silent Night, Holy Night* swelled from the organ. Older heads were bowed, eyes were closed, an occasional tear rolled down a wrinkled cheek - remembering 50, 60, even 70 other Christmases, thankful for the love of God and family, their presents, His presence!"

Little children sat impatiently anticipating the re-creation of the old, old story, their eyes sparkling, reflecting Christmas tree lights, eager to have it all, the Christmas play and, afterward, the dinner and presents, stacked and waiting.

The curtain opened. There it was, as it would be depicted countless times that day, the humble manger scene. Mary was a shy teenager, cheeks flushed with excitement, holding someone's baby doll close in her arms. A young Joseph hovered over her, his smooth face discreetly hidden in old drapery. A beautiful angel glittered and shone, out-brillianced only by the flashing smile for mom and dad in aisle two as her halo slipped to one side. Eleven-year-old shepherds shuffled down the aisle with unmistakable shyness, their jeans peeking out from under dad's old robe.

"The procession halted and the choir sang, *sleep in heavenly peace*. Dr. Luther Mieir (Audrey's brother-in-law) spoke, his voice filled the small church - - *"His Name Is Wonderful,"* he said with his eyes closed and his hands lifted heavenward. And I - I heard the familiar rustling of angel wings. I did not know at that strangely moving moment that a

A Song Is Born

once-in-a-lifetime experience was about to happen. As I grabbed my old Bible and wrote in it, more than with any other of my songs, I felt as if I were only a channel, as if I were not otherwise involved."

Audrey Mieir and her staff shared this moving story with me in the summer of 1996, just days before she lost her husband of 60 years. Four months later, on November 5, 1996, Audrey joined her husband in death. She came into this world Audrey Mae Wagner May 12, 1916, in Leachburg, Pennsylvania, the daughter of Dow C. and Marie Elizabeth (Dorsey) Wagner. Audrey married Charles Mieir in 1936. Amy McPherson, the founder of The FourSquare Gospel Church in Los Angles, CA, performed the service. Both Audrey and Charles were ordained as ministers by Mrs. McPherson and were a part of this group all their lives. Audrey is a musician, not only talented in the art of writing music or poetry, having more than 800 songs to her credit, but she excels greatly in the ability to direct choruses.

Audrey has a tender heart, especially for those forgotten, homeless, or neglected children. In her book, "The Laughter and The Tears," she recalls an event early in her life that had a strong impact upon her. Audrey had been invited to speak at a youth camp in California. Running late, as she often did, she was deep in thought and prayer, often with her eyes closed as they hurried down a busy highway. Audrey never learned to drive a car, so being the passenger she could afford the leisure of closing her eyes. "Suddenly, I saw him! I could hardly believe it! I turned to look again, but the view was blocked by a truck. 'Honey (Charles) we must turn around! There is a child standing at the edge of the road! We turned around and there he stood. A small boy (about three years' old) was standing at the edge of this busy highway intending to cross. Shaking with fear, I pulled him back to safety. His shirt torn, his toes were out of his shoes, his little body was bruised and bleeding. 'Please help me lady, My mommy don't want me. She pushed me out of the car. I got to go home across the street,' the boy said. As I held the dirty little bit of humanity, I thought my heart would burst."

This incident impressed upon her heart the plight of unwanted children. Months later, on a mission trip to Korea, she found hundreds of unwanted, rejected Korean/American children, born to Korean

A Song Is Born

mothers by American servicemen. It became her life's work to seek homes for these unwanted, unloved children. Through the efforts of Audrey and Charles Mieir, two orphan homes were established in Korea and more than 60 Korean/American children have been brought to America and placed in loving homes, including adopting two themselves.

This song was born in 1958 just as the so-called "Jesus Movement" began. At this time there was an effort to better understand the person of Jesus and His presence in our lives. In a time of great darkness, God promised to send a light that would shine on everyone. This message of hope was fulfilled in the birth of Jesus alluded to in Isaiah 9.

Different names have been given to Jesus that allude to His many special roles. Many are found in the book of John, chapter 6. *"Son of Man"* emphasizes His humanity. *"Bread of Life,"* the only source of eternal life. *"Light of the World,"* the symbol of truth and justice. The *"Good Shepherd"* exemplifies the love and guidance He offers us. *"Rock of Ages,"* a symbol of enduring strength, etc. The important issue is not which name we use, but how do you relate to Jesus? Is He your Counselor and Guide? Is He Master of your life or simply another biblical character? One thing is certain, you must decide!

"The song will outlive the chubby human hand chosen to write a few black notes on the five lines and four spaces," Audrey said. "But it will never outlive the original Composer, God, the Father who glories in His Son's name, and glories in our praise of it. His Name is full of awe, and is truly wonderful!"

Therefore God exalted him to the highest place and gave him the name that is above every name, that at the name of Jesus every knee should bow, in heaven and on earth, and every tongue confess that Jesus Christ is Lord. [Philippians 2:9-10]

RJT

A Song Is Born

> *Jesus – withdrew about a stone's throw beyond them, knelt down and prayed.* [Luke 22:41]

KNEEL AT THE CROSS

Charles Earnest Moody was born October 8, 1891, the youngest of eight children, in a log house built before the Civil War, near Tilton, Georgia. Like many small communities, Tilton has just about gone away. While still a small child, the family moved to Tunnel Hill just 15 miles north where Earnest lived until he was thirty-six, and where he wrote his most famous song, *Kneel At The Cross*.

Tunnel Hill, Georgia is an interesting, small community steeped in Civil War history. The town received its name from the railroad tunnel built in 1850, providing an easy way to get across Chetoogeta Mountain. Tunnel Hill was a strategic location for both the north and the south. Early in the War Between the States, the Confederates controlled the tunnel, but later the Union army seized control. General Sherman stayed here before marching through the tunnel on his way to Atlanta and the Gulf in 1864.

When I arrived in Tunnel Hill one morning to research Mr. Moody, I noticed an interesting old abandoned building and a man walking around it, so I parked across the street at the Post Office and engaged him in conversation. Before long, two other men joined us, each with fascinating stories about the building and the town. All were equally interested in my reason for being there. It seems the old building was a grocery store built because the Stevenson couple could not get along. For several years, the husband and wife operated a store together, but a sharp disagreement developed, so the husband went about 300 yards south and built his own store. She continued to operate the original store. It must have been interesting times, to see who bought their groceries from whom!

Bradley Puttman, one of the men who joined our discussion, was quite knowledgeable about the town and was very interested in learning about the research on a former resident, Charles Moody. He took southern hospitality to the max, and for the next five hours Mr. Puttman

A Song Is Born

made appointments for me to meet people, and took me to all the sites of interest regarding Charles E. Moody. Additionally, he remembered that A. J. Showalter wrote his famous song *Leaning On The Everlasting Arms* nearby, and took me to the Stubberfield house where the music was written, and to Stone Church where it was sung for the first time. He even had a key to the famous tunnel, now open only on special occasions, and we walked in the steps of General Sherman.

"Earnest was my great uncle," said Frank Moody. "Although he was much older, I remember him quite well. They lived for a time just across the street in that blue-trimmed house." Charles Moody was interested in music all his life.

"I learned to read music a little," Charles Moody said. "In the meantime I learned to play a few tunes on the banjo and fiddle. Being much interested in the youngest art, I walked three miles up to Ebenezer (Baptist Church) to a singing taught by A. J. Simms of Dalton, Georgia, but was more interested in harmony than voice, so all my time was spent in mastering an easy book of harmony. This was in 1916."

Later that year, he attended the Southern Development Normal in Ashville, North Carolina. F. L. Eiland of Waco, Texas, originated the SDN School of Music. Mr. Moody pursued several studies into the rudiments of music. He taught singing schools, conducted the music at many revivals, and often served as the music director for various churches, both in Tunnel Hill and Calhoun, Georgia.

Charles E. Moody moved to Calhoun in 1927 to sing and record professionally on Victor Records with the Georgia Yellow Hammers. There he met and married Fannie Brownlee, who, along with her brother, owned a 10-cent store in downtown Calhoun. She was also a musician and their union was blessed with three children, all equally talented in music. In 1931, he left the group and returned to keeping books and teaching public school for a time. From 1938 to 1940, they lived in Tunnel Hill again, where he ran a gas station and sold bedspreads along Highway 41, on the corner of his dad's farm. Back in Calhoun, he continued to teach public schools, Singing Schools, and do bookkeeping.

A Song Is Born

Kneel At The Cross was written in 1924 in Tunnel Hill while Charles Earnest Moody was the music director for the local Methodist Church, downtown Tunnel Hill. No doubt he first introduced his new song in the church building now occupied by the Hillcrest Church of Christ.

According to Frank Moody, Earnest worked part-time for his brother in a downtown general store. Earnest left work a little early one day, and walked to the New Hope Baptist church, where a meeting was in process with Reverend Sam Hair. Earnest did a lot of walking, as did many people of his day, but it must have been especially hard for him since he was slightly crippled after having  contracting spinal meningitis at an age three. (The family now believe it might have been polio.) As the minister, Sam Hair concluded his sermon, he said, *"Now let us kneel at the Cross."* This phrase captured the imagination of this young songwriter, and by the next day Mr. Moody had completed the words and music to *Kneel At The Cross*.

Kneeling to pray is not practiced much anymore. It is a symbol of submission and humility. I can still remember as a boy, how when it came time to pray in church, my dad would get off the bench and kneel. When I questioned him about it, he would say "You can stand to pray or you can kneel to pray, but the Bible doesn't say anything about sitting to pray." Kneeling is meant to be an outward expression of an inward humility. Though we seldom practice kneeling, we still sing about this symbolic show of humility. *On Bended Knee, I Come, All Rise* (And as I bowed to kneel with angels I heard the Spirit say;) and *Come Let Us Worship and Bow Down* (Let us kneel down before the Lord) just to name a few contemporary songs that express kneeling.

Our God is an awesome God, and I'm humbled that He would send His Son to die for me. Let us kneel before the cross of Christ and thank God for His redeeming love.

> *But when our time was up, we left and continued on our way. All the disciples and their wives and children accompanied us out of the city, and there on the beach we knelt to pray.* [Acts 21:5]

RJT

A Song Is Born

For our citizenship is in heaven: and we eagerly await a Savior from there, the Lord Jesus Christ. [Philippians 3:20]

O THINK OF THE HOME OVER THERE

The year was 1865. After years of internal conflict and war, the nation found itself strangely at peace after the battle of Appomattox. Then on Good Friday, a bullet from John Wilkes Booth stunned Americans. The assassination of President Abraham Lincoln profoundly saddened and perplexed Dr. D. W. C. Huntington; first, that his beloved leader had been slain, and second that it happened in a theater.

He was born DeWitt Clinton Huntington April 27, 1830, in Vermont. He grew up to become a powerful Methodist Minister, sometimes a political candidate for the Prohibition Party, and later in life the Chancellor and Professor of Bible at Nebraska Wesleyan University. It was often said of Mr. Huntington that he was "well-educated, an eloquent speaker, well informed on all issues, one of the most talented ministers in the country."

Hardly had the nation's pain begun to ease over the untimely death of Abraham Lincoln, when more sorrow came to Mr. Huntington. Mary, his wife, had not been feeling well for weeks and was pregnant with their third child. Horace Davis Huntington was born September 19, 1865, but Mary never recovered and lost her struggle to live 10 months later. Baby Horace was sickly, not expected to live. Mrs. Hiram Davis, a member of the congregation where Dr. Huntington preached, cared for the baby around the clock, night and day for months, and saved the boy.

However, D. W. C. Huntington had not reached the end of his personal sorrow. Two months after his wife died, his father passed away. His suffering was deep, and he was without a home. His children were sent to live with others, growing up not knowing him. Out of these experiences in 1865-66, Dr. Huntington begins a serious study about heaven. *"Everything the New Testament says about the future world can be written on the palm of one's hand,"* he said. From these experiences and this study was born the hymn *O Think Of The Home Over There*.

"The hymn was written wholly during the same week," said Mr. Huntington. "It was written in the winter of 1866. The hymn was never designed for publications; I can only conjecture how it came into print. It was written to relieve myself during the most sorrowful period of my life. My wife had left me for the better world about four months before; my children were scattered into the families of relatives; my father died two months later; and I seemed to have lived life all through. I was, at the time, a homemade singer, and I occasionally sang those verses in the prayer meeting. I never copyrighted the poem, nor have I ever received anything for the production. If it can be a source of pleasure to anyone, or of healthful inspiration to some soul in sorrow, I shall be grateful to Him whose I am."

T. C. O'Kane of Delaware, Ohio, composed the music. He was born Tullius Clinton O'Kane March 10, 1830, in Fairfield County, Ohio. In 1849, he entered Ohio Wesleyan University and graduated in 1852 with A.B. and A.M. degrees. He remained with the University for five years to teach math and affectionately became known as "Professor." His musical talents were also recognized. He was an excellent choir director, but he excelled in leading large congregations in song. It was said of him, *"he sings with spirit and understanding, with due appreciation of both words and music, able to infuse his enthusiasm into his audiences!"*

In 1853, T. C. O'Kane married Laura A. Eaton, the daughter of a prominent family of Delaware. Except for brief periods, Delaware was his home the remainder of his life, which ended February 10, 1912. In 1873, he opened a bookstore, complete with stationery, fine paintings, and wallpapers, and quickly became the leading bookstore in town.

About the song *"Over There"* Mr. O'Kane said, "I cut this hymn out of some newspaper and put, with others in my portfolio, intending sometime when I felt like it to give it a musical setting." One Sunday afternoon, after studying for his Sunday School lesson, he found the poem and something seemed to say, *"Now's your time."*

A Song Is Born

In a strange twist of fate, T. C. O'Kane and D. W. C. Huntington were both born in 1830, they both had the same middle name, "Clinton," and both men died in 1912, just two days apart. While the two men corresponded via mail, there is no evidence that they ever met.

Dr. Huntington made some valuable observations as he reflected upon his personal sorrow. "We must not take trouble hard. Accept it as a part of our inheritance and never once think it does not belong to us. We must not brood over our troubles or talk much about them except to the Lord Jesus. We must pierce the clouds with our prayers and faith, and work on bravely." Dr. Huntington always carried a pocketful of sayings and quotes to fit every situation. One I particularly liked was where he warned against "puffing, stuffing, and blowing." He clarified his comments – that "stuffing" was engaged in for the purpose of getting gain, and that "blowing" was the tooting of one's horn, and that "puffing" was stretching the truth. He urged his colleagues to refrain from exaggerations. Good advice!

If you are part of the younger generation, you may think *O Think Of The Home Over There* is a bit old-fashioned. Songs about heaven have mostly gone away with today's contemporary Christian music. While the song may seem old, the message is timeless, and I assure you that one day, when you lose a parent, or child, or when your health fails and death is eminent, your thoughts will turn to "over there." I do not know what heaven is like, but I know the One who created it, and I trust in his promise made to me and to all those who will follow Him.

People who say such things show that they are looking for a country of their own. If they had been thinking of the country they had left, they would have had opportunity to return. Instead, they were longing for a better country – a heavenly one. Therefore God is not ashamed to be called their God, for he had prepared a city for them. [Hebrews 11:14-16]

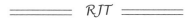

RJT

A Song Is Born

> *"I rejoiced with those who said to me, Let us go to the house of the Lord."* [Psalm 122:1]

THE CHURCH IN THE WILDWOOD

It was noon in Bradford, Iowa, one balmy day in June 1857. A Yankee schoolteacher from southwestern Wisconsin needed to stretch his legs after riding all morning in the cramped stagecoach. W. S. Pitts, a twenty-six year old native of New York was on his way to Fredericksburg, Iowa, to visit his bride-to-be. No doubt he was anxious and excited, but for now it just felt good to walk. He strolled around the dusty streets and crowded buildings until his eyes came to rest on "a spot of rare beauty," he later explained. Beautiful cedar trees stood tall nestled around a natural outcropping of rock on this gentle hill. "What a great spot for a church building," he thought. When he returned to Wisconsin, the thought of a church building located under those ancient cedar trees still lingered in his mind, so he wrote a song and titled it *The Little Brown Church in the Vale*. He put the song away not thinking much about it and went about his task of teaching.

The next year, 1858, William S. Pitts and Ann Elize Warren were united in marriage. They settled down in Rock County, Wisconsin, to raise their family. In June 1862, William and Elize left their home in Wisconsin and moved to Fredericksburg, Iowa, to be near her ailing parents.

Meanwhile, Mr. Pitts was unaware that a Congregational Church had been organized in Bradford in 1855, two years before his brief visit. Then, worship services were conducted in log homes, hotel dining rooms, schoolhouses, abandoned stores, etc. In 1859, a young energetic preacher named John K. Nutting inspired the members to begin building a permanent meeting place. Property was donated, the foundation laid with rock from a nearby quarry, and everything was made ready for the framing. Then the Civil War broke out in 1861 and brought the construction to a halt. John Nutting would not give up. Within a few months, he had assembled enough donated materials and free labor to complete the framing and exterior part of the church building.

In the winter of 1863-64, W. S. Pitts was invited to teach music at

A Song Is Born

the Bradford Academy. This was his first visit back to Bradford since that day in June 1857 when he was inspired to write his yet unpublished song. What a surprise it must have been as he retraced his steps to view that "spot of rare beauty." There among the beautiful cedar trees and natural flowers stood a church building just as he had envisioned. Not only was there a church building located on his "ideal spot," but also the building was painted brown just like in his song.

Five years after construction began, the church building was dedicated on December 29, 1864, and Mr. Pitts sang his song in public for the first time.

Yet this amazing story continues. Bradford, a thriving town of over one thousand people, lost its bid for a railroad to the nearby town of Nausa. By the turn of the century, the town had died, the church was inactive, and its building was in a state of disrepair. High grass and weeds filled the once beautiful grounds. Then in 1910-11, a popular male quartet known as The Weatherwax Brothers included the song, *The Little Brown Church in the Vale* in their programs along with its romantic story. This time the song caught the imagination of thousands, and they all wanted to see the little brown church. Efforts were established to restore the church building and to revive the congregation. Today, nothing remains of Bradford, Iowa, that would remind you of a once thriving town.
No deserted streets. No run down buildings or homes. In fact, only two structures remain from the original town. One is the red brick building formally known as the Bradford Academy where Mr. Pitts taught his music classes, and the other is "The Little Brown Church in the Vale."

The providence of God is a marvelous mystery. A setting of natural beauty inspired a song and provided an ideal location for a church building. Later, the song inspired His followers to overcome all odds and keep the congregation alive even though the town died. I think we all realize that God's Church is not made of sticks and bricks, but is made up of people, Christians who assemble collectively to worship. Yet the place we meet often plays an important part in our growing up. Our childhood memories are filled with the good times we experienced

A Song Is Born

at church. The lessons we learned in Bible Class. The songs we sang in worship. The day we gave our heart to God and promised to obey his word. Remembering places and events can be an effective tool in revitalizing our commitment to God.

And God placed all things under his feet and appointed him to be head over everything for the church, which is his body, the fullness of him who fills everything in every way. [Ephesians 1:22-23]

Text first appeared in a leaflet in 1869.
Tune with Text first appeared in Songs of Devotion by W. H. Doane, 1870

And this is my prayer: that your love may abound more and more in knowledge and depth of insight. [Philippians 1:9]

More Love To Thee, O Christ

A gifted and prolific writer of best sellers, Elizabeth Prentiss was strong in spirit, but frail in body. Throughout her life, she scarcely knew a moment free of pain. Born in Portland, Maine, in 1818, she was the youngest daughter of Edward Payson, a Congregational minister. In 1845, she married George Prentiss, a Presbyterian minister and professor. Their union was blessed with two boys.

During the mid 1850s, while working with a church in New York City, George and Elizabeth Prentiss lost their oldest son in an epidemic. A short time later, the youngest son also died. Elizabeth was almost inconsolable. One evening, she told her husband, *"sometimes I don't think I can stand living for another moment, much less a life time."* George replied, *"but it is in times like these that God loves us all the more. Just as we love our own children more when they are sick or troubled or distressed."* During this period of grief, she meditated upon the story of Jacob, how God met him during his moments of grief. She thought of Sarah Adam's hymn, *Nearer My God To Thee*. She also remembered a comment from her husband's last sermon, *"Love can keep the soul from going blind."*

With this grief and these thoughts, she wrote a poem, but did not think very highly of her work and put it away. Thirteen years later, she rediscovered that poem and showed it to her husband, George. Through his encouragement, the poem we know as *More Love to Thee, O Christ* was published in 1869. Though her best sellers have long been forgotten, the one poem she regarded as inferior has outlived everything she ever wrote.

The more we know about God, the more we understand His love toward us. When grief and tragedy strike our lives, draw closer to God by increasing your study of His word.

Whoever does not love does not know God, because God is love. [1 John 4:8]

RJT

A Song Is Born

"From A Mud hole in West Texas to Glory"

THE GLORYLAND WAY

John Cornelius and Mary Elizabeth (Macauley) Torbett came to Texas in 1869 and eventually settled in Coryell County. They were devout church members, often affectionately called "Singing Methodists," for music was a great part of their Scottish-Irish heritage. John Torbett followed the long-standing family tradition of service, serving in the military, in education, and in the practice of medicine. He served four years in the Civil War – was wounded twice and captured at Gettysburg.

This tradition of service and excellence continued through the children of J. C. and Mary Torbett. Of their seven children, three became doctors and another married a doctor, one was the Chief Engineer of a hospital and yet another was a school teacher. All six children lived and practiced in Marlin, Texas. In fact, their son-in-law, John W. Cook, and their oldest son, J. W. Torbett, Sr. is credited with pioneering the health benefits of the town's mineral water, which the town had considered a curse. In 1898, Mr. Cook and J.W. Torbett built the first major  bathhouse, a beautiful structure called the Bethesda. It stood until 1991 when it was destroyed by fire. In 1908, J. W. Torbett, alone with other investors, built the huge Torbett Sanatorium. This building itself is now gone, but the pavilion which stood in front and covered the original artesian water well is still standing, and the water continues to flow some 100 years later. Advertised as "One of the world's leading health resorts," tens of thousands of visitors came each year, from the average family, to Presidents, to royalty. Today, however, no working bathhouses remain in Marlin.

Years later, when most of the family lived in Marlin, Texas, their father, J. C., would often visit his children, now doctors, in the Sanatorium, just passing the time of day. One day, while recalling his Civil War experiences, he had a bad coughing spell, and coughed up a miniball from his old war wounds. Apparently it had lodged near his lungs and he had carried the miniball for over 50 years without noticeable harm. The doctors loved to tell the story of seeing that miniball.

The contribution of the Torbett family to the Marlin community, to its health care system and to education in general, was tremendous. But what about the seventh child? He was not a doctor – nor a public school teacher. He did not move to Marlin like all the others, but spent his life in Gatesville, Texas. The interesting thing is that if this seventh child had not written a song we love to sing, the accomplishments of the other six children would be left to local historians.

James Samuel Torbett was born March 15, 1868, in Tennessee, but moved to Texas the next year when the Torbett family came west. If J.S. Torbett were alive today, he might say in the spirit of some of our current bumper stickers, "I wasn't born here (Texas) but I got here as fast as I could." Mr. Torbett joined the Methodist Church as a child, but was never active. This is not to say that he was not involved in religious activity, but that he married a young lady who was an active member of the Church of Christ and he always attended church with her. On March 5, 1893, he married Miss Eugenia Wicker of Mound, Texas. They had four children, James Eugene, Annice Amanda (Pierce), Ellen Annez (Rinehart), and Samuel Edwin. "J. S. Torbett's wife, Eugenia Wicker, was an elegant lady of high moral character, and a strong member of the Church of Christ,"  said Wanda Wicker Morgan, a cousin. Wanda's father, Jackson Wicker, was an elder of the Church of Christ for many years. "After Eugenia's father died in 1903, her mother, Missouri Squyers Wicker, was instrumental in bringing many of the old-time gospel preachers into the county, renowned ministers such as Cled Wallace, Foy Wallace Sr., and others, often paying the expenses herself. When the problem of instrumental music and missionary societies came up, Eugenia and her sister Ethel chose to go with the First Christian Church much to the dismay of the Wicker family. About 20 years before Eugenia died in 1949, she returned to the non-instrumental Churches of Christ and spent her last years teaching ladies Bible Class. "J. S. Torbett attended services regularly with his wife" said Wanda.

James S. Torbett was a man of many interests, from all types of music, to business, and even including the search for lost treasure. "I

A Song Is Born

remember he financed several quests for lost treasures," said Wanda. But he was first and always a musician, composing and writing over 100 gospel songs. Songs such as *"Glory-land Way," "Open the Pearly Gates,"* and *"When the Angels Come For Me."* It has been said that "J.S. Torbett taught everyone in Coryell County to sight read and to sing." Others have said "he taught more people to sing than any other in the southwest." He also wrote popular secular songs and taught music, both vocal and instrumental. Jim, as he was often called, played the violin as well as taught many to play it. Mr. Torbett remained in great demand to lead singing at Sunday afternoon singings and at funerals all of his life. He was friends with V. O. Stamps and many other well-known singers and songwriters of his time.

In addition to a lifelong career in music, J. S. Torbett operated a large bookstore on the southwest side of Town Square in Gatesville. He did a thriving business for more than 30 years. According to E. S. Winfield, a local resident who worked for Mr. Torbett in the 20s, "it was more than a bookstore. His slogan was 'Torbett sells everything.'" Wanda, his cousin who also worked for him, recalls, "his store was a veritable fairyland for me as a child. In addition to a huge stock of books, he carried fine candies (especially chocolates) and a huge stock

of toys. His son Edwin was a watchmaker and had his shop in the store also. As a teenager, I worked for Mr. Torbett during the Christmas season. Unfortunately by this time (that she worked for him), age had taken its toll on Mr. Torbett. He didn't restock with new items and the store just withered away." J. S. Torbett retired from the business world around 1937.

From a Mud Hole in Texas to Glory

J. S. Torbett was one of the first to own a car in Coryell County. In the early 1920s, he was hired to teach a singing school in Turnersville, a small town located about twenty-five miles NW of Gatesville. Though the dirt roads were often muddy, he proudly drove his car. As fate would have it, the rains came and he got stuck in the mud in Turnersville. While waiting for a farmer to bring his team of mules and pull him out, Mr. Torbett spent the time writing what became his most popular song, *The Glory-land Way.*

A Song Is Born

J. S. Torbett went to glory May 15, 1941. The list of 25 honorary pall bearers at his funeral reads like a list of who's who among Gospel Music, including people like Frank Stamps, Ernest Rippetoe, etc. James Samuel Torbett and his wife Eugenia are buried in the City Cemetery, Gatesville, TX, along with their son, Samuel Edwin. Funeral services were conducted at the Church of Christ on 10th and Saundens St. The Minister was E. D. Shelton.

A song, inspired and written while stuck in the West Texas mud, provides comfort to those of us who are stuck in the quagmire of life. If we keep our thoughts focused on our real home in glory, the cares of everyday living will go away.

I press on toward the goal to win the prize for which God has called me heavenward in Christ Jesus. [Philippians 3:14]

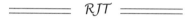

RJT

© Copyright 1982 Integrity's Hosanna! Music. All Rights Reserved. Used by Permission.

A Song Is Born

I said to the Lord, "You are my Lord; apart from you I have no good thing." [Psalm 16:2]

MORE PRECIOUS THAN SILVER

Barbara Lynn DeShazo was born in 1956 in Birmingham, Alabama. She developed an interest in music at an early age, learning to play the guitar by the age of 11. By the time she entered Auburn University, Lynn had already developed an active interest in writing songs, mostly praise and worship material. After graduating from Auburn University in 1978, she continued to pursue the writing of songs and is currently self-employed, writing exclusively for Integrity Music. But before the song writing job opportunities would come, Lynn had to seek employment wherever she could, and for a time she worked at the local McDonalds to support her real interest. It was during this time in her career that Miss DeShazo wrote her very popular praise and worship chorus, *More Precious Than Silver.*

"The Lord gave me *More Precious Than Silver* in July of 1979 during a private time of worship," said Lynn DeShazo. "As I recall, I had gone to my room one Wednesday evening to spend some time worshipping the Lord before a church service I had planned to attend later. While meditating on Proverbs 3:15, and recalling that Christ "Became to us wisdom from God" (1 Cor. 1:30), the words and music came to me. I was amazed at how quickly it came, and thrilled to realize that it was from God Himself. (Receiving songs by the inspiration of the Holy Spirit was still a new experience for me at that time.) I shared the chorus later with my church during a time of open sharing and testimony."

To refresh my memory of that time, I called and talked to some of my friends who were present that night. What they recalled was that I had shared how special the song was to me because the Lord had given it to me after I had "blown" a one-day fast that the whole church was participating in. I was working at McDonalds in Auburn, Alabama, at the time, and was responsible for the french fry station. Well, the temptation of all those golden

fries got to me, and I succumbed! I felt rather badly about it, and I'm sure I must have started out the private worship time that evening by repenting for dipping into the french fries on a fast day! Praise God that the song didn't come out, "Lord, you are much better than french fries!"

Lynn DeShazo has written more than 200 songs to date. Pursuing a contemporary Christian artist career requires constant travel, but Lynn has always embraced the need to be part of a local church, someone to be accountable to. "I've always felt the local church was very important. Among other benefits and needs, it keeps you from getting a big head," Lynn said. She is involved with the worship team at the Liberty Church, Birmingham, Alabama.

A song inspired by someone who broke a promise to God and to her local church continues to inspire millions today to worship God.

We live in a very materialistic society. Everything we have or do is measured by its material or social value. The style or make of our cars, the size of our home, the designer clothes we wear, all are usually measured by how much they cost. How do you measure your love and commitment to God? Is God more precious to you than money? More precious than your time? Is God more precious than silver or gold to you? We are foolish if our main concern in life is self. The love and respect we have of God and our fellowman should be the measure of a person's true wealth.

Happy is the man who finds wisdom, and the man who gains understanding; For her proceeds are better than the profits of silver, and her gain than fine gold. She is more precious than rubies, and all the things you may desire cannot compare with her.
[Proverbs 3:13-15]

═══ RJT ═══

A Song Is Born

No temptation has seized you except what is common to man. And God is faithful: he will not let you be tempted beyond what you can bear. [1 Corinthians 10:13]

SOMETIME WE'LL UNDERSTAND

Maxwell Newton Cornelius was born July 30, 1842, on a farm in western Pennsylvania. He left the farm at an early age to earn a living in the building and construction trade. He was very successful and soon established his own company. While building a house in Pittsburgh, Pennsylvania, Mr. Cornelius suffered a tragic accident, severely mangling his leg. The doctors decided that the damaged leg must be amputated. He withstood the operation well, but felt his house building career was ended. He then decided to enter college and obtain an education. After graduating with honors, he entered the Presbyterian Ministry in 1871, and remained in the East for several years. Because of his wife's poor health, they moved to Pasadena, California, in 1885. There he established an effective ministry, taking a struggling church of 100 members to 1000 members in less than three years, even though hampered at times with an unexpected economic collapse.

While struggling to meet the financial obligations on the new church building during this economic downturn, and at the same time caring for his wife's rapidly declining health that required much more of his time, Mr. Cornelius wondered why God had permitted so many tragic events to occur in one person's life, especially since he was striving to serve Him! He was suddenly filled with remorse, feeling his load was too great to bear.

Then he began to think about "God's better land," beyond the reach of sorrow and tears, where God's children would understand the reasons for the tears. With these thoughts heavy on his mind, he was inspired to write his one and only poem, which still stands today as an affirmation of his faith in God, no matter what trials may come his way.

His wife died shortly after he wrote the poem, and he preached the funeral. At the conclusion, he read his newly written poem. Both the words to his poem and the sermon were printed in the newspaper, where evangelist Major Whittle discovered the poem. Impressed by its beauty,

A Song Is Born

he wrote the chorus and encouraged James McGranahan to compose the music we still use today.

The answer to life's suffering can not be explained by human logic, but someday, in God's own time and place, we'll understand. In the meantime, heed the admonition added by Mr. Whittle in the chorus, as he summarized the thoughts of Maxwell Cornelius,

> *Then trust in God through all the days,*
> *Fear not for he doth hold thy hand.*
> *Though dark thy way still sing and praise,*
> *Sometime, sometime we'll understand."*

Dear friends, do not be surprised at the painful trial you are suffering, as though something strange were happening to you. But rejoice that you participate in the sufferings of Christ, so that you may be overjoyed when his glory is revealed. [1 Peter 4:12-13]

RJT

Text first appeared in Fawcett's Hymns adapted to the Circumstances of Public Worship, England 1782
The tune, DENNIS, appeared in The Psaltery edited by Lowell Mason and George J. Webb, 1845.
Original tune found in Nageli's Christliches Gesangbuch, 1828.

A Song Is Born

Finally, all of you live in harmony with one another; be sympathetic, love as brothers, be compassionate and humble. [1 Peter 3:8]

BLEST BE THE TIE THAT BINDS

John Fawcett had been left an orphan when he was 12 years old. He had to work long fourteen-hour days in a sweatshop to make ends meet, leaving little time for formal training. He learned to read by candlelight. At the age of sixteen, he was greatly impressed with the preaching of George Whitefield. In 1758, at the age of 18, he married Susannah Skirrow, and within five years they had four children. The same year he married, he joined the Baptist Church and, by 1765, had become the preacher at Wainsgate, a small Yorkshire village.

By the summer of 1772, John Fawcett's family had increased but his salary of less than $200 per year, paid partly in potatoes and wool, was not increasing as fast as his expenses. After seven years with the Wainsgate church, a congregation of less than 100 people, he received an invitation to preach for a much larger, more affluent church in London England. John was overcome with joy and immediately made preparations to move. The invitation had been formally accepted. The farewell sermon had been preached and the packing begun with the help of the Wainsgate members, even though they could not hide their reluctance and disappointment.

It is reported that the wagons had arrived and the loading begun, until there were only a few items remaining. He and his wife stood nearby in silence and deep thought, until she asked, *"Do you think we are doing the right thing? I do not know how to leave."* He thought for a moment, walked to the porch and exclaimed, *"unload the wagons, we are staying."* The Fawcett's never left the small church in Wainsgate, England. He remained there until his death in 1817, a total of 52 years even though there were more offers to relocate for better wages.

John and Susannah Fawcett gave up their ambitions and increased income to remain with a little congregation who needed them. The church family tie was stronger than wealth and fame. Sometime after

A Song Is Born

this event, John wrote the hymn poem we have sung for over 200 years. "*Blest be the tie that binds, our hearts in Christian love.*"

The tie that binds us as Christians is not social, economical, racial, or national. It is divine; it is spiritual and eternal, and not lightly broken. To be in fellowship with God we must be in fellowship with our brothers and sisters in Christ. You cannot be godly and ignore the bond between fellow Christians. This bond involves *caring*, *sharing*, and *bearing* each other's burdens. Fellowship and brotherly love will cost us time and energy, but we must be involved in the lives of others. Mr. Fawcett sacrificed ambition and personal gain for the fellowship of those he loved. A great example for each to follow.

Anyone who claims to be in the light but hates his brother is still in the darkness. Whoever loves his brother lives in the light—. [1 John 2:9-10]

Brethren, if a man be overtaken in a fault, ye which are spiritual restore such a one in the spirit of meekness; considering thyself, lest thou also be tempted. Bear ye one another's burdens and so fulfill the law of Christ. [Galatians 6:1-2]

RJT

A Song Is Born

One Day At A Time

You, Just give me the strength to do ev-'ry day what I have to do; Yes-ter-day's gone, sweet Je-sus, and to-mor-row may nev-er be mine, Lord, help me to-day, show me the way one day at a time.

Live a life worthy of the Lord, and please him in every way: bearing fruit in every good work, growing in knowledge of God.
[Colossians 1:10]

ONE DAY AT A TIME

This is the story about a native Texan who somehow survived the death of her father just before High School graduation, the death of her first husband in WW II, a broken second and third marriage, the magnetic pull of drugs and alcohol in the "Nashville scene," and emerged to become a top-notch singer and songwriter of popular music. She produced such great secular hits as *Waterloo, PT-109*. Additionally, this devout Baptist lady became an inspiration by writing spiritual songs such as *One Day At A Time, The Scars in the Hands of Jesus* (currently in many hymnals), and many more.

She was born Marijohn Melson July 14, 1920, in Kemp Texas. Marijohn moved with her family to Sanger, Texas, at the tender age of three. It was here that her father, Earnest Melson, opened the *"Veribest Bakery."* Mr. Melson's generosity quickly became well-known. Hobos, drifters, and anyone looking for free grub during the Depression Era knew about this place, because Mr. Melson would give free day-old bread to anyone if they would listen while he read the scriptures to them.

The only child of a relatively prosperous businessman, Marijohn never wanted for any material things early in life, but as she approached her last years in Sanger High School, things begin to change. Her dad developed cancer and died, leaving the bakery in the hands of Marijohn and her mother, Karla. After some delay, she was able to attend college, first at Baylor, then at Hardin Simmons University in Abilene, Texas. Here, she became a member of the renowned *"Cowboy Band,"* the first and only female member at that time of this prestigious musical troupe. Marijohn's performances gained her considerable attention. W. Lee (Pappy) O'Danel, a popular governor of Texas, enlisted her to tour with his campaign for re-election. Her beautiful low alto voice and savvy stage presence helped her to earn a living, even though it never was her desire to be a performer.

While at Hardin Simmons she met, courted, and later married Bedford Russell, the son of a medical doctor. He was a football letterman and a newly commissioned military pilot. Marijohn willingly gave up a movie contract and a promising career in music, content to settle down as a mother and housewife. The newlyweds left Abilene, a town with minimal violence and virtually no alcohol, to a military life where nightclubs and drinking were a way of life. Tragedy struck quickly! Bedford was killed shortly after reaching the war's front lines. His death seemed to destroy her lifetime dream of family, home, and children. She took a job teaching sixth grade, not singing, not playing the piano, no music, just teaching. Her drinking increased as she plunged deeper into sorrow and depression. Marijohn knew from the beginning that her second marriage was a mistake. To this union was born one son, John Buck, on April 26, 1946, ten years to the day after her father had died. Bucky, as he became known by, has become a top-notch songwriter himself, writing such hits as *GTO, All-American Girl, Sandy,* and many more.

Now, in 1949 at the age of 29, a widow and a divorcee supporting her son and her mother, she once again felt the need to develop a lasting relationship, and soon married Art Wilkin. Marijohn was always endowed with more strength and fortitude than most. She began to write songs to provide original material for her boy's choir, and this set her on an unparalleled career of songwriting. After a short period of nightclub singing to support the family, something she still feels uncomfortable with, Marijohn moved to Nashville and devoted herself full time to writing country songs. She wrote with and for such noted performers as Jimmy Dean, Kris Kristofferson, Lefty Frizzell, Les Paul and Mary Ford, Stonewall Jackson, Mel Tillis, Webb Pierce, and the list goes on. Her hits number many, like *Waterloo, Long Black Veil, Shanghaied, Mary Don't You Weep, PT 109* just to name a few. In addition to writing, she sang backup on hundreds of hit records with the Jordanaires, Anita Kerr Singers, Johnny Cash, Glen Campbell, Hank Locklin (including the unforgettable *Please Help Me I'm Falling).*

Even with this remarkable success, she was not satisfied. She never felt that writing country songs was her calling. "I never felt that I belonged," said Marijohn. "To be believable, country songwriters must bear their soul, something I was taught not to do. Also, country songs try to say 'I can't live without someone.' I could and had made it on my own." The year 1964 was especially hard on Marijohn. Her personal life was in a mess, her third marriage was crumbling, her job of six years with Cedarwood Music was now over and her mentor, Jim Denny, suffered and died of cancer much the same way as her dad. By Thanksgiving of 1964, she was at the end of her emotional rope. Now drinking heavily again, she tried to end her life with pills. Two friends, Mel Tillis and Red Foley, by chance or by the providence of God happened by to rescue her. After once more trying to end it all, Marijohn slowly begin to reason "Lord, I think you're trying to tell me something." Thus began a long, long journey back to God.

"Bookstores are filled with dramatic accounts of people turning or returning to God," Marijohn said, "Unfortunately, readers are often led to believe that as soon as one makes a decision for God, everything jumps into focus. This simply is not true." Marijohn began to search for religious satisfaction through yoga, cards, seances, Buddhism, and even took a trip to Israel to learn more about Judaism. *"It was a slow transition away from God and a slow process back to Him,"* she said. Once again death of someone close really affected her. (Losing those close to her had always set off tragic emotions in the past.) This time, it was her mother who died, and also a close friend and business partner, Hubert Long. Once again Marijohn was heartbroken, but this time she reacted with a new sense of understanding. Back in Texas again for a brief time, amid childhood memories and newfound wisdom, Marijohn began to reclaim some of her heritage, herself, and her God.

"I had not been to church in many years," Marijohn indicated. "Finally, back in Nashville, I said, 'I've got to have some help; it's more than I can handle!' I dialed a prayer number found in the phone book. As I drove (to meet the minister) in my brand new Cadillac and expensive clothing, I thought, How ironic that I need help!' But I did. The minister saw my distress. He told me to thank God for the problems and to let God handle them." Her questions and doubt about prayer began years before when Baptists all over Texas prayed for her father, yet he still died. From that time until now, her communication with God had been very erratic. "I didn't realize that prayer and praying was to help me - not necessarily to change the situation. I finally understood; I prayed: 'Lord change me so I can accept the situation.' When I prayed this, even I was totally amazed," said Marijohn.

After praying with the minister from the prayer hotline, she went home. As she prayed in the quiet of her home, Marijohn began to write her now famous song *One Day at A Time.* Her thoughts must have been, "Lord just help me make it this day. Tomorrow, I'll talk to you again about that day." As the years have passed since *One Day at A Time* was jotted down on paper by a weeping, conquered lady in Nashville, this prayer song just becomes more incredible. It is a BMI Award winner. It won the 1975 Gospel Music Association Dove Award. It has been recorded at least 200 times.

We too can benefit from the lesson learned by Marijohn over a lifetime, and expressed through her beautiful song, *One Day at a Time.* You can face the ever-changing, unbelievable pressures of life if you just take it one step at a time, one day at a time, and let the Lord be your guide. We live in a world that demands instant results or instant

A Song Is Born

gratification. I think it's time to revisit the wisdom of the Psalmist who said *"Be still and know that I am God."* (Psalm 46:10) Take time each day for a quiet talk with God and to exalt the Lord in Praise.

Life certainly has not been kind to this quiet lady from Texas. More and more demands are placed upon her already burgeoning schedule. There is the endless clanging of important incoming telephone calls. I might add that she is one of a very few celebrities who will return your call. As I, a complete stranger, wanting to know more about her and her songs, she took the time to call, to write, and to offer me encouragement. Marijohn's story is unique. It is an account of pain and glory that few people have experienced. Her music, a beautiful gift from God, will stand as her monument. I close with some very fitting words, taken from her song, *Lord, Let Me Leave a Song*.

> *Some folks leave wealth of silver and gold,*
> *Some leave letters like Paul*
> *But the saddest story that's ever been told*
> *Is the man who leaves nothing at all.*
>
> *Like a shadow that's cast on the sidewalks of time,*
> *In one fleeting moment it's gone;*
> *Let me leave something real, something, Lord, that will last*
> *Lord, let me leave a song.*
>
> *Lord let me be a servant to man*
> *Even after I'm gone;*
> *In the language of love we all understand*
> *Lord, let me leave a song.*
>
> *So give me a song the whole world will sing*
> *After my spirit has flown;*
> *Let the words inspire some soul to climb higher*
> *Lord, let me leave a song*
>
> Marijohn Wilkin

But the Counselor, the Holy Spirit, whom the Father will send in my name, will teach you all things and will remind you of everything I have said to you. Peace I leave with you; my peace I give you. - - Do not let your hearts be troubled and do not be afraid. [John 14:26-27]

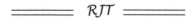

A Song Is Born

Brighten The Corner

And let us consider one another in order to stir up love and good works. [Hebrews 10:24]

BRIGHTEN THE CORNER

The song, *Brighten the Corner,* was written almost a century ago, but its message is timeless. Do what you can today with the talent and resources available, and don't wait for some great event to show your love for Christ and others.

As the twentieth Century draws rapidly to a close, there are new songs in the air, songs like *Majesty, Glorify Thy Name, As the Deer, Awesome God, Shout to the Lord, Thank you Lord,* etc. The verdict is still out on how long these new songs will last, or if any of them have the staying power to become classics – capturing the spirit of our needs as we begin the twenty-first Century. But without a doubt, one of the most popular gospel songs during the first half of the twentieth Century was *Brighten the Corner Where You Are.*

Homer Rodeheaver, the masterful songleader for evangelist Billy Sunday, first introduced the song in 1913. This was the same year in which George Bennard wrote his famous song *The Old Rugged Cross.* Just three short years later, *Brighten the Corner* was so well known that Theodore Roosevelt used it to begin each political rally. During World War I, the song could be heard throughout the war trenches of France. By 1925, its popularity had extended to most foreign countries including China where the Nanking Baseball Team used *Brighten the Corner* as their official team song. It was sung before each game.

A Song Is Born

Mrs. Ina Duley Ogdon, the author of *Brighten the Corner*, lived all her life in Toledo, Ohio (1872-1964). Mrs. Ogdon was a gifted speaker as well as a talented singer. This devout Christian lady had a lifelong burning desire to influence thousands for Christ. She dreamed of being a missionary, helping the poor and needy souls in our large cities. She had visions of traveling to foreign lands, carrying the message of the Gospel to many, and had spent time planing and preparing herself well for this noble career. Many friends recognized her talents and predicted a great future. *"With a beautiful voice and her winning personality, she'll go a long way,"* neighbors were known to say.

Suddenly in 1912, her visions and dreams of greatness came to an abrupt end. She received word that her father had suffered a severe stroke and was in need of help. Mrs. Ogdon, with little thought about sacrificing her personal ambition and promising career, returned home to care for her invalid father. Gradually she learned to put aside her desires and in time, her resentment, accepting her new role of caretaker. As she wrote the words *"To the many duties ever near you now be true,"* she was busy washing dishes, cleaning house, bathing and feeding her invalid father, while at the same time being a wife and a mother to her eleven-year old son.

Then one day as she shared her dreams and disappointments with a neighbor, another hard working mother and housewife, the friend told her that the hours which she spent in her quiet home were the bright spots in her life. From that time on, Mrs. Ogdon began to view her task with a different attitude. She set about to become an inspiration to those around her.

Later, as she reflected back upon the experience, she said *"I had visions of speaking to thousands, but God had other plans. He put me back here (home) and commanded me to let my light shine before my family."* Mrs. Ogdon dreamed of speaking to thousands, but God used her song to inspire millions.

It's ironic that as *Brighten the Corner* begin to lose favor in the 1950s, we as a nation and as a people became more self-centered, overly concerned about our rights. The message is simple! Do what you can today with the talent and resources available. Don't wait for some great event to show your love. Many dream about greatness and often wait

A Song Is Born

for it before ever doing what they can, but true greatness begins at home. The words *"if"* and *"when"* often rob us of doing little acts of kindness that mean so much. *"If only I had the talent to speak!"* *"If only people would listen to my ideas!"* Or *"When I win the lotto I'm going to be so generous!"*

Some years' back, I remember a bumper sticker that caused a mild stir. It read *"Practice random acts of kindness."* I'm sure it was developed to counter the overused phrase, "Random Acts of Violence," but the underlying message was clear. During the Presidential campaign of George Bush (the first George), he talked of the need for many to perform small humanitarian acts of kindness and when put together, they would represent *"A thousand points of lights."*

There are so many scriptures using the phrase *"one another,"* we must conclude that concern and caring for each other is the center of Christianity. *Love one another* John 13:34; *Spur one another on toward love and good deeds,* Hebrews 10:24, just to mention two. Let's take a fresh look at the words of this great gospel song:

> *Do not wait until some deed of greatness you may do,*
> *Do not wait to shed your light afar,*
> *To the many duties ever near you now be true,*
> *Brighten the corner where you are."*

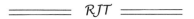

========= RJT =========

A Song Is Born

A Song Is Born

As a prisoner for the Lord, then, I urge you to live a life worthy of the calling you have received. Be completely humble and gentle; be patient, bearing with one another in love. Make every effort to keep the unity of the Spirit through the bond of peace. [Ephesians 4:1-3]

CAN HE DEPEND ON YOU

Sometimes we become so engrossed in our everyday activities that we lose sight of our purpose in life. We often use the expression; "We can't see the forest for the trees." How true! There comes a time when we should pause, and reflect upon the direction our life is going. Wilkin Bacon, affectionately known as "Big Chief," came home one night after a quartet concert reflecting on some of these same thoughts. *"I am supposed to be a child of God, but I am letting the demands of the quartet keep me away from many of the services of the church,"* he said. Brother Bacon changed his life. He left the quartet and became a minister for the Lord's kingdom. The song *Can He Depend on You* was written during this time. He had two purposes for writing it: A direct question to himself and to cause others to ponder the same question. *"For us He died that for Him we might live, Can He depend on you?"*

Wilkin Bacon, a Choctaw Indian, was born in Talihina, Oklahoma, in 1908. Most of his early life was spent teaching and singing. He spent a few years in the early 1940s, singing with the Stamps Quartet in and around Dallas, Texas. About 1944, he quit the full time quartet singing and became a minister of the Gospel, working for congregations of the Churches of Christ in Dallas, Corsicana, and Arlington, Texas, Duncan and Talihina, Oklahoma. The last 10 or 11 years of his active preaching career was for his hometown congregation in Talihina.

He never lost his love for singing and was always part of singing groups or quartets. In 1946, the *"Bacon Male Quartet"* was formed consisting of Paul Epps, Tex Stevens, Ray Wood, and Wilkin Bacon. He also sang in quartets with L.O. Sanderson and his son, Leon, Lowell and Nancy Brown, and V.E. Howard.

A Song Is Born

"The song was written in February 1945," Mary Bacon said. "We were living in Dallas. I remember he sat at our dining room table and wrote the words one night, staying up till 3 a.m. He wrote the music the following week. The thing that prompted the writing of this song, I am sure, was the death of our five-year-old daughter Barbara, in January 1945 (one month earlier). It was at that time that he left the Stamps Quartet and started doing full-time work for the Lord's church. He said at the time, 'The Lord could depend on him to do his will here on earth because heaven seemed so much sweeter now that Barbara was there.'"

Every relationship in life that is worthwhile involves responsibilities. Marriage, home, parenthood, school, work, church, serving God -- all of these depend on a commitment, a personal responsibility.

Sometimes we become so engrossed in everyday activities that we lose sight of our purpose in life. There comes a time when we must pause and reflect upon our purpose for living and on our commitments. Jesus gave His life so that you and I might follow Him. Can He depend on you to tell others the story of love?

More than 200 years ago, in 1762, Charles Wesley expressed some of the same thoughts of personal responsibility in another hymn:

"A charge to keep I have,
A God to glorify.
A never dying soul to save
And fit it for the sky."

―― *RJT* ――

A Song Is Born

> *The eternal God is your refuge, and underneath are the everlasting arms.* — [Deuteronomy 33:27]

SAFE IN THE ARMS OF JESUS

*H*ave you ever tried to be creative or tried to solve a problem while someone is rushing you? Have you tried to meet a deadline, while the boss is standing impatiently beside you? *Safe in the Arms of Jesus* was developed under these kinds of pressures. Frances Jane (Fanny) Crosby was born in Putman County (Southeast), New York, on March 24, 1820. The house is still there on Foggintown Road, looking much like it did more than 160 years ago. When she was six weeks old, she caught a cold, and a country doctor unwittingly prescribed a hot mustard poultice for her inflamed eyes. With the exception of being able to distinguish between day and night, she was totally blind for life. Soon afterward, her father John Crosby, died and her mother Mercy had to work to provide a living. It was Fanny's grandmother, Eunice, who provided  much of her early training. Fanny Crosby was a marvelous lady who never felt a moment of bitterness or remorse for her blindness or her plight in life. No doubt the results of a wise grandmother. When Fanny was about eight years old, she wrote:

> *"Oh, what a happy child I am, Although I cannot see!*
> *I am resolved that in this world, contented I will be."*

This poem was printed in the Saturday Evening Post. Later in life, she would remark "If I could ever meet him (the country doctor), I would tell him that unwittingly he did me the greatest favor in the world. By being blind on earth, when my sight is restored in Heaven, the first sight my eyes would behold would be that of my Savior." Fanny Crosby attended the New York Institute for the Blind for many years before becoming one of their instructors, teaching language and history. On March 5, 1858, she married Alexander Van Alstyne, a blind Methodist minister, musician, and fellow teacher. Because of the Institute's rules regarding husbands and wives working together, Fanny was dismissed.

A Song Is Born

The Van Alstynes had one child born the following year, who evidently died in early infancy. Alexander died on June 18, 1902. Fanny would seldom discuss her marriage or their child throughout her lifetime.

One afternoon during the summer of 1868, William Doane, a song writer as well as a successful businessman, visited Fanny Crosby, known affectionately as Aunt Fanny. Mr. Doane hurriedly explained "There is to be a state-wide Sunday School convention in Cincinnati with many young people and children, and I want a new hymn to capture their hearts." He went on to say that he had only 40 minutes, and then he must catch a train home. Fanny knew, having worked with Mr. Doane many times and because of her own intuition, that he had already composed the tune. She listened as William Doane played his new tune in a rousing and stirring manner on her piano, all the time encouraging Fanny to hurry so he could catch the train. Quickly she dictated the words to a friend and handed him the paper. In such a hurry, Doane folded the paper, put it in his pocket and rushed to meet his train. Once seated on board, he unfolded the paper and read:

> *"Safe in the arms of Jesus, Safe on His gentle breast:*
> *There by His love o'ershaded, Sweetly my soul shall rest.*
> *Hark! 'Tis the voice of angels, Borne on a song to me-*
> *Over the fields of glory, Over the Jasper sea. —"*

After writing more than 8000 poems, many of which are hymns that we sing today, *Safe in the Arms of Jesus* was to become Fanny Crosby's favorite. Fanny J. Crosby never let the circumstances of life affect her disposition. Life is what you make it. The difference between a life of usefulness and uselessness is attitude.

Safety and security are the most sought after feelings in life today. We hear horror stories about people working years for a company, only to lose their entire pension just short of retirement. No longer can we leave our homes unlocked or walk down the streets of our large cities without feeling uneasy or insecure. The only true safety and security is in the arms of God.

> *Fear of man will prove to be a snare, but whoever trusts in the Lord is kept safe.* [Proverbs 29:25]

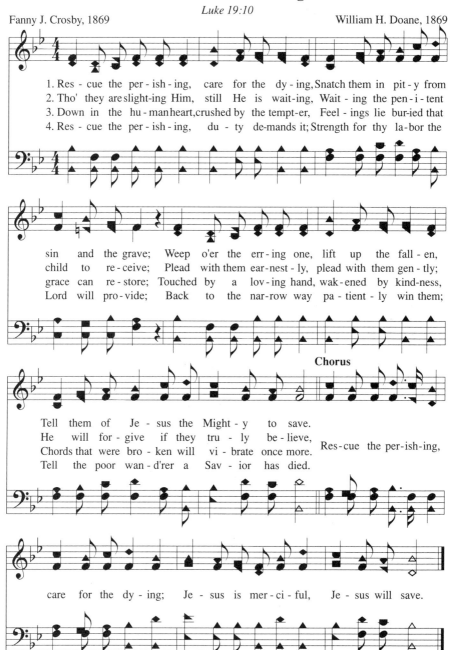

A Song Is Born

And the Lord said unto the servant, Go out into the highways and hedges, and compel them to come in, that my house may be filled. [Luke 14:23]

RESCUE THE PERISHING

Every large city has always had its place where the downtrodden, derelicts, drunks, out of work, and out of luck people congregate. Usually, there is a mission where meals and overnight lodging are available. Houston has the Star of Hope Mission; New York had the Bowery Mission.

Sometimes we feel very uncomfortable in this environment and stay clear of these areas. It could be that we doubt our own spiritual strength, faith, or ability to help. Others feel they might tarnish their reputation. Many may just fear the elements or surroundings.

For years, a tiny blind lady (less than five feet tall, weighing under 100 pounds), made regular visits to the New York Bowery Mission, speaking to them often. Fanny J. Crosby herself relates the following story of one such visit in 1869:

"I was addressing a large company of working men one hot summer evening, when the thought kept forcing itself on my mind that some mother's boy must be rescued that night or not at all. I made a pressing plea that if there were a boy present who had wandered from his mother's home and teaching, he would come to me at the close of the service. A young man of eighteen came forward and said, 'Did you mean me? I promised my mother to meet her in heaven, but as I am now living, that will be impossible.'"

A few days before, William H. Doane had sent me the subject suggestion, "Rescue the Perishing," and while I sat there that evening, the line came to me. "Rescue the Perishing, care for the dying." I could think of nothing else that night. When I arrived home, I went to work on the hymn and, before I retired, it was ready for the melody."

A Song Is Born

Our inner cities are filled with souls who need the message of God. I praise those with the strength and zeal to carry God's banner to them. Verse three seems to convey the message very well:

Down in the human heart, crushed by the tempter,
Feelings lie buried that grace can restore;
Touched by a loving hand, wakened by kindness,
Chords that were broken will vibrate once more.

Therefore go and make disciples of all nations, baptizing them in the name of the Father and of the Son and of the Holy Spirit. [Matthew 28:19-20

RJT

Rock of Ages

Augustus M. Toplady, 1776 — Thomas Hastings, 1830

1. Rock of Ages, cleft for me, Let me hide my-self in Thee, Let the wa-ter and the blood, From Thy wound-ed side which flowed; Be of sin the dou-ble cure, Save from wrath and make me pure.
2. Could my tears for-ev-er flow, Could my zeal no lan-guor know, These for sin could not a-tone, Thou must save, and Thou a-lone; In my hands no price I bring, Sim-ply to Thy cross I cling.
3. While I draw this fleet-ing breath, While my eyes shall close in death, When I rise to world's un-known, And be-hold Thee on Thy throne; Rock of A-ges, cleft for me, Let me hide my-self in Thee.

Text frist appeared in *The Gospel Magazine*, 1775 titled "Life a Journey."
Tune first appeared in *Spiritual Songs for Social Worship*, 1832.

A Song Is Born

For I do not want you to be ignorant of the fact, brothers, that our forefathers were all under the cloud and that they all passed through the sea — for they drank from the spiritual rock that accompanied them, and that rock was Christ. [1 Corinthians 10:1,4]

ROCK OF AGES

One day as Augustus Toplady was walking though the Barrington Coombs of England, he was caught in a sudden storm. Looking for shelter, he found a huge overhang or cleft and took refuge. As the storm raged, the words began to come to him. Looking for something to write on, the only thing available was a playing card. This popular legend about the writing of *Rock of Ages* may not be true, even though it is reportedly recorded in two standard British encyclopedias.

Augustus Toplady was converted to the Methodist belief at the age of 16, but later condemned its teachings and its founder, John Wesley, with great vigor. Wesley taught that man could live without sinning and that God's grace was free to all. Toplady, a strong follower of John Calvin's teachings, believed that all mankind were born lost, and that God saved only the elect. For years, Toplady poured out resentment and criticism in a series of sermons, pamphlets, letters, and printed materials. While Preaching in London, he became the editor of a religious publication "The Gospel Magazine." In March 1776, he wrote an article on the spiritual improvement and the national debt (of England). He sought to prove that man was as helpless to pay his debt of sin as was England able to liquidate her national debt. At one sin per second, Toplady figured one would accumulate 1 1/2 billion sins in 50 years and 2 1/2 billion in 80 years. He concluded, "Since no one can pay off such a debt, we rely on Christ alone to redeem us." At the end of this article, he placed a poem entitled *"A Living and Dying Prayer for the Holiest Believer in the World."* We know the poem as *Rock of Ages*. Many hymns have been written out of some deep personal need or experience. However, this hymn evidently was born out of spiritual controversy. It is possible that Toplady was inspired by a sudden storm, to recall the words of a sermon he had listened to sometime before, on the subject of

A Song Is Born

"O Rock of Israel, Rock of Salvation, Rock cleft for me." According to Toplady's own words, "he was so stirred by these thoughts that he could not shake them from his memory." It is likely that Toplady, having previously written the poem, used the scathing article against Calvinism to publish the hymn text we now sing.

Augustus Toplady died at age of 38, only two years after this poem was published. In spite of the original belligerent intent behind the publication of this text, God has, in His providence, preserved the hymn for more than 200 years. Perhaps it is because of the truths the hymn expresses, through the thoughts that, without being washed by the saving blood of Jesus Christ, we are spiritually dead. Nothing we can do merits the salvation God has promised, even if our zeal never becomes weak (Languor). "Vile," that is without Christ we are worth little, yet we can run to the "Fountain" that is Christ, for our source of life.

He is the stone you builders rejected, which has become the capstone. Salvation is found in no one else; for there is no other name under heaven given to men by which we must be saved. [Acts 4:11-12]

RJT

A Song Is Born

They were longing for a better country – a heavenly one. Therefore God is not ashamed to be called their God, for he has prepared a city for them. [Hebrews 11:16]

How Beautiful Heaven Must Be

An obscure choir member from a small country church wrote the words of this famous old hymn. The church's clerk and choir director wrote the music. Mr. Bland, himself a farmer and sawmill worker by trade, composed the tune for this memorable hymn. From such humble beginnings comes this popular hymn that no doubt has been sung at more funerals than almost any other song.

After repeated unsuccessful efforts to locate A. P. Bland in the central Alabama area, our search led us to Cullman, Alabama, the county seat for Cullman County. A search through the Public Library records provided no answers, but we did notice a large number of Blands had lived in the little town of Hanceville, just 10 miles south. We drove to Hanceville and began walking cemeteries and asking questions. At a little country store, the elderly owner said, "You need to talk to Thelma Jackson," and handed me the phone. She turned out to be a daughter of A. P. Bland.

Andy Pickens Bland was born November 13, 1876, in Dallas, Texas. His parents, James Elgin and Allie, lived there about six years before moving back to Alabama where they farmed in the black lands near Hanceville, living in a small house with no doors. This is more amazing after hearing stories from the children how granddad (Mr. James Elgin Bland) would plow the fields always carrying an ax to protect them from predators. One day Allie (their grandmother) was picking berries along the edge of the field when she spotted a small bear. She set the pail down and ran to tell grandpa. By the time he returned the bear had eaten the berries and left.

A. P. Bland often jokingly referred to himself as Apple Pie Bland. Even though he was born in Texas, he grew up near Hanceville, Alabama. There he farmed about 100 acres of land and often worked in a local sawmill. On July 1, 1900, A. P. married Array Jane Abercramb. They had seven children before she died in 1918 during childbirth. He then married Anne Jane Smith and to this union four girls were born. Thelma Jackson and Charleen Nelson, both still living in Hanceville, were children of A. P. and Anne Jane. In addition to farming, Mr. Bland served as choir director at the Bethlehem Baptist Church until his health began to fail. He always enjoyed singing and taught a few singing schools. Many of his approximately 30 songs were published by the J.M. Henson Music Company. Andy Pickens Bland died January 30, 1938, and is buried in the Bethlehem Church cemetery.

Mrs. A. S. Bridgewater, Cordie, was born around 1873 in North Carolina. She married A. Samuel Bridgewater from Tennessee and they lived near Hanceville, Alabama, from 1909 to 1917, where he farmed. It was during this time that she wrote the words to *How Beautiful Heaven Must Be*. The Bridgewaters left Hanceville about 1917, and no other records of them have been found.

In 1937, Roy Acuff sung *How Beautiful Heaven Must Be* at a performance, and Asher Sizemore of the Grand Ole Opry liked what he heard. He set out to locate A. P. Bland and traveled to his home for a visit. Thelma can still remember the excitement of this visit. Mr. Sizemore purchased the copyrights and went on the make the song famous. This enduring hymn, written by simple, down-to-earth, hardworking country folks will forever be etched into our minds and into the hearts of generations yet to come.

What is your mental picture of heaven? There is one thing sure about life, it will not last. Someday we will leave this home and take up residence elsewhere. Can you picture heaven?

> *The city does not need the sun or the moon to shine on it, for the glory of God gives it light, and the Lamb is its lamp. The nations will walk by its light, and the kings of the earth will bring their splendor into it. On no day will its gates ever be shut, for there will be no night there. The glory and honor of the nations will be brought into it. Nothing impure will ever enter it, nor will anyone who does what is shameful or deceitful, but only those whose names are written in the Lamb's book of life.* [Revelation 21:23-27]

A Song Is Born

Not to us, O Lord, not to us but to your name be the glory, because of your love and faithfulness. [Psalm 115:1]

TO GOD BE THE GLORY

The hymn, *To God Be the Glory,* was written in 1875 and made its first appearance in *Brightest and Best*, a Sunday School collection of songs. Other songs making their first appearance in the same book were *All the Way My Savior Leads Me; I am Thine, O Lord; Savior, More Than Life to Me,* etc. However, *To God be the Glory* was almost lost and forgotten here in the states, but it survived in Great Britain. In 1952, Cliff Barrows, a music director for Billy Graham, heard the song and included it in their London Crusade Songbook. Upon their return to the states in 1954, at a crusade in Nashville, Tennessee, it was reintroduced to the American people.

It is strange that neither Fanny Crosby nor W. H. Doane ever mentioned this hymn in any of their writings. And given its popularity over the last fifty years, it is odd that it was not included in the historic songbook *"Gospel Hymns"* by Ira Sankey in 1875.

Much has been written about Fanny Crosby, the author, including stories in this book, but little has been said about the composer.

William H. Doane was an ingenious, multitalented young man. While working for his dad, he developed a knack for accounting and bookkeeping. Quickly he put this talent to work when he was hired by the J. A. Fay Company, a large manufacturer of woodworking machinery with plants in four states. He soon was placed in charge of their entire bookkeeping systems and became what we call today the CFO, Chief Financial Officer. It wasn't long before his management skills were also recognized and Mr. Doane became the President and General Manager, or CEO. Mr. Doane had a third skill, that of engineering, and was the holder of at least 70 patents on woodworking machinery. His engineering expertise was widely recognized in America and the entire world. These skills earned him a very good living and considerable recognition, but today he is not remembered for any of these skills. It is his fourth talent for which we remember William H. Doane - - his ability to write beautiful, lasting hymn tunes.

Mr. Doane moved to Cincinnati, Ohio, in 1860 and moved into a beautiful Italian style home, which still stands today. The outside remains about the same as when it was built, but the inside has been converted into a multi-level medical clinic. Only one room remains virtually untouched from its original design. I recently had the opportunity to visit the Doane House, as it's still called, and was able to convince the doctor to let his nurse give me a tour of the last remaining original room. It was in this house, and perhaps the the very room where I stood, that William H. Doane wrote the music for *More Love to Thee, O Christ, Rescue the Perishing, Take the Name of Jesus with You, Safe in the Arms of Jesus, To God be the Glory,* and many more of his 2300 Gospel Hymns. Fanny Crosby was a frequent guest in this house, and they often collaborated on many hymns.

We are free to work, to play, to gain fame and fortune like Mr. Doane, but the only thing that will last is what we do for the Lord. How fitting the words of this almost forgotten hymn by Fanny Crosby and William H. Doane, "To God be the Glory" in everything we do!

The message of this song should resound in the heart of every Christian. The reason for man's creation and the whole purpose of his living is to express praise to God, both with our lips and with our lives. We give God glory because of His love, a love that provided redemption for us.

Ascribe to the Lord, O mighty ones, ascribe to the Lord glory and strength. Ascribe to the Lord the glory due his name; worship the Lord in the splendor of his holiness. [Psalm 29:1-2]

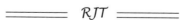

A Song Is Born

> *I no longer call you servants, because a servant does not know his master's business. Instead, I have called you friends.* [John 15:15]

WHAT A FRIEND WE HAVE IN JESUS

Joseph Scriven began his life full of promise and with high expectations. He had ambitions to pursue a military career like his dad, Captain John Scriven of the Royal Marines, but had to abandon those plans after struggling for two years with poor health. He could not take the rigors of military life. After receiving his BA degree from Trinity College, Dublin, Ireland, he was all set to make it in the business world. At this time he became engaged to marry a beautiful Irish lass, but his bride-to-be accidentally drowned the evening before their wedding. When Scriven saw the body taken from the waters, he suffered a shock that was to stay with him forever. After this tragic death, Mr. Scriven left Ireland to find solace in Canada. He spent the rest of his life in the small towns of Port Hope and Lake Rice, Ontario.

Some thought Joseph Scriven rather strange and eccentric, but to the many he helped, he was God's answer to prayer. He was a true friend to the needy and the underprivileged. Joseph would seek out orphans and those underdeveloped to help, he would cut firewood and do carpentry work for widows, but he would never hire out to work for those able to pay. Joseph never owned a home! He lived with friends, basically with the two families whom he served as a private tutor.

It was in a guest room of the Sackville home sometime in 1857 where he tutored their children and where he was inspired to write a poem for his grief-stricken mother who was back in Ireland. He titled the poem *"A Friend Who Understands"*. The poem was never intended for anyone else to see, other than his mother. But in fact, it was being sung as a hymn some 10 years before Scriven knew it, or before anyone else knew who wrote the poem. How the poem got printed, we can't say for sure. When a friend, who was taking care of him during a prolonged period of ill health, noticed the poem among his writings, he asked Mr. Scriven if it was his. He replied *"The Lord and I wrote it between us."*

A Song Is Born

Falling in love for a second time some 16 years after his first attempt to marry ended with the death of his bride-to-be, he became engaged again, this time to Miss Eliza Catherine Roche. However, she contracted pneumonia and died in 1860 before they could complete the wedding. The inscription on the grave marker simply reads, Scriven's Sweetheart.

With failing health, meager income, and fear of becoming helpless, he became greatly depressed. While ill and in his delirium, he staggered from bed and stumbled, exhausted, into a little creek and drowned. After his death, the citizens of Port Hope, Ontario, Canada, erected a monument on the Port Hope - Peterborough highway with these words "Four miles north, in Pengally's cemetery, lies the philanthropist and author of this great masterpiece, written at Port Hope, 1857."

Ira Sankey discovered the hymn in 1875, while he and Phillip Bliss were gathering songs for the first Sankey's Gospel Hymnbook. Later he wrote "The last hymn, which went into the book, became one of the first in favor."

Henry Brooks Adams (1838-1918) once said "One friend in a lifetime is much; two are many; three are hardly possible." Most of us have several we call friends. How many of our friendships are dependent upon social position or financial status? If we were to openly reveal our insecurities and prejudices, we would probably lose contact with many we consider friends. You see, some of us believe that if a friend gets into trouble, or falls into sin, they must be dropped, lest our reputations be soiled. Also, if a friend asks too often for a favor or fails to reciprocate adequately, or fails to call us often enough, the relationship could be jeopardized.

A friend is a person who knows all about us, yet loves us just the same. Jesus is that kind of true friend. He will never leave nor forsake us. *"What a friend we have in Jesus - -Can we find a friend so faithful - Jesus knows our every weakness."*

The power of speech is a beautiful gift from God. It is a source of joy, comfort, and intellectual power. This is only available to those who use it. Unless we pray, we have no contact with God. "Men ought always to pray." Prayer is not designed to help God, but for man's spiri-

A Song Is Born

tual growth. *What a friend we have in Jesus* admonishes us to take advantage of this special gift from God.

We have this assurance in approaching God, that if we ask anything according to his will, he hears us. And if we know that he hears us - whatever we ask - we know that we have what we asked of him. [1 John 5:14-15]

RJT

What Will Your Answer Be?
Romans 14:12
Tillit S. Teddlie, 1935 — Tillit S. Teddlie, 1935

1. Some day you'll stand at the bar on high, Some day your re-cord you'll see;
2. Sad - ly you'll stand if you're un-pre-pared, Trem-bling, you'll fall on your knees;
3. Now is the time to pre-pare, my friend, Make your soul spot-less and free;

Some day you'll an-swer the ques-tion of life, What will your an-swer be?
Fac - ing the sen-tence of life or of death, What will that sen-tence be?
Washed in the blood of the Cru-ci-fied One, He will your an-swer be.

Chorus
What will it be? What will it be? Where will you spend your e-ter-ni-ty?
What will it be, O what will it be? What will your an-swer be?
what will it be?

A Song Is Born

So then every one shall give account of himself to God.
[Romans 14:12]

WHAT WILL YOUR ANSWER BE

From time to time, most of us are attracted to the scene of an accident or a disaster. There seems to be something in our nature, which compels us to want a close up look. In days gone by, towns and courtrooms were often filled to capacity when a murder trial was in session, especially if the judge might pass out a death sentence. Such were the events that prompted the writing of the hymn, *What will your Answer Be,* in 1936.

Tillit Sidney Teddlie was born in Swan, Texas, in 1885. At the age of 18, he began teaching singing schools at night while picking cotton in the daytime. By 1923, Brother Teddlie begin preaching for the Churches of Christ in Texas and Oklahoma, and continued for more than fifty years. He tells the story about the inspiration for this hymn.

"I'd been holding a meeting in West Texas. On the way back home, I stopped in Vernon, Texas, where I'd formerly lived, and I learned that Brother Horace Busby was holding a meeting there. I decided to wait overnight and hear him preach. They told me that the court was in session and the judge was going to pass the death sentence on a young man from Amarillo. He was on trial for murder; accused of killing a mother and her baby, and burying them in a field. Well, I'd never been in a courtroom where they did that (pass the death sentence), and I thought I would just go and see what it was like. It was just about sundown as I walked in. The judge asked the large audience to rise. I bowed my head while he was giving out that sentence. It just sent a chill through the whole audience and me. You could just feel something terrible. I thought I'd just write something about that.

My mind was diverted for a month or two. Then one Sunday afternoon, while living in Electra, Texas, I sat down to write the song, but had no music paper. I drew the lines and spaces on some copy paper, and wrote all three verses, melody, and harmony. After playing it on the piano to check the harmony, I folded it up and sent

A Song Is Born

it to Stamps-Baxter, and they got it the next day."

Picture the final judgment, with God on His throne and Christ by his side. You stand there before the great Creator, unprepared, never knowing Christ, or worse yet, Christ denies any knowledge of you, as He hands out eternity sentences. A solemn thought!

And I saw the dead, great and small, standing before the throne, and books were opened. Another book was opened, which is the book of life. The dead were judged according to what they had done as recorded in the books. If anyone's name was not found written in the book of life, he was thrown into the lake of fire. [Revelation 20:12,15]

RJT

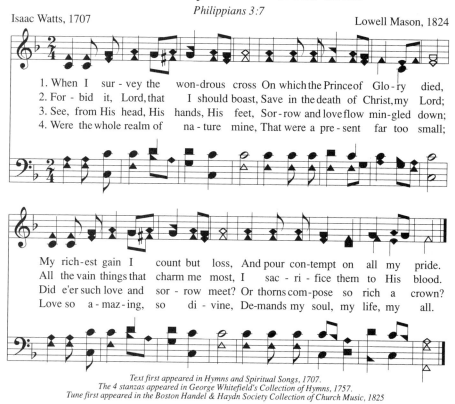

When I Survey The Wondrous Cross

Philippians 3:7

Isaac Watts, 1707 — Lowell Mason, 1824

1. When I sur-vey the won-drous cross On which the Prince of Glo-ry died,
   My rich-est gain I count but loss, And pour con-tempt on all my pride.
2. For-bid it, Lord, that I should boast, Save in the death of Christ, my Lord;
   All the vain things that charm me most, I sac-ri-fice them to His blood.
3. See, from His head, His hands, His feet, Sor-row and love flow min-gled down;
   Did e'er such love and sor-row meet? Or thorns com-pose so rich a crown?
4. Were the whole realm of na-ture mine, That were a pre-sent far too small;
   Love so a-maz-ing, so di-vine, De-mands my soul, my life, my all.

Text first appeared in Hymns and Spiritual Songs, 1707.
The 4 stanzas appeared in George Whitefield's Collection of Hymns, 1757.
Tune first appeared in the Boston Handel & Haydn Society Collection of Church Music, 1825

A Song Is Born

May I never boast except in the cross. [Galatians 6:14]

WHEN I SURVEY THE WONDROUS CROSS

A father and his teenage son were on their way home from church when a heated discussion developed about participation in worship. "Son," the father said, "I'm disappointed that you did not sing during worship." "Oh, dad, the songs are so boring and out-of-date," the teen replied. "Well, if you think you can write better songs, then I'll see to it that we sing them," the father challenged his rebellious son thinking he would surely silence him. The next Sunday and for each Sunday for over two years, Isaac Watts met that challenge with new songs. Songs like *Joy To the World, Alas! And Did My Savior Bleed, We're Marching To Zion,* and *When I Survey The Wondrous Cross.* Many have declared this last hymn to be the finest hymn in the English language.

This is the first known hymn in the English language to include the personal pronoun "I," and the first to express the experience of Christian faith. In this hymn by Isaac Watts, it was not acceptable to merely look at the cross or to gaze with wonder upon it, but he chose to survey its implications, to deliberate upon its applications to life. Let's use Isaac Watts' 18th Century approach and survey the cross using 21st Century language.

When I survey the wondrous Cross
On which the Prince of glory died,
My richest gain I count but loss,
And pour contempt on all my pride.

When I study the implications of the cross upon which the Prince of Glory was sacrificed, I find that there is nothing that is mine or of myself I can consider with any degree of pride. Who of us can truly say "we pour contempt on any kind of pride?" We are a proud people, proud of our family tree, our nationality, our position at work or in the community. We are proud of our education, our degrees from Universities, our religious beliefs, etc. We cultivate pride. When I think about the cross on which Christ gave his life for me, I realize just how small my best

A Song Is Born

efforts must be by comparison. There is nothing; nothing I can do of which I should be proud.

> *Forbid it, Lord, that I should boast,*
> *save in the death of Christ, my God.*
> *All the vain things that charm me most,*
> *I sacrifice them to His blood.*

Lord, stop me from bragging about anything, except the fact that Jesus died for me. Gladly will I give up the foolish things of this world, since I remember that His precious blood was shed for me, for my sins.

> *See, from His head, His hands, His feet,*
> *sorrow and love flow mingled down.*
> *Did e'vr such love and sorrow meet,*
> *or thorns compose so rich a crown?*

No other words could better describe His sacrifice. Picture, if you can, Jesus hanging on that cross. Nails in His hands and in His feet. Blood flowing freely from the crown of thorns on his head. Is there any greater love?

> *Were the whole realm of nature mine,*
> *that were a present far too small.*
> *Love so amazing, so divine,*
> *demands my soul, my life, my all.*

If I owned the whole world, if I win the lottery and gave it all to Him it would be a gift far too small to offer the Lord. The amazing truth is that even with such love as Christ has shown, no earthly gift is required. Just my soul, my life, just me! Believe in Him today, and obey His commands.

> *But whatever was to my profit I now consider loss for the sake of Christ. What is more, I consider everything a loss compared to the surpassing greatness of knowing Christ Jesus my Lord, for whose sake I have lost all things. I consider them rubbish, that I may gain Christ and be found in him.* [Philippians 3:7-9]

===== *RJT* =====

A Song Is Born

Every good and perfect gift is from above, coming down from the Father of the heavenly lights, who does not change like shifting shadows. [James 1:17]

WE LIVE IN A CHANGING WORLD

We live in a changing world. Truer words could not be spoken today, even though they were penned in this hymn nearly 30 years ago. I remember a popular saying in my younger days which said "The only thing certain in this world is change." In the last few years, this cliche has been modified to say, "Even change is changing, nothing is certain." That is, even the very nature of change and how we interact with it, has changed. Today, we make purchases, especially electronic components, knowing full well that they will be obsolete the next day. Such is the rapid pace of change. I recently attended a seminar where the speaker made a comment that tells you just how things will continue to change. "Of all the technology we have today, from personal computers, space travel, planes, phones, etc., only 1% of it will still be in use in the year 2050."

Melvin Stanton, the author of this timely hymn, was born August 31, 1930, near Centralia, MO. He was the last of seven children born to James and Bettie (McLane) Stanton of Centralia. Melvin grew up on the farm, helping his dad and uncle to care for several acres of farmland. On September 23, 1948, he was convicted to obey the Gospel and was baptized by Searcy White. With some encouragement by Searcy White and J. C. Roady, Melvin started preaching two years later. During his lifetime, he attended Bible schools in Hutchinson, Kansas; Bloomington, Indiana; Moberly and Jamesport, Missouri; but for the most part he considered himself a "self-made" minister.

On August 29, 1953, Melvin married Ella May Edgar. To this union were born three children: Solomon, Naomi, and Bettie. Melvin Stanton's preaching took him into ten states. According to his own records, in his lifetime he presided over 600 funerals, conducted nearly 100 weddings, and assisted in 200 baptisms. "I have preached in meeting houses without screens and some without electric fans," Mr. Stanton said. "When I first started preaching, there was no air-conditioning used and very few public

A Song Is Born

address systems." In his book *"Thirty-five Years of Preaching and Personal Work,"* he relates one humorous event that occurred when he first started preaching in 1952. "When I gave the invitation and everyone stood, an elderly man came down the aisle and looked right at me. I said to myself this is an elderly man and he's coming forward the first service. He came up to me and shook my hand and went right on past me to a door behind me and went outside to a restroom. I later learned he did that each Sunday." In the early 1980s, Melvin developed a brain tumor. The tumor was removed and he continued preaching on a limited basis although he was never able to fully regain his health. Melvin Stanton died September 14, 1996, and is buried in Centralia. On his tombstone are the words *"O Lord Thou Art Forever,"* another song he had written in 1972, and *"We Live in a Changing World,"* which brings me back to the development of this hymn.

As I began my search for Mr. Stanton, the only thing I knew was that he lived in Jamesport, Missouri, in 1971, the time this hymn was published. In the summer of 1998, I set out for Jamesport. It is a quaint little town located in the north-central part of Missouri. The first things you notice are the hitching post and the numerous horse-drawn vehicles around town. In 1953, the Amish people came to this area. Since then, it has grown to be one of the largest settlements of the Amish in Missouri with more than 165 families living on farms nearby. The Old Order Amish are direct descendants of the Mennonite Anabaptist, a group that formed during the Reformation in Germany and Switzerland. The Amish live in modest homes on rural farms and travel by means of horse-drawn buggies. Their religion forbids any reliance upon technology so they usually do not use electricity, and farm work is done without motorized implements.

Mr. Stanton never documented why or what had motivated him to write this poem. I learned from Ella, his widow, that her father had died two years before he wrote this poem, and that his mother had just died the previous year. No doubt these events had an impact upon him as he wrote, *"The faces once known have silently gone."* Yet, as I walked around Jamesport that hot, July day in 1998, it became clear to me that there were other factors which influenced Mr. Stanton to pen these words. When Melvin Stanton wrote *"We Live In A Changing World,"* he was the minister for the Church of Christ in Jamesport. All around him were

A Song Is Born

good, honest, hard-working people, many whose beliefs could not accept change. For them, change was evil. Anything new was suspect as being from the Devil. As I reflect upon this subject of change, it seems to me to be a two-edged sword. On the one hand, most of us resist change, preferring that everything remain the same as it has always been. Yet, on the other hand, few of us would be willing to give up our gadgets that modern technology has brought to us. Change is not inherently evil, but it does present us with a challenge to *"search the Scriptures daily,"* to evaluate the change in society's beliefs against God's Holy Book, the standard. The message Mr. Stanton wanted to give was that the world is constantly changing, but that's okay. The important thing is that God never changes.

Melvin Stanton was a simple hometown boy who loved people. His talents went far beyond preaching. As I walked around Jamesport, inquiring if anyone knew Melvin Stanton, I was impressed with their response. *"I remember him. He was a good man, always helping those in need. I think he was a minister for the Church of Christ."* It seemed that Melvin was known for always helping his neighbors. When it came time to spray the fruit trees, he was there. If someone was sick, he was there. If the children had a ballgame, he was there. What a marvelous testimony to the life of this fine Christian.

God's promises are unchanging and trustworthy because God is unchanging and trustworthy. You don't need to wonder if He will change His plans. Our hope is secure and immovable, anchored in God.

God also bound himself with an oath, so that those he promised to help would be perfectly sure and never need to wonder whether he might change his plans. He has given us both his promise and his oath, two things we can completely count on, for it is impossible for God to tell a lie. Now all those who flee to him to save them can take new courage when they hear such assurances from God; now they can know without doubt that he will give them the salvation he has promised them. (Living Word) [Hebrews 6:17-18]

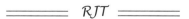

Text and tune appeared in *Hymns Old and New*, 1887, Fleming H. Revell Co.

A Song Is Born

> *By grace are you saved through faith.* [Ephesians. 2:8] *If a man claims to have faith, but has no deeds? Can such faith save him?* [James 2:14]

TRUST AND OBEY

The inspiration for this hymn came in 1886, when D.B. Towner was leading the singing for the noted evangelist, Dwight Moody. Mr. Moody was conducting a series of meetings in Brockton, Massachusetts. A young man responded to the call of Christ during one of the meetings and made the candid remark, "I'm not quite sure how — but I'm going to trust and I am going to obey." Mr. Towner was impressed with the comment, and jotted down the phrase "trust and obey." He sent it to J.H. Sammis of New York, a Presbyterian minister who wrote the verses we now sing, and returned the poem to Mr. Towner.

Daniel Towner wrote the music, but was not happy with the results, wadded up the paper and threw it away. Mrs. Towner was cleaning her husband's study when she saw the discarded crumpled paper and read it. She sang it over and over, and felt compelled to leave it out for Daniel to see again. When questioned, she told him the melody was just what was needed to carry the message. Her instinct and intuition were right.

This song blends together perfectly our responsibility to faith and works. Theory and practice in religion are inseparably connected. Truth must always exhibit itself in obedience. Dawson Trotman once said it's like "TNT," Trust-n-Tackle." To be a Christian, we must have a child-like confidence in God. With this we can tackle any challenge set before us.

> *Although he was a son, he learned obedience from what he suffered and, once made perfect, he became the source of eternal salvation for all who obey him.* [Hebrews 5:8-9]

═══ *RJT* ═══

A Song Is Born

I will praise you, O Lord, among the nations; I will sing of you among the peoples. For great is your love, reaching to the heavens; [Psalm 57:9-10]

THE STEADFAST LOVE OF THE LORD

The study of hymnology is fascinating! I am constantly amazed at how God's providence works through so many different people, all with different cultural backgrounds and occupational training. Throughout history there have been gifted songwriters who have written thousands of song texts, many of which are still in use today. Fanny Crosby wrote more than 8000 hymn texts. We still sing many of her great songs today, songs like: *Blessed Assurance, I Am Thine O Lord, To God be The Glory,* etc. There are other dedicated poets and musicians who have written hundreds of songs, only to have one survive. J. B. F. Wright wrote more than 500 songs, but *Precious Memories* is the only one sung today. Occasionally, someone will come along who is neither a songwriter nor a musician, but somehow the words or music or both are laid upon their hearts. Amy Bessire falls into this last category.

Amy Karen Bessire was born in Abilene, Texas, in the 1950s. Her parents were Milton Carl and Aileen Bessire. After completing high school, she went on to receive a B. S. degree in Social Work at Abilene Christian University in 1973. Later, in 1982, she obtained an Associate degree in Dental Hygiene at Bee County College, Beeville, Texas and continues to follow a career in Dentistry today. Amy, a member of the Church of Christ, grew up around singing both in church and at school where she was part of a singing group called the "Choralaires." However, writing music was never part of Amy's plans.

"I didn't sit down to write a song," said Miss Bessire recently, " I wasn't considered to be a songwriter. I was merely reading an assignment given by a guy at church who was teaching 'The Prophets.' As I read Lamentations 3:22-24 (RSV), it had a syncopation - like trumpets sounding in a royal court when a throne was approached. I could visualize a red carpet and long trumpets held across the aisle to make an arch for a king's entry - it sounded like a French horn concerto!"

A Song Is Born

Amy wasn't feeling well that day so she had stayed home from work. As the day went by, she felt a little better and was doing some light housework when these images seemed to develop in her mind. She tried to ignore the images in her mind for a while, thinking she was just hallucinating, but they persisted. Finally, she sat down and made some notes of the words and tune. "I suppose God was merely giving me 'dictation' for a song He wanted to be sung," Amy said. Not knowing how to write out songs or music notes, I used a small tape recorder to sing into."

Miss Bessire continues, "I took the recorder to the church building and told the class teacher what had happened. He listened while I sang with myself *"The Steadfast Love of the Lord,"* echoing the part at the beginning. He was amazed, along with me - and encouraged me to have someone else we both knew write it down with three parts - - Alto, Soprano, and Tenor, which I did. However, when it was shared with the youth groups and began to spread from Abilene to Saint Louis, only two parts were sung and only two parts are printed in most hymnals."

Her song first appeared sometime in 1978 in the little red songbook called "Rejoice" with words only. Young people from all over the nation fell in love with the song, and it quickly spread through numerous youth rallies. It now appears with the music in most Church of Christ hymnals. Miss Bessire concludes by saying, *The Steadfast Love of the Lord* was God's song, one I didn't intend to write. So all the credit - all the credit goes to Him!"

The Lord's loving kindness indeed never cease, for His compassions never fail. They are new every morning; great is Thy faithfulness. The Lord is my portion says my soul therefore I will hope in him. (ASV) [Lamentations 3:22-24]

A Song Is Born

Victory In Jesus
1 Corinthians 15:57

E. M. Bartlett
E. M. Bartlett

1. I heard an old, old story How a Savior came from glory, How He gave His life on Calvary To save a wretch like me; I heard about His groaning, Of His precious blood's atoning, Then I repented of my sins And won the victory.

2. I heard about His healing, Of His cleansing pow'r revealing, How He made the lame to walk again And caused the blind to see; And then I cried "dear Jesus; Come and heal my broken spir-it," And somehow Jesus came and bro't To me the victory.

3. I heard about a mansion He has built for me in glory, And I heard about the streets of gold Beyond the crystal sea; About the angels singing, And the old redemption story, And some sweet day I'll sing up there The song of victory.

Chorus

O victory in Jesus, My Savior, forever, He

© Copyright 1939, Renewed 1967 by Albert E. Brumley and Sons. All Rights Reserved.

A Song Is Born

Victory In Jesus

But thanks be to God! He gives us the victory through our Lord Jesus Christ. [1 Corinthians 15: 57]

VICTORY IN JESUS

The song *Victory in Jesus* has become the favorite of many Christians, and perhaps one of the most popular gospel songs in the world. Another gospel song with the same popularity, and another contender for the most popular song, is *I'll Fly Away* written by Mr. Bartletts' longtime friend, Albert E. Brumley. An interesting footnote, when E. M. Bartlett, Sr., passed away, he left instructions that the copyrights to *Victory in Jesus* be given to his friend, Albert E. Brumley. As a result, Mr. Brumley owned two of the most popular southern gospel songs of our day.

Eugene Monroe Bartlett, Sr., was born December 24, 1884 in Waynesville, Missouri. He spent his life teaching singing schools,

A Song Is Born

promoting gospel music, and singing God's praises. He established the Hartford Music Company in 1919 in Hartford, Arkansas.

During the 1930s and at the height of the depression, money was hard to come by. Mr. Bartlett's son, Gene Bartlett, Jr., enrolled in the Shenandoah Conservatory of Music. The elder Mr. Bartlett had to sell the publishing rights on two of his popular songs, *Just a Little While to Stay Here* and *Everybody will be Happy Over There* just to help pay the tuition. Soon afterwards, he sold the company to his partner, John A. McClung. Mr. Bartlett then moved his family to Dallas, Texas, to work for the Stamps Baxter Music Company, singing for one of their quartets while promoting book sales and teaching singing schools. It was at one of these singing schools in Tulsa, Oklahoma, that E. M. Bartlett suffered a stroke in 1936. He was staying in the home of Malvin Dalton at the time. Dalton's friend, Cedric Weehunt, a regular on the old "Lum and Abner" radio show, is credited with saving Mr. Bartlett's life. The stroke left his speech impaired and his right side paralyzed.

Late in 1939, when this song was written, Mr. Bartlett was confined to his bed, never to leave it again. As his earthly body grew weaker, he began to think of heaven and his resurrected body. There he would have no more sickness, so he wrote, *"I heard about his healing."* He thought about the beauty of heaven and wrote *"- I heard about the streets of gold beyond the crystal sea."* He looked forward to being released from his pain, and wrote *"And some sweet day I'll sing up there the song of victory."* This was the last song he wrote before he died in 1941. Gene Bartlett, his oldest son, called this song "a fitting postlude to a great Christian life."

Many moral and spiritual battles are lost when we trust in our own wisdom and strength. Christ overcame the temptations of the devil by simply answering, "It is written." We, too, must respond by letting the words of Christ dwell in us today, and we will have the promised victory in Jesus.

I have told you these things, so that in me you may have peace. In this world you will have trouble. But take heart! I have overcome the world. [John 16:33]

RJT

First appeared in Pentecostal Praise by William J. Kirkpatrick and H. L. Gilmour, 1898

A Song Is Born

> *But I, when I am lifted up from the earth, will draw all men unto me.* [John 12:32]

NEARER, STILL NEARER

*I*t had been a year since the War Between the States had erupted. The topic of discussion on street corners and in local stores everwhere was the battle of Shiloh – fought just the week before. It was one of the bloodiest battles of the Civil War. More than 23,000 men lost their lives in this two-day encounter between Northern and Southern troops. As to be expected, the lives of every citizen of this young nation were consumed with thoughts of the Civil War.

But in one home in Pennsville, Ohio, a woman was fighting her own battle – the battle every mother must fight, that of giving birth to a child. Olivia Naylor gave birth that night to a child who one day would bring comfort to millions. Today, talk of the Civil War is mostly left to historians, but the hymns of this new child born in the midst of choas are still on our lips and in our hearts.

She was born Lelia Naylor, April 15, 1862, to Olivia and John T. Naylor. When her father returned from the war in 1866, they moved from Pennsville to Malta, Ohio, just ten miles north. Shortly after establishing their home, John Naylor died, leaving his wife and their family of seven children to struggle for survival. *"I can remember no carefree childhood day. Always there was work to be done and every penny stretched,"* Lelia recalled in later years. Lelia, another sister and their mother opened a millinery shop, first in Malta then in McConnelsville across the Muskingum River from the twin city of Malta.

Olivia Naylor faithfully took her children to church and taught them the principles of Christian living. Lelia, even as a young girl, felt the need for a Savior. She grew up longing to be close to God. At age ten, she proclaimed publicly her belief in Jesus. At age eleven, she felt the need to repeat the public confession and again at age twelve. Though always active in church, even playing the organ for prayer meetings and singing in the choir, she did not have a feeling of closeness to God. It wasn't until many years later (1892) – at age thirty, after having a family

A Song Is Born

of her own and having been introduced to the Methodist Holiness Movement, that Lelia began to feel the closeness she had always desired, and she could write:

Nearer, still nearer, close to my heart
Draw me my Savior so precious thou art

Just a few years later, in 1900, Lelia Naylor Morris would again write about the closeness she yearned for.

Sweet will of God, still fold me closer,
Till I am wholly lost in Thee.

We often experience various levels of closeness to God. There are times we are involved in countless religious activities, yet don't have a sense of nearness to God. We can talk the talk but have difficulty walking the walk. How do we draw nearer to God? One way is to humble yourself before God in prayer, asking Him to rule your thoughts and actions. Become a student of His Word so that you might know the will of God. Pride often keeps a lot of people away from Christ. We sometimes think, "Will I have any friends if I seek Christ?" What will my friends think of me? None of this really matters! Remember, God is as close to you today as He was the first time you came to know Him. If you don't feel the closeness, remember, God does not move away, we do!

Mrs. C. H. (Lelia Naylor) Morris wrote more than 1500 songs of various styles, including both words and music, but this early hymn has been a favorite of millions for generations. To learn more about Mrs. C. H. Morris, see the hymns *Let Jesus Come Into Your Heart* and *Sweeter As The Years Go By*, also in this book.

The righteous cry out, and the Lord hears them; he delivers them from all their troubles. The Lord is close to the brokenhearted and saves those who are crushed in spirit. [Psalm 34:17-18]

RJT

A Song Is Born

> *Sing and make music in your heart to the Lord. [Ephesians 5:19]*

SING AND BE HAPPY

If the skies above you are gray, you are feeling so blue;
If your cares and burdens seem great all the whole day thru,
There's a silver lining that shines in the heavenly land,
Look by faith and see it my friend, trust in His promises grand.

How many times have I sung these lines and wondered who the person might be that wrote them? What was their life like? Just by chance, or rather by the providence of God, I stumbled upon a granddaughter of Mr. Peck while researching another author. Emory Speer Peck was born, January 19, 1893, in Lumpkin County, Georgia, but lived most of his life in Gainesville, Georgia. His parents were hard working tenant farmers, too poor to own their farm or home. Emory never cared much for the farm life. His interest was in music. Even from an early age, he could play just about any instrument with ease. His parents, especially his father, thought that music was a waste of time and pursuing it would never amount to much. He tried to force Emory to become interested in farming, or some other worthwhile vocation. He even went as far as locking up the family organ so that Emory could not waste his time.

In 1914, Emory Peck entered Shenandoah Collegiate Institute (SCI) in Dayton, Virginia. This conservatory has an interesting and important history. After the Civil War, Aldine S. Kieffer (who fought for the south) and his brother-in-law Ephrain Ruebush (who fought for the Union) teamed together and reopened the Singers Glen print shop established by Joseph Funk. The Kieffer/Ruebush Publishing House became the driving influence for shape-note songbooks for the next fifty years. In 1875, Aldine Kieffer established Shenandoah Conservatory with its primary emphasis on musical education. From this school, which became SCI, came some of the most influential songwriters and publishers of the 20th century, names like A. J. Showalter, J. D. Vaughan, J. H. Hall just to name a few. Emory Peck was certainly in good company. He received a Bachelor of Arts degree from SCI and also learned the skills of piano tuning, a vocation that would serve him well in years to come.

After graduating, he entered WWI and served in the US Army, 116th Infantry as a musician and a band director. After receiving his discharge, he remained in Europe for a time to tour and play in a band.

Once back in the States, he served as band director for Chicopee, New Holland and Gainesville Mills Schools in Georgia. In the early part of the 20th century, large companies like the cotton mills, would build complete towns for their employees, including family housing, medical care, general stores, and schools. The company would provide the doctors and teachers and all things necessary for their employees to live. What a forward-thinking idea!

About 1940, Emory S. Peck became a music professor of theory and music education and the band director for Brenau College, a woman's college located in Gainesville, Georgia. Emory held this position for the remainder of his life, except for the times he left to further his  education. He received a Bachelor of Science degree and later a Master degree in Music from the prestigious Columbia University of New York. He also took several classes at the famous Julliard University of New York.

Emory Peck began writing songs at the age of 15. Later, in the 1930s, his songs were written and published mostly in the Stamps Baxter shape note songbooks. After attending Columbia and Julliard Universities, he wrote a very different style of song and had some success from this effort. Popular songs like *Moon Walkin'*, *Monday Mornin' Blues*, *Swanee River Moon,* and *Down Where the Chattahooche River Flows* just to name a few.

In 1921 at the age of 28, Mr. Peck met the girl of his dreams, Lou Emma Whitmire. She was the lovely daughter of the local Postmaster and a very influential family in the social life of Gainesville. Lou Emma was some nine years younger than Emory. In 1922, their marriage was blessed with a beautiful daughter, Marguerite, but in 1925, tragedy struck. Lou Emma died of pneumonia, a worldwide epidemic at the time. *"Her death had a profound impact on Emory,"* said Lynn Lathem, a granddaughter. Emory never remarried, and as far as we know, he

A Song Is Born

never even dated. Mr. Peck turned his full attention to music for his comfort and to his faith in God to sustain his life.

Of all the songs Emory S. Peck wrote, *Sing And Be Happy* is by far the most popular. Even if you disregard the success of the Stamps Baxter books that first introduced this song, *Sing And Be Happy* has appeared in all major hymnals of the Churches of Christ since 1956. This amounts to more than 8 million copies being sold over the last 50 years, not to mention how many times the song has been sung. Even today it remains a favorite of youth, promising to extend its popularity for generations to come.

You might say that *Sing And Be Happy* became the biography of Emory Peck's life. Perhaps the popularity of his song is within it; he provides the formula for a positive Christian life. When events in his life made him blue, or sad, or troubled, he simply turned to music. With a song in his heart and a passion to be near God, he could face each new day refreshed, able to withstand any problem.

An interesting side note, from the proceeds of his occupation in music, Mr. Peck purchased a farm for his parents, providing them with the only place to call their own in their lifetime. Also, in addition to putting his daughter through college, he paid all the expenses for his four grandchildren to complete college, and all of this without one dime of royalty from his most popular song, *Sing and Be Happy*. Not bad for the son of a tenant farmer who simply loved music.

Be filled with the Spirit. Speak to one another with psalms, hymns and spiritual songs. Sing and make music in your heart to the Lord, always giving thanks to God the Father for everything, in the name of our Lord, Jesus Christ. [Ephesians 5:18-20]

A Song Is Born

> *May I never boast except in the cross of our Lord Jesus Christ, through which the world has been crucified to me, and I to the world.* [Galatians 6:14]

THE OLD RUGGED CROSS

One of the most popular gospel songs of the twentieth century has been *The Old Rugged Cross*. Though often despised by hymnologists, and considered too personal, too corny, too sentimental, or just too popular for others, it remains a favorite.

George Bennard, the son of a coal miner, was born in Youngstown, Ohio, in 1873, but his parents soon moved to Iowa where he grew up. His father died when he was sixteen, and George became the sole supporter of his mother and four sisters. Mr. Bennard served for a time as an officer in the Salvation Army. Later, he became a minister for the Methodist Episcopal Church, a position he continued to fill until his death in 1985. Mr. Bennard describes the experience that inspired his popular hymn.

"I was studying about the cross, seeing it central in Christianity. I saw Christ and the cross inseparable. The Christ of the cross became more than a symbol. John 3:16 had always been my favorite verse and the more I studied it, the more it became alive. Always there was with it a vision of a cross. Not one of gold, but a rough and rugged cross, stained with the blood of God's only Son. Then I remembered an old wooden cross I once had seen. Suddenly, the first ten words and a melody came to me, *'On a hill far away stood an old rugged Cross.'* Something within me prevented the completion of the song at that time."

Sometime later, after returning to Michigan from a series of meetings in New York, Mr. Bennard passed through a trying experience that caused him to reflect more closely upon the cross. Now it seems he was able to complete the hymn. "Every word just fell into place," George said. He sent the manuscript to Charles Gabriel, a well-known composer of gospel songs, for review. Mr. Gabriel returned the song after making some minor corrections, and penned this note; "You will hear from this song."

A Song Is Born

At the heart of our Christian faith is the cross. I know we do not worship the cross, but rather the Christ of the cross. Yet one can not understand the Gospel plan and Christ's atonement without feeling the power and glory of the cross. Paul understood this as he wrote *"God forbid that I should glory save in the cross of our Lord Jesus Christ"* Galatians 6:14. When we assemble to worship and especially when we commune with our Lord, what thoughts come into your mind? Can you picture that "hill far away?" Can you by faith see your Savior hanging on that "old rugged cross?"

Picture in your mind the scene on that awful day, the day they crucified our Lord. Outside Jerusalem was a hill called Golgotha, an ugly hill that from a distance looked like a skull. Christ had been taken from the garden the night before and tried by the Roman governor. He was ridiculed, mocked, humiliated, despised, and beaten until the blood ran from the wounds. Then he was forced to carry the cross, upon which he was to die, up that hill to Golgotha. There on that cross, suspended in mid-air by the nails in His hands and feet, our Savior suffered and died.

The beauty of a hymn is not in its unique poetry, outstanding melody, or perfect harmony, but in the images it creates in our minds. This simple song helps us to recreate an image of Calvary, and the cross upon which our Savior died. Although his hymn won international fame, George Bennard continued his itinerant ministry with very little recognition. He wrote more than 350 hymns in his lifetime, but only this song has survived.

—Because Christ suffered for you, leaving you an example, that you should follow in his steps. He committed no sin, and no deceit was found in his mouth. When they hurled their insults at him, he did not retaliate; when he suffered, he made no threats. Instead, he entrusted himself to him who judges justly. He himself bore our sins in his body on the cross, so that we might die to sins and live for righteousness; — [1 Peter 2:21-24]

RJT

A Song Is Born

Sing Me A Song About Jesus

A Song Is Born

> *Sing praises to the Lord, enthroned in Zion proclaim among the nations what he has done.* [Psalm 9:11]

SING ME A SONG ABOUT JESUS

Today's gospel music industry owes much of its existence to James D. Vaughan. Many others have had an active part in the history of gospel music, but Mr. Vaughan's innovative ideas in marketing and sales techniques blazed the trail. In the early 1900s, he hit upon the idea of forming singing groups and sending them around the country promoting his songbooks. At one time in the 1920's, sixteen all-male quartets traveled under the sponsorship of the James D. Vaughan Music Company.

G. T. Speer, author of Sing *Me A Song About Jesus,* once sang in a Vaughan quartet, but in 1921, he formed his own group called "The Singing Speer Family." It was a unique group in that it consisted of both men and women's voices, something unheard of for southern Gospel groups in the 1920s. The first Speer Family group consisted of G. T. Speer (dad), his wife, Lena Speer (mom), his sister, Pearl, and brother-in-law, Logan Claborn. In 1925, their oldest son, Brock, and his sister, Rosa Nell, joined the group. Later, Ben and sister, Mary Tom, began to sing with them. In 1948, Brock's wife, Faye, joined the family. Mom and Dad Speer died in the 1960s, but the group continues to sing today and have recorded over 65 albums. They recently gained new popularity with number one hits like: *Saved To The Uttermost* and *He's Still In The Fire.* The Speers, as the group is known today, have had many personnel changes over their long seventy-year history, but have always maintained their unique sound.

George Thomas Speer was born in Fayetteville, Georgia, March 10, 1891. He was the fourth of eighteen children, and spent most of his youth living in Alabama. Family circumstances didn't give him much of a chance at a formal education. He served 20 months as a combat soldier in WWI. Back home from the war, he settled down on an Alabama cotton farm. In addition to singing in groups, Mr. Speer taught hundreds of singing schools and composed more than 600 songs. At one time, he was a member of the faculty of The Vaughan School of Music.

A Song Is Born

One day in the 1950s, Mr. Speer took a casual walk along the sidewalks of downtown Nashville, Tennessee. Everywhere he went the radios were playing, and it seemed all he could hear was the current very popular song, *"How much is the doggie in the window, the one with the straggly tail."* This song, *The Doggie In the Window*, was recorded on Mercury Records, and released by Patty Page in 1953. It stayed on the pop charts for twenty-one weeks, eventually become number one. As Mr. Speer listened to the words, he thought to himself, *"If that's all they have to write songs about, I'm going to write a better song."* This he surely did, as he composed the wonderful uplifting words and music titled *Sing Me A Song About Jesus*.

Through Jesus, therefore, let us continually offer to God a sacrifice of praise – the fruit of lips that confess his name. And do not forget to do good and to share with others, for with such sacrifices God is pleased. [Hebrews 13:15-16]

RJT

A Song Is Born

Christ's Love Is All I Need

243

A Song Is Born

And we know and rely on the love God has for us. God is love. Whoever lives in love lives in God, and God in him. [1 John 4:16]

Christ's Love Is All I Need

*I*n the fall of 1992, Barbara and I set out on a research trip through three southern states. I am constantly amazed how the providence of God continues to lead us as we uncover the history of our songs, and the lives of the writers. This is a story of how our research develops.

Our first destination on this trip was Smithville, Mississippi, a small town located about twenty-five miles east of Tupelo. The object of our search was George W. Sides, the author and composer of the song, *Christ's Love Is All I Need.* The only information we knew was that he once signed this song as: "Geo. W. Sides owner, Smithville, Miss., 1924." On Sunday afternoon, we left our campsite at the beautiful Elvis Presley Lake and Campground near Tupelo and drove to Smithville. This small community consisted of five or six stores (mostly empty), a couple of service stations and several churches. Our first place to look on this day was the community cemetery. We found nothing, even after talking to a long-time local resident who was also visiting the cemetery.

As we drove around town looking for clues, Barbara noticed two older men sitting in their car in the parking lot of the Church of Christ. *"I remember Mr. Sides,"* brother Rolland Ausborn explained to me, *"He and my dad used to sing together all of the time. He's buried about eight miles east of town in the New Hope Community Cemetery."* At last a real clue! Armed with this information and directions, we found New Hope Cemetery out in the country. After searching the cemetery at length without success, I was beginning to get discouraged. Then we discovered a second section of the cemetery about one-quarter mile up the road and over the hill.

There we located the gravesite of George William Sides, born August 29, 1880, and died, November 3, 1956. Next to him was apparently his wife, Alice Pearl (Ray) Sides, born December 14, 1889, and died September 30, 1968. Also buried beside them in a freshly dug grave, was Mary Sides. This gave me an idea that some of the family might still be alive, but where? I walked across the street to an older house, and inquired if they might know or have known the Sides. *"I attended a singing school taught by Mr. Sides right here in this house, which was once a community school,"* Mrs. Little explained to me, *"but that was in the 20s and I don't know what happen to him after that."* It turned out that Mrs. Little was a member of the nearby Church of Christ. Other inquiries around there and with older residents of Smithville failed to provide any additional information about Mr. Sides or any living relatives. It was clear that none of the Sides family lived in the area now, but where had Mary lived?

Since the tombstone listed his wife's maiden name as Ray, we noticed a large group of them buried nearby, and jotted down their information, which proved to be very helpful later. Also on the new grave site of Mary Sides was a small metal marker indicating the name of Boone Funeral Home, Greenville, Mississippi (about 100 miles West of Smithville). Monday, I went to Avory, a much larger town about ten miles south of Smithville. In the library there I found a small family record of Alice Pearl Ray who married a George W. Sides. Three children were born to this union; Mary Sides, George W. Sides, Jr., and Jenny Lynn Sides. Also we found where her dad, James Curry Ray had moved to Leland, MS (near Greenville), to live with one of the twelve children.

Upon arriving in Greenville, Mississippi, I called the Boone Funeral Home. From their records, they gave me the name of Lynn Dolliver who lived nearby. She was a sister to Mary Sides. Now I was excited! Here was the name of a living relative of George W. Sides. I called Lynn but she was unwilling to talk about the family history, other than to confirm that she was his daughter. This was the first time in four years of research that someone had not been excited to discuss the family history. My curiosity was aroused. Why had she not wanted to talk about her dad? Had there been family problems? How was I going to continue the research? Here I was so close, yet so far away from obtaining additional information. Then I remembered my notes on the Ray family, the family of Mr. Sides' wife, Alice. I located a distant cousin living nearby, and he was very helpful, filling in many of blanks.

The Sides family moved to the Mississippi Delta in 1929, shortly after the great flood destroyed much of that area. He purchased several acres of the rich land and spent most of his time farming. In addition to

A Song Is Born

farming, Mr. Sides drove a school bus while his wife taught school. In his later years, George became the Justice of the Peace for Avon, MS. *"It is doubtful that he ever was a member of any church, although he attended many,"* said his cousin. *"After leaving the Smithville area, George probably never wrote any more songs."* There is still much to uncover about George William Sides. Where did he obtain his training? How many other songs had he written, etc.? The search continues!

As we walk along the road of life, from its mountain peaks of joy through the dark valleys of despair, we often wonder why it must be so. Life is full of things we can't understand nor explain, full of trials, heartaches, and disappointments. Unless the love of Christ is in you, you may easily be overwhelmed. Jesus came to give you strength that is greater than all the forces of evil. Whether you are a teenager or a senior citizen, Jesus can make you a new person. All the wrinkles on your soul can be smoothed away. He died to make this possible. His love is all you need to give your life purpose and meaning.

Praise be to the God and Father of our Lord Jesus Christ! In his great mercy he has given us new birth into a living hope through the resurrection of Jesus Christ from the dead, and into an inheritance that can never perish, spoil or fade – Cast all your anxiety on him because he cares for you. [1 Peter 1:3-4; 5:7]

A Song Is Born

> *I have fought the good fight, I have finished the race, I have kept the faith. Now there is in store for me the crown of righteousness which the Lord, the righteous Judge, will award to me on that day, and not only to me, but also to all who have longed for his appearing.* [2 Timothy 4:7-8]

FROM THE CROSS TO THE CROWN

The history of southern gospel music is filled with many great songwriters, but only a few have aspired to true greatness. The names of James D. Vaughan, V. O. Stamps, J. R. Baxter, and Albert Brumley quickly come to mind. I believe the name of F. L. Eiland should be included in this exclusive list. Each of these talented songwriters was also a great leader in the gospel music business.

Franklin Lycurgus Eiland, a self-taught musician with less than six months of formal schooling, was considered a musical genius. George W. Winningham, a former student of Mr. Eiland and a Texas State Senator, spoke of him as *"A poet and musician who breathed into his songs such beauty, eloquence, and pathos that they persuaded more sinners to repentance than the songs of any other writer of his generation."* Mr. Eiland was a natural poet, comedian, and storyteller whose mannerisms have been compared to Tennessee Ernie Ford. This devoted Christian, with his sweet, unassuming personality and love for music, wrote or composed more than 200 gospel songs that have inspired many. F. L. Eiland, along with H. W. Elliott and Emmett S. Dean, established the Trio Music Company in 1896. Two years later they established the Southern Development Normal (SDN), one of the first schools designed for the training of singing school teachers.

His marriage to Mary Nesbett in 1884, his constant companion, co-worker and sweetheart for nearly ten years, ended when she died in 1893. Two years later he married Ella Tolen, who died from a ruptured appendix only 10 days after the marriage. From this experience, he was inspired to write the song *From the Cross to the Crown*. Shortly after the death of his second wife, Mr. Eiland, accompanied by his niece, Florence Massey, resumed the work of establishing singing schools. One such school was in Carlton, Texas, in September 1895. Florence recalls a glowing account of how she and "Uncle Frank," as she called him, left Carlton just before dawn, driving in their one horse buggy to another school opening in Hamilton County, Texas. Somewhere along the way, Mr. Eiland stopped the buggy, handed her the lines, and walked to a large rock by the roadside for prayer and meditation. Shortly after sunrise, he returned to the buggy humming his newly written song, *From the Cross to the Crown.*

There is an interesting footnote to the legacy of F. L. Eiland. Cindy Walker, born in 1918, is a noted songwriter from Mexia, Texas. Her career began in the 1950s when Bing Crosby recorded one of her songs. Ms. Walker has written songs for movies and has been a recording artist for over five decades. More than 500 of her songs have been recorded, songs like *Dream Baby* by Roy Orbison, *You Don't Know Me* by Eddie Arnold, *In the Misty Moon Light* by Dean Martin, *When My Blue Moon Turns to Gold Again* by Elvis Presley, just to name four. Cindy Walker is the granddaughter of F. L. Eiland and seems to possess the same talent and zeal for music.

The "cross" Mr. Eiland speaks of is our personal cross of trials, heartaches, and burdens we suffer as we journey through life. We can clearly see his own sorrow in verse two as he wrote, *"Though the burdens of life may be heavy to bear, and your crosses and trials severe; - -."*

If we focus our thoughts on the conflicts, battles, and struggles of life, we will quickly become burdened down with care. The message within this hymn is for you and I to focus our thoughts upon heaven and the promised crown of life, rather than the struggles and trials of everyday living. F. L. Eiland was able to continue his work with the same sweet spirit and hope because his eyes were set upon heaven and not his daily crosses.

I press on toward the goal to win the prize for which God has called me heavenward in Christ Jesus. [Philippians 3:14]

RJT

A Song Is Born

Men cry out under a load of oppression; they plead for relief from the arm of the powerful. But no one says, "Where is God, my Maker, who gives songs in the night. [Job 35:9-10]

GOD LEADS US ALONG

*T*he search for hymn writers and the history of their songs is a never-ending process. For some time now, I've been intrigued with the song *God Leads Us Along* and have spent countless hours trying to locate the author, George A. Young. I have been able to uncover the fascinating story of this song as written by Haldor Lillenas, songwriter and founder of the Lillenas Publishing Company. I've also talked with several hymnologists, including the late Dr. Al Smith, who shared with me his first hand information from Mr. Lillenas. Unfortunately, both men are now deceased. After several years of inquiries and trips to other states for information, I still have not been able to locate detailed information about the author. But while the search continues, I want to share this remarkable story with you. Dr. Lillenas tells how he came to know the story some time before 1940.

"I began to make inquiries and soon learned that Mr. Young had passed away – but some thought his widow was still alive. I soon located her address and on one morning bright and early, I started off from Kansas City. It was quite a drive and when I came to the small town in which the woman lived, I pulled into a service station. I showed the attendant the address and his face became clouded. 'Why sir, that's the county poor house up that road about 3 miles – and mister, when I say poor house I really mean it.' I almost said to him 'Fill up my gas tank, I've got to get back to Kansas City,' but something seemed to say 'Haldor, you've come all this way so you had better go.' After we had been introduced, she said 'Why you're Dr. Lillenas, and you've come all the way from Kansas City to see little me?' Then she smiled and straightened her 4'10" frame and said 'Of course, that's just the way our blessed Lord leads, doesn't He?' She continued, 'you know, Doctor; I came to know Jesus Christ when I was a young girl. One day I met a young man who also was a Christian. We soon fell in love. Together we pledged that we would go anywhere and do anything that the Lord Jesus would want us to. God would do the leading and we would do the following.'"

A Song Is Born

George A. Young was a lay preacher who dedicated his life to ministering for poor congregations who often were unable to pay for his services. George was also a skilled carpenter and earned most of his living doing carpentry work. After many years of living from hand to hand and in borrowed houses, the Young's were finally able to build their first home. By working many extra hours at his trade, and by the family often doing without, they were able to save enough money to purchase a piece of land. The small house would take several additional years of sacrifice and dreaming to complete, but at last the day came when the Young's moved into their own home. What a happy day that must have been.

Then disaster struck. While George and his family were away holding meetings, the home burned to the ground. It is thought that someone who was unhappy with his preaching set the fire. When the family returned, all that was left was a heap of ashes. The home, the clothing, cherished personal items, and a lifetime of memories all gone! As he viewed the smoldering ashes, words begin to form in his mind:

> *Thro' sorrows befall us and Satan oppose,*
> *God leads His dear children along*
> *Some thro' the waters, some thro' the flood*
> *Some thro' the fire, but all thro' the blood*
> *Some thro' great sorrow, but God gives a song*
> *In the night season and all the day long.*

Later, he would complete the other verses and the song was published in 1903. It has been said that from this tragic event, George A. Young wrote perhaps his only song – a song that would lift the burdens of thousands and give encouragement to Christians as they experience trials along life's pathway. The Psalmist David wrote, *"The Lord is My Shepherd, I shall not want. He leadeth me beside the still waters."*

Whether you are experiencing a period of "night" in your life, or feeling like you are enjoying a mountaintop experience, God is in control. How marvelous it is to be led by the Master!

> *Yet I am always with you; you hold me by my right hand. You guide me with your counsel, and afterward you will take me into glory.* [Psalm 73:23-24]

RJT

A Song Is Born

> *In my Father's house are many mansions - - I go to prepare a place for you. And if I go and prepare a place for you, I will come again, and receive you unto myself; that where I am, there ye may be also.* [John 14:2-3]

MANSION OVER THE HILLTOP

Ira F. Stanphill was born in Bellvue, New Mexico. His parents moved there briefly, partly to be near Ira's maternal grandparents, and also to escape the wrath of his mother's rejected suitor. It seems the disturbed suitor had slipped into the Stanphill's Arkansas home after they had been married for just a while and mixed poison with the flour. When Ira's mother baked the biscuits, neither she, nor his dad liked the taste and threw them outside. Within minutes, chickens were dead and the dogs were violently ill. The Stanphills later settled in Coffeyville, Kansas, where Ira graduated from high school during the great depression, in 1932. Ira began to pick up music very early. At the age of five, he learned to play the piano from a blind pianist, but it was with his ukulele that earned him his own radio program at the age of 15 in 1929. Ira wrote his first song while still in high school. Some years later, he showed Frank Stamps some of the songs he had written such as, *Move Forward, After the Showers,* and *There's a Savior Who Cares.* Mr. Stamps turned them down, saying they didn't fit the southern gospel mold. Also, Haldor Lillenas, another song publisher, rejected them, saying "you need additional instructions in harmony and composition". Rather than change his style, Ira began to publish his own sheet music. How grateful we are that Mr. Stanphill did not heed their advice, for we surely would miss such songs as *Room at the Cross, I Know Who Holds Tomorrow,* and *Follow Me,* just to name a few. Interestingly enough, this song, *Mansion Over the Hilltop,* does seem to fit the southern gospel style. In his book, "This side of Heaven," Ira Stanphill tells how he was inspired to write *Mansion Over The Hilltop* after hearing the following story in 1949, told by a visiting preacher, Gene Martin, in Dallas Texas:

"A man of considerable means, facing imminent bankruptcy, took a driving trip through a rural part of the country. Here, one particular

A Song Is Born

house caught his attention. It was badly in need of paint and repairs of every kind. Most of the windows had oil paper to replace the broken glass. Parts of the roof and shingles were missing. He wondered how the house was still standing. Out front, playing in the yard, was a young girl about 8 or 9, who was poorly dressed. The traveler felt an urge to stop and talk. During the conversation, he mentioned how sorry he was that the young lady had to live in such poor surroundings. The young girl replied, "Why, haven't you heard? My daddy just inherited a fortune and he's building us a mansion just over that hill over there. Don't know when it will be done, but I won't have to live in this house forever."

As Ira wrote the song, he was reminded of the parallel between our struggling existence here on this earth, while at the same time, God is preparing a mansion in Heaven for us. Through the words of an innocent, imaginative child, a lesson in contentment was given, and a song was born. The apostle Paul has much to say about being content:

I am not saying this because I am in need, for I have learned to be content whatever the circumstances. I know what it is to be in need, and I know what it is to have plenty. I have learned the secret of being content in any and every situation — [Philippians 4:11-12]

A Song Is Born

Majesty

Thine, O Lord, is the greatness, and the power, and the glory, and the victory, and the majesty . . [1 Chronicles 29:11]

MAJESTY

For two weeks, Jack Hayford and his wife Anna, explored the corners of Scotland, Wales, and England in their tiny rental car. It was the summer of 1986. The people were enjoying a kind of regal festive period as the silver anniversary of Elizabeth's coronation as Queen was being anticipated. After fulfilling a preaching engagement in Denmark, the Hayfords began their journey, sampling the variety of climates, customs, cuisine, and clothing styles in Great Britain. "By the time we arrived in London, a special sense of wonder had overtaken us," Mr. Hayford said. "An illusive sense of the grand, the regal, and the noble caught my imagination and defied my efforts at definition. I thought millions of common folk of ordinary means were enthused and excited about celebrating one woman's royal ascent a quarter of a century earlier. The entire kingdom possessed a general mood of personal and national significance. And it seems inescapably linked in some mystical way to the fact that each one perceived themselves linked with and personally represented by the one who wears the crown and bears the scepter."

Then a second thought came to Mr. Hayford. "This was the essence of the relationship Jesus wants us to have with His church." As he gently squeezed Anna's hand, he said "Honey, I can hardly describe to you all the things which this setting evokes in me. There is something of a majesty in all this."

Majesty, the word was crisp in his mind. Majesty, he thought! It's the quality of Christ's royalty and kingdom glory that not only displays His excellence, but which lifts us by His grace and power. As they drove along the narrow highways, the road took them from one breathtaking view to another. Mr. Hayford said to Anna, his wife, "Take a notebook and write down some words!" With that he began to dictate not only the lyrics, but the key, the musical notes, and the time value of each.

What a great thought. You and I, though unworthy, are part of royalty. Through Christ we have a direct link to the throne of God, the King of Kings. We believe and we serve Jesus Christ, not because of what some preacher has said, but because we honor Him as our Savior, our Lord, and our King. We need to sense the presence of God as we worship His Majesty. A worship service is convened to serve God with our praise and to serve people's need with His sufficiency. Worship is a gift to bless us rather than a chore to fulfill.

The Son is the radiance of God's glory - - After he had provided purification for sins, he sat down at the right hand of the Majesty in heaven. [Hebrews 1:3]

A Song Is Born

My Eyes Are Dry
Psalm 25:5

Keith Green　　　　　　　　　　　　　　　　　　　　　　　　　　　　Keith Green

My eyes are dry, My faith is old, My heart is hard, My pray'rs are cold. And I know how I ought to be, A-live to You and dead to me. What can be done to an old heart like mine? Soft-en it up with oil and wine. The oil is You, Your spir-it of love. Please wash me a-new in the wine of your blood.

© 1978 by Ears to Hear Music/Birdwing Music/Cherry Lane Music. All Rights Reserved.

A Song Is Born

> *These people honor me with their lips, but their hearts are far from me.* [Matthew 15:8]

My Eyes Are Dry

Keith Green spent years struggling to succeed as a musician, singing in cheap nightclubs and suffering through many second-rate recording contracts. He finally became a recording star, yet when this success came it was not in the secular music field for which he had trained, but as a contemporary Christian artist. Keith came from a very musical family. His mother studied voice at Carnegie Hall. At the age of two, Keith won his first talent show by singing "Love and Marriage." By the time he was five, he could play anything he heard on his ukulele. He was seven when he did his first television commercial. By the age of eleven, Keith had published his first song and began making television appearances on "The Jack Benny Show," "The Joey Bishop Show," and others. "Our whole life revolved around Keith's drive to make it big in the music business," said his wife, Melody Green, in her book "No Compromise." In the early 1970s, Keith had a "New Birth" experience. He now had dedicated his whole life to Christ and with this conversion a whole new world of fame and fortune opened up to him. Keith Green was well known for his talent to sing and to write songs. Songs like *O Lord You're Beautiful, There Is A Redeemer, My Eyes Are Dry,* and many others.

Keith had mixed feelings about his newfound popularity. It was great to be successful, but he struggled to make sure that the message of Christ for which he so deeply believed was being heard, and not just the music of his artistry. The song, *My Eyes Are Dry,* was born from one such internal conflict. It was the summer of 1978. Keith was invited to sing at a festival called "Jesus Northwest," in Oregon. It normally drew about 20,000 people, but because of Keith's popularity, they expected more than 35,000.

The campsites were overflowing. Traffic jams clogged the roads for miles. Because of the heat and large crowds, people had stripped down to the bare minimum. Keith and Melody remarked how it looked like a

A Song Is Born

mini-Woodstock. It was great that so many people were there enjoying the concert and each other, but something seemed to be missing.

On the last evening of this seven-day event, several gathered in Keith's trailer to pray before he went on stage. They were troubled – not about what had happened, but what hadn't happened. The emphasis of the festival had been on music, lots of it, and loud, but it seemed, at least to Keith, that God had not spoken. About this time a knock came from the door. A young girl in tears wanted to express her concerns. "Excuse me," she said in a timid but determined voice, "I've felt a little grieved during this festival, because it doesn't seem like God has been given a chance to speak." Keith wept. He, too, was feeling the same burden. Before the young visitor had left, she handed them a small piece of paper on which was a scripture. When Keith read it, his mouth dropped open. Here was the direction and motivation he needed for going on stage that night.

When it came time for him to sing in the concert that last evening, he spoke to the crowd. "Have you ever felt the Lord was sad?" Keith said. "Well, tonight I was praying and I kind of felt the Lord inside me, weeping. So I started to cry. And I got to thinking about all the people that give God one day a week. How would you like it if your wife gave you one day a week?" The crowd seemed restless but he continued. "In the Old Testament it says, *'These people draw near with their words and honor me with their lips, but they remove their hearts far from me.'* If you praise Jesus with your mouth but your life does not, there's something wrong," Keith exhorted.

Keith went on, "I want to share a scripture with you from Amos. (Amos 5:21-24) *'Thus saith the Lord, I hate, I reject your festivals, nor do I delight in your solemn assemblies, even though you offer up to Me burnt offerings – I will not accept them – Take away from me the noise of your songs. I will not listen to the sound of your harps. But let justice roll down like waters, and righteousness like an ever-flowing stream.'* "Does anyone understand what that means" Keith asked?

The crowd sat in stunned silence as he continued. "How many of us care about the people living next door to us? How many of your neighbors have never seen anything more than a little fish on your car? As for me, I repent of ever having made a record or ever having sung a song unless it has provoked people to follow Jesus, to lay down their

A Song Is Born

whole life before Him. –Unless you become a broken vessel, Jesus can't put you back together the way He wants," said Keith as he concluded his remarks. After a couple of more songs, he ended that concert by teaching them a new song he had just written.

> *My eyes are dry, my faith is old,*
> *My heart is hard, my prayers are cold.*
> *And I know how I ought to be,*
> *Alive to You and dead to me.*
> *What can be done with an old heart like mine?*
> *Soften it up with oil and wine!*
> *The oil is You, Your Spirit of love,*
> *Please wash me anew in the wine of Your blood.*

Keith concluded that memorable event with a challenge, one we might all do well to heed. "I challenge everybody who calls himself a Christian to live as Jesus did. Because when someone is born again, they get excited! It changes the way they live, what they do, how they speak, how they act, etc. If in a few months your family or friends can't tell that you're born again, if your relatives can't see a change, if your teacher can't see that you're a Christian, you're probably not!"

I'm reminded of the words to the Laodicean church in Revelation 3:16. *"So then because you are lukewarm, and neither cold nor hot, I will vomit you out of My mouth."* Cold water is refreshing; hot water is useful for medical purposes. Lukewarm water is neither. This is a very vivid picture of how the Lord will react to the halfhearted efforts of self-satisfied Christians.

If you have no tears in your eyes for the sin and moral decay taking over our nation, if you feel no compassion in your heart for those with emotional and material needs, then you need to accept the challenge Keith Green offered that day in 1978. If you call yourself a Christian, then act like it!

> *Create in me a pure heart, O God, and renew a steadfast spirit within me. - Restore to me the joy of your salvation and grant me a willing spirit, to sustain me.* [Psalm 51:10-12]

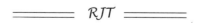

I am the way, the truth, the life. No one comes to the Father except through me. [John 14:6]

LET JESUS COME INTO YOUR HEART

She was born Lelia Naylor in 1862, during the early days of the Civil War. By the time she was five, her father had died leaving a large family to be cared for. As soon as Lelia Naylor was old enough to help her mother in their millinery shop, she was compelled to quit school. Lelia was always a willing and cheerful helper and contributed greatly to the support of the Naylor family. However, she still found time to pursue her first love, music. By the age of ten, she had learned to play the piano, and with the help of a kind neighbor who owned a piano, she was able to take piano lessons and to practice.

While working in her mother's millinery shop, Lelia met and dated Charles H. Morris, the only son of a well-known, well-respected, and some say well-to-do family in McConnelsville. In 1881, at the age of 19, she became Mrs. C. H. Morris, a name soon to become widely known in hymnody. Charles was a popular, active young man who worked at the family business of hardware, plumbing, and metal fabrication. But his avocation was ornithology, the study of wild life, mainly birds.

Soon after their marriage, "Father Morris," the father of Charles, built the young family a new home on Kennebec Ave. Lelia and Charles lived there for the next forty-seven years, until poor health forced them to move in with one of their children in 1928. Lelia and the Naylor family were Methodist Protestant while the Morris family was Methodist Episcopal. After her marriage, Lelia moved her membership to the Trinity Methodist Episcopal Church and remained an active member all her life.

This remarkable lady – saddled with adult responsibilities at such an early age - taught herself the art of music, including harmony. Lelia began to write hymns, both the words and the music while still raising her young family of four children. At first, she composed them secretly

A Song Is Born

and sang or played them in private. Little by little she began to share them with her closest friends, who encouraged her to have them published.

In 1892, at the age of thirty, Mrs. C. H. Morris went to Mountain Lake Park, Maryland, to attend a Methodist camp meeting. There she met H. L. Gilmour, a songwriter and publisher. A lasting friendship developed and he encouraged her to continue writing songs.

A few years later, in 1898, during a revival service in Mountain Lake Park, she was inspired to write one of her most popular invitation songs, *Let Jesus Come Into Your Heart*. Before I tell you the inspiring story of the birth of this hymn, let me explain a little about Mountain Lake Park, Maryland.

Towns usually are established or develop along strategic locations. Chicago by the Lake Shore; San Francisco by the Bay, and many others by rivers. Mountain Lake Park was founded partly because of the clean mountain air but mostly upon idealism. In 1881, four men from Wheeling, WV, all prominent Methodists, inspired by the summer climate and beauty of the region, bought 800 acres of land in far western Maryland. They resolved to build a Methodist Summer Resort, much like Chautauqua in upstate New York. The new town was to be known as Mountain Lake Park. The fact that there was not a lake didn't bother them - they would just build one. Their concern was that the town should have high moral tones. The town charter prohibited dancing, card playing, drinking, and gambling among other restrictions, not just in public places but in private homes. Violation could lead to forfeiture of their land and home.

There are some who indicated that while these four men were working out the details of a new town, a fifth man quietly purchased land across the railroad tracts and built the Loch Lynn Hotel. It had a swimming pool, pool hall, and ballroom and also allowed card playing and drinking. A popular saying soon developed:

> "If you want to sin, go to Loch Lynn,
> For Jesus sake, go to Mountain Lake."

The resort town of Mountain Lake Park flourished. In 1882, the Assembly Hall was built on a 10-acre plot known as Chautauqua Park, and by 1894 it had to be expanded. By 1900, a new Assembly Hall

 capable of sitting 5000 was erected to accommodate the crowds. People came from everywhere to enjoy the clean mountain air and to partake in the many educational and spiritual sessions. Even President W. H. Taft came in 1911. Hundreds of small town lots were sold and summer cottages began to spring up everywhere. A lake was built and in time ballparks, tennis courts, and other recreational facilities, plus many hotels were built.

But the emphasis was always on the mental and spiritual development with courses in Liberal Arts, Fine Arts, Natural Sciences, and Spiritual Revivals. To understand the attraction of such resorts, one must remember what life was like in America in the late 1800s. It was the day of one-room schoolhouses that provided limited education to the masses. Mountain Lake Park, and other places like it, provided opportunities for more advance studies in many fields. Plus, it provided a wholesome atmosphere for learning and recreation.

Today, Mountain Lake Park Resort is mostly just a memory, though the town and many structures still exist. Many factors caused the unraveling of the Park. Development of the car and better roads made travel easier and more flexible. People became tourists, not summer residents. New inventions such as movies, radio, TV, etc., brought entertainment into the homes. The wars and the Great Depression led to the decline of resorts in general. But no doubt a major cause for the demise of Mountain Lake Park was the idyllic standards imposed upon property owners – making the selling of the property nearly impossible.

One Sunday morning in the Assembly Hall at Mountain Lake Park, visiting Evangelist L. H. Baker delivered a soul-stirring message on "Repentance." Among the many who had responded to the invitation was a woman whose dress and manner suggested refinement. Mrs. C. H. Morris, the well-known gospel song composer, was present at the meeting. Observing that the woman was having difficulty, she began to talk with her. Mrs. Morris discovered that her problem was one of fear that God would not receive her. Putting her arm around her, Mrs. Morris exclaimed, *"Just now your doubtings give o'er."* The song leader, H. L. Gilmour, had been watching the struggle. He got to his knees beside the women and added, *"Just now reject Him no more."* Evangelist Baker,

A Song Is Born

who had also gathered in the circle, replied, *"Just now throw open the door,"* and then Mrs. Morris added a last appeal, *"Let Jesus Come Into Your Heart."* The woman's needs were met, and in a most unusual way the chorus of a very popular invitation song was born.

Before the close of the camp meeting that week, Mrs. C. H. Morris had written a complete set of stanzas and the music. To learn more about Mrs. C. H. Morris, see hymns *Nearer, Still Nearer* and *Sweeter As The Years Go By*, also in this book.

We are living in a world filled with hatred, and it often comes in the name of religion. To know Jesus is to love one another, and to be loved. To know Jesus is to value life and to respect the life of others even if they have different religious views. To know Jesus is to know God, the one true God who created all mankind, the God of love, the God of eternal salvation. Now, more than ever, we need to introduce our neighbors, our friends, and all nations to Jesus!

I have been crucified with Christ and I no longer live, but Christ lives in me. The life I live in the body, I live by faith in the Son of God, who loved me and gave himself for me. [Galatians 2:20]

A Song Is Born

You have been a refuge for the poor, a refuge for the needy in his distress, a shelter from the storm. [Isaiah 25:4]

MASTER, THE TEMPEST IS RAGING

H. R. Palmer, the noted composer of such popular tunes as *O Lord, Our Lord* and *Yield Not To Temptation*, asked Mary Baker to write several hymn texts for Sunday School lessons. Miss Baker did not feel very much like writing hymns. In fact, she was feeling very despondent and somewhat rebellious since her brother had recently died, but the providence of God was at work to heal her broken spirit and to provide inspiration to others. One text subject given to her by Mr. Palmer was Mark 4: 37-39, where Christ rebuked the storms. Miss Baker gives the account of those events.

"A very dear and only brother, a young man of loveliness and promise of character, had been laid to rest in his grave, dying of the same disease that had already taken our mother and father. His death occurred under distressing circumstances because he was a thousand miles away from home, seeking the warmer airs of the South to help heal his condition. Suddenly, he grew worse, and I was too ill to go and be with him. For two weeks, we kept in touch by telegraph, until he passed from this earth.

We mourned, not as those without hope, for I had believed in Christ in early childhood and had always desired to give the Master a consecrated and obedient life, but I had become wickedly rebellious. But the Master's voice stilled the tempest in my heart and brought it to the calm of a deeper faith and a more perfect trust. Since then, I have come to feel a keen sense of gratitude for the sweet memories left of my departed brother, and know God's way is best."

With a heart full of grief, heartache and woe, Mary A. Baker called upon her own personal experiences to write the poem she called *"Peace Be Still"* that served to restore her faith and trust in the Lord.

The hymn did not achieve popularity until some seven years later, when a President of the United States was assassinated. James A. Garfield had been President just four months when he left the White

A Song Is Born

House en route to his college class reunion at William's College. A disgruntled office seeker, Charles Guiteau, struck him down as he walked through the train station in Washington, DC. For weeks he lingered near death, which finally came, September 19, 1881. During this time, people discovered the hymn *Master the Tempest Is Raging,* and Christians throughout this land sang it over and over again as they expressed concern for their President and their country. From that time on, it has won a place in most hymnals, and also a place in our hearts.

Recent destructive forces unleashed by hurricanes that devastated the Eastern coast of South Carolina and Florida, and the deadly earthquake which destroyed buildings and freeways in California, graphically point out the awesome power of nature. Yet, we often fail to realize that when our lives are filled with grief, heartache, and suffering, it creates powerful destructive forces within us that work to destroy the very fiber of our soul. Miss Baker realized that the same Lord who could still the tempest of nature, could calm the storms in our lives.

There is comfort in knowing that our Savior not only controls the forces of nature, but he can calm the troubled heart. Christ provides a place of refuge from the tempest of life and a rest for the weary soul. He is a friend who cares.

> *Without warning, a furious storm came up on the lake, so that the waves swept over the boat. But Jesus was sleeping. The disciples went and woke him, saying 'Lord, save us! We're going to drown.' He replied, 'You of little faith, why are you so afraid?' Then he got up and rebuked the winds and the waves, and it was completely calm.*
> [Matthew 8:24-26]

RJT

Text and Tune First appeared in Songs for Young People published by Excell, 1897

A Song Is Born

Count Your Blessings

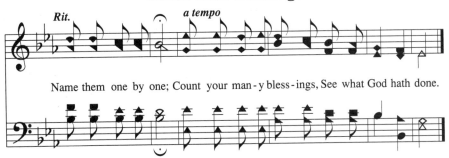

Praise be to the God and Father of our Lord Jesus Christ, who has blessed us in the heavenly realms with every spiritual blessing. [Ephesians 1:3]

COUNT YOUR BLESSINGS

Johnson Oatman, Sr., had a rich, powerful voice. This local merchant of Lumberton, New Jersey, was considered the *"best singer in the state."* His son loved to hear his dad sing and would always sit beside him in church. Johnson Oatman, Jr., remembers thinking at age nine, *"When I grow up, I'm going to sing like my daddy,"* but as he reached adulthood it was obvious he did not have the musical talents of his dad. Though disappointed, he thought, *"If I can not sing like my dad, I'll become a powerful preacher and reach thousands with the message of Christ."* So off to the Seminary he went. After several years of study, he was licensed to preach and went from pulpit to pulpit as a local preacher, but he never felt his talents would allow him to become a full time minister.

After years of frustration trying to be like his dad, Johnson Oatman, Jr. discovered that what he really wanted was to contribute something back to their faith. While searching for some way to contribute, he began to write poems and within three short years, the world was singing his songs. Hymns like *Higher Ground, No, Not One, Sweeter Than All,* and *Count Your Blessings.*

Soon after Mr. Oatman, Jr., began to write hymn text, one poem stands out as perhaps best expressing his feelings having finally found his calling in life; it was *Count Your Blessings!* If he could not sing like his dad, he could write the songs for others to sing. While he dreamed of reaching thousands with the message of Christ through preaching, he reached millions through his songs. Rather than reflecting on what he could not do, he focused on what he could do, and counted his blessings.

By the time of his death in 1922 at the age of 66, Johnson Oatman, Jr., had written over 5000 hymn texts. He was reluctant to accept money for the things he wrote, but when publishers insisted that a price be set on his works, it is reported that he would not accept more than one dollar per song.

Gratitude is at the heart of thanksgiving. Sometimes our ambitions and goals in life do not match the results. We are disappointed, let down, and feel sorry for ourselves. We sometimes let our thoughts linger much too long on these disappointments of life, allowing them to hide all the positive, good things that have come our way, making it difficult to count our blessings. Someone once said: *"Hem your blessings with thanks or they will unravel."*

Sometimes when we are feeling low, we quickly notice the negatives in every event or in another person. A Christians' life should not be filled with pessimism and despair. We have everything to live for and even more hope in death. Be optimistic! Count your blessings rather than your failures and you will be happy. Set your mind on things above. It's all about attitude!

In everything by prayer and supplication, with thanksgiving, let your request be made known to God. [Philippians 4:6] *In everything give thanks; for this is God's will for you in Christ Jesus.* [1 Thessalonians 5:18]

A Song Is Born

> *Peace I leave you; my peace I give you. I do not give to you as the world gives. Do not let your hearts be troubled and do not be afraid.* [John 14:27]

IT IS WELL WITH MY SOUL

Sometimes the problems of life seem to swell around us like great ocean waves. We are tempted to give up and let depression weaken our faith or sidetrack our resolve to overcome. We tend to feel that something or someone "has it in for me." We often rationalize, "no one else could possibly suffer as much, or give up more, than I." Mr. Spafford, the author of this hymn, could have easily taken this attitude.

During the 1860s, Horatio Gates Spafford had developed a successful law practice in Chicago. Several months prior to the great Chicago fire of 1871, he had invested heavily in real estate. That fire wiped out all these holdings plus his law office. Mile after mile of wooden buildings, homes, stores, bridges, and sidewalks burned out of control for days. Human emotion and conduct were also out of control. In a city lawless with panic, confusion and death, the brutality and horror were sickening.

Mr. Spafford was in Indiana on this fateful day October 8, 1871, attempting to establish a sale for the lakeshore property that burned. His wife Anna, however, witnessed the tragic event. Left alone with four small children and house servants, she was not alarmed for their safety at first and while viewing the great inferno from her porch she began

preparing to receive refugees. Old acquaintances and perfect strangers began to arrive, with burns, blisters, and eyes blinded from the fire. No sooner had she made them all comfortable, when word arrived that some near-by trees were on fire. Now Anna, her children, servants, and added house guests had to move out, leaving one faithful employee who constantly poured water on the house and grounds. The home was saved from destruction.

A Song Is Born

Sometime later, upon the advice of their family physician, the Spaffords planned a European trip, mostly for the sake of Anna who had witnessed so much pain, sorrow, and death in that fire. Because of last minute business, Mr. Spafford sent them on ahead, planning to join them in a few weeks.

On their way over, the French Liner, "Ville du Havre," was struck by an English sailing ship, the "Lochearn." Within minutes, the huge French Liner sank, killing some 226 people. Mrs. Spafford survived, but their four daughters, Maggie, Tanetta, Annie, and Bessie all died. Upon hearing of the tragedy, Mr. Spafford walked the floor all night in anguish. Toward morning, he turned to devoted friends, and said: "I am glad to trust the Lord when it will cost me something." He booked passage on the next available ship for Europe.

Adding to Mr. Spafford's personal grief was a spiritual conflict. It was universally accepted by Christians everywhere that sickness or sorrow were the result of sin in your life. All around him people were asking the unspoken question, what had he or Anna done to be punished like this? Mr. Spafford did not accept this view of scripture, that sickness or tragedy was a result of sin, and as a result he was removed from the church rolls. Ten years later, the church changed its position but by this time the Spafford's were living in Jerusalem.

It is reported that as they passed near where the accident occurred, the Captain indicated the general location to Mr. Spafford. In the dark of the night, heavy with grief and pain, but filled with faith and hope, he wrote:

> *When peace like a river attendeth my way*
> *When sorrows like sea billows roll*
> *What ever my lot, thou hast taught me to say*
> *It is well with my soul.*

I like the transition Mr. Spafford made, as he wrote the second verse, turning his thoughts toward Christ and the sacrifice that He made for us. Then he concludes in verse three with the hope of a speedy second coming

A Song Is Born

of our Savior.

A personal tragedy became the inspiration for the text of this great hymn, but the story does not end there. Philip Bliss, the renowned composer, agreed to set the poem to music, and near the end of November 1876, Mr. Bliss introduced the new hymn. Ironically, within a month, Philip Bliss and his wife were both killed in a tragic fiery train accident near Ashtabula, Ohio. Neither the Spafford's four children, nor Mr. and Mrs. Bliss, have an earthly grave. Their bodies have never been recovered.

It has been said that "Only those who suffer greatly have the opportunity to demonstrate great faith." Horatio and Anna Spafford demonstrated great faith as they continued to serve God. Paul declared, "I have learned to be content whatever the circumstance." We are in this old world for only a short time when compared to eternity. The things we experience or suffer will hurt because we are human. But, never, never, never let anything weaken your faith in God or turn your eyes away from Heaven.

And we know that in all things God works for the good of those who love him, who have been called according to his purpose. [Romans 8:28]

A Song Is Born

> *Cast all your care upon Him for He careth for you.* [1 Peter 5:7]

DOES JESUS CARE?

*E*very sincere Christian at some point in their life feels like the words of a great Afro-American spiritual *"Sometimes I'm up, sometimes I'm down, sometimes I'm almost to the ground"*. We often find ourselves confessing Christ as our Savior one moment only to have Satan rule our lives the next. Even Peter, the Apostle, experienced this internal struggle with Satan. Some unknown author has written:

> *"Only those people are capable of great faith who have known tremendous doubt and find spiritual certainty only after having passed through the dark valley of questioning."*

Is God present and concerned during my times of hurt? Does He care when the burdens weigh heavy on my thoughts? Does He care when I can no longer resist some strong temptation? These questions and doubts are common to nearly all of God's children at some point in their lives, just as they were to Mr. Graeff.

Frank Graeff was born in Tamaqua, Pennsylvania, in 1860. He became a Methodist Minister and was often referred to as the *"Spiritual Optimists"* and the *"Sunshine Minister."* He was a great friend of children and the author of several children's stories. Those who knew him spoke often and tenderly of his devotion to little children. This was a great characteristic in view of the fact that he and his wife were never able to have children of their own.

Even with these years of optimism, at one point in his life, Frank Graeff became very despondent, questioning the very truths he had believed and taught others, doubting the goodness of God. During those long trying days, as he sought solace and strength, he turned once again to the scriptures. Out of this period of darkness in his life he wrote the poem *Does Jesus Care* which not only helped lead him back to Christ's love and renewed optimism, but has comforted millions of Christians through the years.

RJT

A Song Is Born

> *This is how we know what love is: Jesus Christ laid down his life for us.* [1 John 3:16]

THERE IS A REDEEMER

On the evening of July 28, 1982, Keith Green was eager to show his friends around the Last Days Ministries ranch near Lindale, Texas. Melody, his wife who was pregnant with their fourth child, declined to go on the short airplane ride in their leased Cessna 414. Only moments had passed when the phone rang. "Our plane just went down!" reported an office girl. "I'm going to call an ambulance, but I wanted to tell Keith first. Will you please tell Keith?" the caller requested. The problem, unknown to the caller, was that Keith was on that plane along with two of the Green's children plus nine friends, twelve in all. There were no survivors. Thus ended the short, tremulous but productive 28-year life of Keith Green.

Keith Green was born, October 21, 1952, in Camino, CA. Spiritual roots ran deep in his family. His grandfather had been a Christian Scientist for 60 years and Keith's father followed suit. Keith was raised in a good, moral atmosphere, but when he became a teenager he began to rebel. "Organized religion" started to feel dead to him. He struggled with some inherited beliefs such as there's no literal hell, or that only certain parts of the Bible are the inspired Word of God. By the end of 1972, Keith had scratched so many things off his spiritual search list that he barely had anything left. He had narrowed things down quite a bit and spent a lot of time reading two books, "The Bible" and "Science and Health." For a few weeks he thought he'd get totally into Christian Science. He wrote, "I dig the teachings, but the organized machine scares me." He began to struggle with the person and concept of Jesus. Who was He? Was He God? How could God be three persons?

About this time he met Melody Steiner, seven years his senior. Melody was born to Helen and Charles Steiner, in Hollywood California. Her mother was Jewish and her father a Methodist, though neither were active in their beliefs. By the time she was twelve, her parents had divorced. Soon afterwards, her dad had a stroke and lived out his life in a VA

A Song Is Born

hospital. Melody and her mother tried to keep in touch for a while, but soon they both stopped visiting. He died and was buried without Melody's knowledge, which caused her deep anxiety for many years. "I was left to wonder why so much of what I really wanted in life had been taken away from me," Melody said later. "I never had the family or the home I wanted. I tried all forms of religion but nothing seemed to have any reality. My Buddhist experience was a flop. Now my father was dead." So hurt from this combination of events that she never visited his grave.

Keith and Melody were married on Christmas day, 1973. *"Keith and I had both been caught up in a search to find our "spiritual identities" for some time,"* Melody said. "We were looking for truth – whatever it was – and our search for light had taken us both on many strange paths, from Buddhism to stuff like astral projection and, of course, drugs. We were both convinced "the truth" was hidden out there somewhere like a pearl in the ocean, and that when we found it, it would fill an empty spot in our hearts. We had been looking into Jesus Christ. We weren't Christians and the Church concept was a dead institution to us. But Jesus did seem to be a spiritual Master of some sort."

There Is A Redeemer was recorded and released the same year of Keith's death, 1982, but it was written some five years earlier during their search and acceptance of Jesus as their Savior. Melody had written verse one, the chorus and the music, but when Keith recorded it, he added the second and third verses. To make this statement about Jesus may seem simple, contrite, and unnecessary to some of us, but to Melody and Keith, it was a conviction born out of an earnest quest to know Jesus, to understand His teachings and meaning in their lives. This was not a statement taken lightly, nor without a commitment. From this commitment, they established the Last Days Ministries, an organization devoted to helping people. Keith not only believed in Jesus and His teachings, but he tried with all of his heart to practice what he preached. He had little tolerance for those who sought financial gain through Christian merchandising or even charging for Christian concerts. *"The ticket prices for concerts are a nail in Jesus' hand,"* he once wrote. *"Unbelievers aren't going to pay to hear about Jesus."*

"Keith was a spiritual revolutionary," said Leonard Ravenhill. "He wasn't just a performer or preacher, he was a crusader." Keith was

A Song Is Born

intense in his faith, outspoken in his opinions, and very strong in his convictions. He was also a deeply talented musician, a young man seemingly out of step with his generation. "He was intense," said Melody, his wife, in her book "No Compromise." "He questioned everything and everyone about life, reality, and religious beliefs, but once he found the answer, nothing could turn him." And Keith believed in Jesus as the Redeemer of mankind.

A ransom was the price paid to release a slave from bondage. Jesus often told His disciples that He must die, but in Matthew 20:28, He told them why; *"to redeem all people from the bondage of sin and death."* Jesus has willingly done His part. He has paid the price for our salvation. What remains now is for you and I to commit our lives to Jesus – not only in word but also in deed.

In Him we have redemption through his blood, the forgiveness of sins, in accordance with the riches of God's grace that he lavished on us with all wisdom and understanding. [Ephesians 1:7]

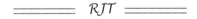

RJT

The Family Of God
Ephesians 3:14-15

William J. Gaither, 1970   William J. and Gloria Gaither, 1970

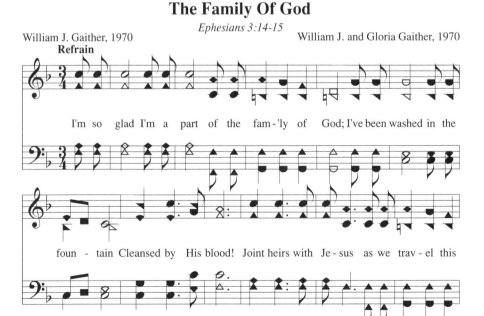

I'm so glad I'm a part of the fam-'ly of God; I've been washed in the foun-tain Cleansed by His blood! Joint heirs with Je-sus as we trav-el this

A Song Is Born

© Copyright 1970 by William J. Gaither. All Rights Reserved. Used by Permission.

A Song Is Born

> *Now the body is not made up of one part but of many.- - If one part suffers, every part suffers with it.* [1 Corinthians 12:14; 26]

THE FAMILY OF GOD

*F*rom her book, "Fully Alive," Gloria Gaither provides most of the details for the background of their song. Ron and Darlene Garner are a young couple with three children in their fellowship. It was on the Saturday after Good Friday that Ron, a mechanic, went in to work. He was working alone that day, making up time for having taken his little daughter in for tests prior to the anticipated heart surgery. With the operation coming up, he knew they would need the money for hospital and doctor bills. Ron was working with combustible materials and there was an explosion. He managed to crash his way through the large double doors before the building blew apart, but he was severely burned.

The news from the emergency room was pessimistic: Ron was alive but not expected to make it through the night. It was only a matter of minutes before a chain of telephone calls alerted the whole church, and they began to pray for Ron. All day long they prayed. In little groups, in bigger groups, in homes, at the church, over the phone - all over town people who were related to Ron and Darlene because of their belief in Jesus, prayed. By evening the word came that, although the doctors gave no hope, Ron was still alive. Possibly, if he could make it until morning, there was a chance, just a chance.

The believers kept on praying. The church building was kept open, and lights burned all through the night as a steady stream of folks who cared and loved came to talk to Jesus about this young father.

"The sun streamed in the windows that Easter morning on an assembly filled with the most weary, bleary-eyed congregation you've ever seen," said Gloria Gaither. "There were very few Easter bonnets or bright new outfits. We were just there, drawn together closer than we had ever been before by the reality we had been sharing, that when one part of the Body suffers, we all suffer with it. Nobody felt much like

A Song Is Born

celebrating. There was hurt and pain in the Body. About twenty minutes into the service, the minister came in with a report from the hospital. Although he had gone without sleep to be with the Garner family, there was sunshine in his eyes. 'Ron has outlived the deadline. The doctors say he has a chance. They are going to begin treatment.'"

Tears of joy! Tears of praise! They all knew it would be a long road back for Ron, many pints of blood, expensive hospital bills, meals for the family, etc. The congregation was thankful for the life spared, and was up to the challenge ahead. "Today" Gloria said, "Ron is a healthy basketball coach and a strong witness to the power of Christ."

On the way home from church that Easter morning, Bill and Gloria were overwhelmed with what they had witnessed. As Gloria prepared dinner, Bill sat down at the piano. A hymn was born!

We assemble together to praise God, to worship our Redeemer, and to share our faith. These are important functions of the church and serve to strengthen us as we go about our daily task. But the body of Christ is not just an organization; it is a living organism. We feel the joy when a member celebrates, and we feel the pain when a member suffers. This is how a healthy body functions.

Be devoted to one another in brotherly love. Honor one another above yourselves. [Romans 12:10]

A Song Is Born

Thanks be to God for his indescribable gift! [2 Corinthians 9:15]

Thank You, Lord

The Sounds of Glory Quartet, with C. D. Davis, Lenier Stevens, Charles Davis, and Dale Underwood, once wrote and recorded a song titled "Prodigal Son." It was inspired by the true story of a young man who had Aids, contacted from a sinful life of homosexuality. As this young man faced the irreversible physical consequences of his life style, he sought to correct his spiritual life – but the fear of people's response made it difficult for him to "come home." He approached the Elders with some reservation. To his amazement, the leadership and the whole congregation embraced this prodigal son with forgiveness and love, making his last days on this earth as peaceful as possible.

I tell you this story partly to show the difficulty many Christians have with this sin of homosexuality, and also because one of the most prolific writers of contemporary Christian music today was once caught up in this life style. His name is Dennis Jernigan, the author of our song *Thank You, Lord*. He has also written *All in All, Rushing Wind, Nobody Fills my Heart Like Jesus, I am a Sheep, Jesus Flow Like a River,* and countless others.

He was born Dennis L. Jernigan, February 9, 1959, in Boynton, Oklahoma. After completing high school there, he graduated from the Baptist University. He and his lovely wife Melinda have nine children. They currently attend the New Community Church in Muskogee, Oklahoma, where he is the Worship Leader. Mr. Jernigan has written over 1000 songs, and has been nominated for several Dove Awards.

At an early age, Dennis became involved in homosexuality. "The reasons were many," he said "but I simply believed a lot of lies – about my father – about myself – and about God." It was during this time in his life that he discovered his musical talent. He had been the church pianist from the age of nine. While Dennis knew that his sexual immorality was a sin, he just did not know how to overcome it.

The church people and its leaders did not seem to be the ones to talk to, for all that he heard from them were harsh rebukes for homosexuals.

A Song Is Born

"—Ship them all to another country – they all belong in hell — etc." He reasoned that if God's people were like that, then God must also be unapproachable, harsh, and disgusted with him. After college, his life hit bottom. It was there that he met God, the God of forgiveness, and the God of love and compassion. In his own words, Dennis Jernigan explains the birth of this song.

> "*Thank You, Lord* came as the Lord began having me share concerning my deliverance from sodomy (the world calls this homosexuality) in 1981. The things we think will be the most devastating to us, like sharing who we once were, God wants to use to affect the lives of others who have believed a lie. When you begin to declare what He has done for you, people begin to receive hope, but Satan also begins to work. The world needs to see that there is a way – but how will they see if those who were once blind don't tell about their healing? The truth is this; we have all fallen into the depravity of sin no matter how "innocent" your past may seem in comparison to mine.'

Dennis Jernigan concludes his comments by saying, "This song, *Thank You, Lord,* is my thanks to Jesus for taking a trashed out life and making a vessel for His glory out of it. It's also meant to be a boast in the face of Satan and a weapon to break down hardened hearts."

Thank you, have a nice day! How often have you heard this parting remark? It sounds nice, but often seems so shallow. We usually respond with "you, too." It is one thing to say thank you when politeness is expected, but quite another to say thank you when receiving a blessing. How do we really say thanks? It must come from an honest heart – a grateful heart – from one that truly feels someone has given them something they could not give themselves. For many, that's difficult to do in this self-centered, self-satisfying, and seemingly self-made world we live in.

Thanks be to God for his indescribable gift! [2 Corinthians 9:15] Give thanks to the Father, who has qualified you to share in the inheritance of the saints - - For He has rescued us from the dominion of darkness and brought us into the kingdom of the Son he loves. [Colossians 1:12-13] Give thanks in all circumstances, for this is God's will for you

A Song Is Born

in Christ Jesus! [1 Thessalonians 5:18] Without God's grace, without the gift of Jesus dying on the cross for us, what hope would we have? Those who are redeemed must cry out "Thank You."

And I thank Christ Jesus our Lord who has enabled me, because He counted me faithful, putting me into the ministry, although I was formerly a blasphemer, a persecutor, and an insolent man; but I obtained mercy because I did it ignorantly in unbelief. – This is a faithful saying and worthy of all acceptance, that Christ Jesus came into the world to save sinners, of whom I am chief. However, for this reason I obtained mercy, that in me first Jesus Christ might show all longsuffering, as a pattern to those who are going to believe. [1 Timothy 1:12-16]

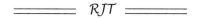

RJT

A Song Is Born

A Song Is Born

> *Yea, I have loved thee with an everlasting love: therefore with loving kindness have I drawn thee.* [Jeremiah 31:3]

THE LOVE OF GOD

*F*rederick Martin Lehman was born in Germany, August 7, 1868. The family moved to the United States in 1872 and settled on farmland in Iowa. While still in his youth, he became a believer and follower of Christ. As Frederich grew up, he followed the family tradition of farming until he was in his late 20s. He then begins a long career as a preacher, religious editor, and music publisher.

The first six years of his ministry were spent as a circuit rider, traveling from town to town in a horse-drawn buggy. In 1911, Mr. Lehman moved to Kansas City and helped to establish the Nazarene Publishing House. In 1914 we find him in Pasadena, California, continuing to preach and where he lived until his death in 1953.

Within just three short years after moving to California in 1917, something had gone drastically wrong. An unnamed misfortune had caused the Lehmans to lose everything, forcing him to hard, physical labor in a lemon-packing house. It was under these trying circumstances that the hymn *The Love of God* was born.

"This song was written during the interim while waiting on eight women lemon-sorters in a Pasadena packing house, carrying to them boxes of lemons and taking away from them the finished trays," Mr. Lehman said. He would carry crates of lemons to the women for inspection and sorting, then carry the finished product away for shipping, lifting as much as 30 tons each day. There were short periods of time in-between these two tasks, and this is when Mr. Lehman penciled down the words to stanzas one and two and the music to *The Love of God*. To write of God's love with such warmth and feeling at perhaps the lowest time in his life is truly amazing. But what about stanza three?

> *Could we with ink the ocean fill*
> *And were the skies of parchment made,*
> *Were every stalk on earth a quill,*
> *And every man a scribe by trade,*
> *To write the love of God above*
> *Would drain the ocean dry,*

> *Nor could the scroll contain the whole*
> *Tho stretched from sky to sky.*

Mr. Lehman did not write this stanza, yet the poetic beauty of this verse was the inspiration! While attending a camp meeting early in his preaching career, Mr. Lehman heard an evangelist use this poem to conclude his sermon. So impressed with the poem, he was moved to preserve the words until additional stanzas could be written, a period of nearly twenty years.

It was commonly believed that the author of these profound lines was a patient in a mental institution. The story goes that the words were found written on a wall in an institution for the insane nearly 200 years earlier. After the person died, the painters came to repaint the room and found these words on the wall. They were so impressed with the poem, that they took the time to copy and preserve it before repainting. No one remembers who the person was, or how they could have written such profound lines was unknown.

A few years back, it was determined that stanza three was actually written by a Jewish rabbi hundreds of years before. The book titled *A Book of Jewish Thoughts* by Herman Hertz contains the poem *Hadamut*, written by Meir Ben Isaac Nehoria in the year 1096. It is believed that the third stanza of *The Love of God* was adapted from this poem, which reads:

> *Were the sky of parchment made,*
> *A quill each reed, each twig and blade,*
> *Could we with ink the oceans fill,*
> *Were every man a scribe of skill,*
> *The marvelous story Of God's great glory*
> *Would still remain untold:*
> *For He, most high the earth and sky*
> *Created alone of old.*

If the poetic words we sing as stanza three in the hymn *The Love of God* were adapted from this poem written over 900 years ago, then who made the adaptation? Who translated the words from Hebrew to English? Was it the troubled mental patient? Or was it the camp meeting

A Song Is Born

evangelist around the turn of the twentieth century? Or was it Mr. Lehman himself? We simply do not know.

What are the odds? That a 900-year-old Jewish poem could etch its beauty upon the heart of one mentally challenged. Be preserved by house painters to live again in a sermon in rural America only to remain a note on paper for 20 years, until Mr. Lehman had lost everything and be inspired to write other verses and fitting music. Perhaps only the providence of God can explain the tangled web of events that provided the birth of this great song.

Throughout the hymn, the theme of God's eternal love and concern for His people is evident. What an awesome God we have!

Who shall separate us from the love of God? Shall trouble or hardship or persecution or famine or nakedness or danger or sword? – No, in all these things we are more than conquerors through him who loved us. [Romans 8:35-37]

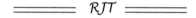

RJT

A Song Is Born

A Song Is Born

> *Be joyful in hope, patient in affliction, faithful in prayer.* [Romans 12:12]

WHISPERING HOPE

*T*he author of this hymn was once considered to be one of the most popular, prolific composers of the 19th century. His youthful song Der Deitcher's Dog, better known as *"Oh where, oh where is mine little dog gone,"* is sometimes still sung today. One of his songs in 1862 so enraged the Secretary of War that he was arrested and could not be released until he promised to stop selling the song and destroy all copies. The most popular of his well-known songs sold over 20 million copies. What is the popular song? Who was the author? What hymn did he write?

The name Alice Hawthorne often appeared on the hymn credits, but the song *Whispering Hope* was actually written and composed by Septimus Winner. He was born May 11, 1827, and died November 22, 1902, in Philadelphia, PA. Mr. Winner was a prolific composer, teacher, and publisher producing more than 200 volumes of music. His parents were Joseph Eastburn Winner, a violin maker, and Mary Ann (Hawthorne) Winner. Though largely self-educated in music, Septimus Winner learned to play several instruments. By the age of 20 he was teaching guitar, banjo, violin, and other instruments. Around 1845 he became a music publisher, opening a music store with his brother, Joseph E. Winner.

Septimus Winner is best known for his enormously successful secular songs, which he issued under the pseudonym Alice Hawthorne. His popular song, *Listen To The Mocking Bird* (1855) was one of the greatest successes of the century. Within 50 years of its first publication, the song had sold 20 million copies. However, like so many others of his day, Mr. Winner did not profit from his success. He had sold the copyright for $5! The basis for the tune came from Dick Milburn, known as "Whistling Dick", a black youth who ran errands at Winner's store.

The event that so enraged the Secretary of War and landed Mr. Winner in jail, occurred in 1862. When General George B. McClellan was discharged as commander of the Army of the Potomac, Mr. Winner composed and published a protest song titled "Give us back our old commander: Little Mac, the people's pride." The song quickly won a huge following and so provoked Edwin M. Stanton, then the Secretary of War that Union soldiers were forbidden to sing it under threat of court martial. Mr. Winner was arrested for treason and was not released until he destroyed all remaining copies of the song and promised to stop selling it. Ironically, two years later when George McClellan became the Democratic candidate for president, the song was used in his election campaign.

Whispering Hope was first published in 1868. Those who knew him said that Mr. Winner did not regard this composition as a religious song. In fact he was amused and amazed that its great popularity was achieved as a religious song. After all, God, Christ, or the Holy Spirit are not addressed anywhere in the text. It is also interesting to note that Winner's brother, Joseph E. Winner (who wrote under the pseudonym R. E. Eastburn) was somewhat jealous of his brother's success with *Whispering Hope*. Joseph attempted to outdo his brother by writing and publishing a novel song about "drinking." That song was *Little Brown Jug* (1869). It was very successful but remains to be a dubious comparison to *Whispering Hope*.

Whatever Septimus Winner's intentions were, *Whispering Hope* achieved instant popularity and has been published continuously by hymnbook publishers ever since. The song's strength lies in the message of hope it gives. The inspirational power of this song can be justified by the assurance that Paul stated in Romans 5:5 *"And hope does not disappoint us, because God has poured out his love into our hearts by the Holy Spirit."*

We sing of hope in so many of our beautiful hymns: *My hope is built on Jesus'*, *Oh God our help in ages past, our hope for years to come,* to name just two. The Biblical definition of faith as being the substance of things hoped for is reason enough to find strength in the power of hope. In the beautiful song, *Whispering Hope,* several tender expressions allude to the quiet comfort that children of God can find in hope: *"Hope whispers her comforting word. . hope as an anchor so steadfast."* May we always be reassured in our faith by singing this wonderful chorus: *"Whispering hope, O how welcome thy voice. Making my heart in its sorrow rejoice. . .O blessed hope!"*

We have this hope as an anchor for the soul, firm and secure.
[Hebrews 6:19]

RJT

A Song Is Born

The Scars In The Hands Of Jesus

A Song Is Born

Then he said to Thomas, "Put your finger here; see my hands. Reach out your hand and put it into my side. Stop doubting and believe." [John 20:27]

THE SCARS IN THE HANDS OF JESUS

Marijohn Wilkin has lived a remarkable life. For more details about Marijohn, see the story for *One Day At A Time*. This song, The Scars In The Hands Of Jesus, was inspired while flying in a small plane. The Lord replaced her fear of flying with a song. Listen as she tells the story.

"The title *Scars in the Hands of Jesus* was given in kind of a backwards way. Barbara Fairchild had been talking to me one day, and had given me the line *"the only thing in heaven made by man would be the scars in Jesus' hand,"* almost like an assignment to write the song for her. The beauty of the thought kept running through my head, but no words came in my devotional times.

One day, the University of Tennessee sent their private plane to take me to Knoxville to work with their singers. It was a single prop plane with five of us in there. I was scared to death before we took off anyway, but when we got up in the air, I suddenly got panicky. "Wait," I said to myself; "I've got this new faith I've been talking and writing about. How 'bout me using it?"

So, in order to keep my mind off flying, I started thinking of the title Barbara had given me. I looked out of the plane's window at the snow on the Smoky Mountains near Gatlinburg. I was in the back seat and began writing on my ledger pad;

> *When I see a mountain covered with snow*
> *that's fallen from heaven above,*
> *It makes me feel small - hardly nothing at all –*
> *to know I'll be a part of That mansion world*
> *where the gates of pearl are opened by an angel band.*
> *And the only thing there that's been made by man*
> *are the Scars in the hands of Jesus."*

——— RJT ———

A Song Is Born

Get up, be baptized and wash your sins away, calling on his name. [Acts 22:16]

O Happy Day

Sometimes a tune comes along that is so distinctive it catches the imagination of everyone. This was especially true of tunes created during the camp meeting era of the Nineteenth Century. A large number of radio and television commercial jingles used today are created using similar catchy tunes. The instant we hear them, we can recall the words or message. This is true for the tune, *O Happy Day,* indelibly linked to our hymn for this discussion.

There is an interesting kaleidoscope of events that took place to bring us this enduring hymn. A distinguished theologian, Philip Doddridge, wrote the words. An equally talented and renowned musician, Edward Rimbault, composed the chorus. Yet the writer of the tune that has sustained its popularity, remains anonymous.

Philip Doddridge was born in London, England, in 1702, the youngest of twenty children, eighteen of which died in infancy. Even he was laid aside at birth believing that he had been still born. His parents died by the time he was thirteen. Physically he was a frail child in poor health most of his short life. As a talented young man, he was given the offer of a free education at Cambridge University if, upon completion, he would become a minister for the Church of England. He refused, choosing rather to study and become a minister for the Congregational Church. Philip went on to become a brilliant scholar, writing volumes of theological treatise including a New Testament commentary. He also wrote about 400 hymns. *O Happy Day* was written by Mr. Doddridge sometime before his death in 1751. He titled this poem "Rejoice in Our Covenant Engagement to God."

The tune we use for *O Happy Day* was created by anonymous musicians, and has often been criticized as not worthy of the text it carries. Furthermore, it has been abused when someone made it the tune of a dismal drunk "How Dry I Am," yet the melody has been and continues to be the vehicle for the success of Mr. Doddridge' poem. The

A Song Is Born

chorus was written by Edward F. Rimbault. This talented Englishman was not only a distinguished composer, but he was also well known as an organist, author, editor, and lecturer. He received many honorary degrees of music from universities in the East, as well as having the honorary LLD degree conferred upon him by Harvard.

Philip Doddridge's poem was originally published in 1755 with another tune. However, it did not become popular until some 100 years later, when in 1854 the words were married to the current tune and the chorus composed by Edward F. Rimbault. This combination became an instant hit at revivals and camp meetings in America. It received new popularity some 100 years later, when in 1969 the Walter Hawkins Singers developed and recorded an arrangement based upon the black gospel music style. Their arrangement became a best seller, and stayed on the pop charts for ten weeks.

The words of this song remind us of our beginnings of grace. Mr. Doddridge is looking back to his conversion, both with amazement and gratitude. What is conversion? It involves a deep, personal choice, a spiritual transaction between God, and us a covenant relationship. It is a beginning, not an ending. Can you recall the precise happy day of your conversion?

So often we lose sight of that joyous moment of conversion, a time when the love of Christ and the love for Him was so real and very much alive in our hearts. To be converted to Christ involves a personal choice, a time when inwardly and outwardly we freely acknowledge Jesus as our Savior, pledging to follow him all the days of our life. The words of Mr. Doddridge not only remind us of our glorious beginning, but also remind us that it involves a commitment to Christ, a commitment for life not just to serve but to accept the joy of our salvation.

And all Judah rejoiced at the oath; For they had sworn with all their heart, and sought Him with their whole desire; and He was found of them; and the Lord gave them rest round about.
[2 Chronicles 15:15]

A Song Is Born

Sweeter As The Years Go By

How sweet are your words to my taste, sweeter than honey to my mouth. [Psalm 119:103]

SWEETER AS THE YEARS GO BY

The name Mrs. C. H. Morris, has appeared on hymns in hymnals for over 100 years, yet few have known that for nearly half of her 37-year song writing career, she was blind. I believe that at least two of her finest hymns were written after her blindness, *Sweeter As The Years Go By* and *'Tis Marvelous and Wonderful*. This latter song has not been as widely known as her other works, but the Lillenas Company recently recorded a beautiful rendition of this great song.

This remarkable lady, who was born Lelia Naylor in 1862, wrote more that 1500 hymns, both words and music. Though she had limited musical training, or for that matter limited formal education, her hymns offer a depth of spirituality and variety of musical styles not often found from one writer. Her education was cut short from the death of her father and the need to work to help support the family.

A Song Is Born

In 1912, Mrs. Morris realized she was rapidly going blind. One of her sons, Bill, built a large, 28-foot blackboard and placed it in a sunny room of there home on Kennebec Ave. in McConnelsville. Lines were cut into the huge blackboard representing the staff and, for a short time, she was able to continue her song writing, but within a year her sight was virtually gone. Through a government agency, she learned to use a special typewriter for the blind, but the music had to remain in her mind until her daughter, Fannie Lunk, could come from New York once a year and write them down.

A spiritual healer once offered to make the attempt to cure her blindness, but she refused reportedly saying, *"The Lord had seen fit to take away her sight. If He desired for her to see, He would restore it. She would not question His purpose."* Such was the disposition of this sweet, unassuming housewife and mother of four. Although her fame was worldwide and she was known by most of the leading evangelists of her day, and her songs were sought by the leading publishers, she was content to let her light shine through her hymns without even many of her neighbors aware of her talent.

The beauty of this great lady was that she never believed she was different or special. Her days were filled with the normal household chores such as cooking, sewing, cleaning, etc. In fact, she once said of her blindness, *"Learning to write songs without sight was not so great a task as learning to do housework."* When asked how she could find the time to think up all those words and tunes, she said *"Oh, I get both words and music when I am about my household tasks, and then when I have a little time I write them down."*

Lelia Naylor Morris had a cheerful disposition from her childhood all through her years of blindness. She knew well how to be friendly and to make everyone her friend. As the years passed and the infirmity of blindness came, and as cares and trials pressed more heavily, there never was any hardness or rebellious feelings; she still looked up through clouded eyes and sang:

> *Sweet will of God, still fold me closer,*
> *Till I am wholly lost in Thee.*

Or she would write in 1912, even knowing that she was going blind:

> *Sweeter as the years go by*
> *Richer, fuller, deeper,*
> *Jesus love is sweeter,*
> *Sweeter as the years go by.*

Still later, when her son Bill died in 1919, after devoting his life to helping her write songs, she could still write:

> *The Savior has come in His mighty power*
> *And spoken peace to my soul*
> *And all of my life from that very hour*
> *Has yielded to His control - -*
> *It is marvelous and wonderful,*
> *What Jesus has done for this soul of mine!*
> *The half has never been told.*

Lelia Naylor Morris (Mrs. C. H. Morris) truly felt her life was "richer, fuller, and deeper" because of the love of Jesus, in spite of her hardships. On July 23, 1929, she passed from this world while living with her daughter, Mrs. Fannie Lunk, in Auburn, New York. A cousin, Mrs. Ralston, was living in the Morris house in McConnelsville at the time, and she insisted that Lelia be brought back to her home of more  than forty years where friends could pay their last respects. To learn more about Mrs. C. H. Morris, see hymns *Let Jesus Come Into Your Heart* and *Nearer, Still Nearer*, also in this book.

True love must go beyond the passion of the moment, or the romantic feeling of a period, and find a life-long attachment. It is when we give ourselves completely to the principles of Christ's love that we can understand how it gets sweeter as the years continue.

> *And I pray that you, being rooted and established in love, may have power, together with all the saints, to grasp how wide and long and high and deep is the love of Christ, and to know this love that surpasses knowledge.* [Ephesians 3:17-19]

RJT

A Song Is Born

Teach Me, Lord, To Wait

But they that wait upon the Lord shall renew their strength; they shall mount up with wings as eagles; they shall run, and not be weary; and they shall walk, and not faint. (KJV) [Isaiah 40:31]

TEACH ME, LORD, TO WAIT

*F*rom the pen of this cowboy turned movie star and radio personality have come some of the most truly inspirational gospel songs. Stuart Hamblen was born in the small west Texas town of Kellyville. He began his illustrious career as a country western singer, composer, and radio-movie personality in 1926, from station KAYO in Abilene, Texas. Keep in mind that from 1920 to about 1950, all radio programs were produced live, without the benefit of prerecorded material. Mr. Hamblen was not just an announcer, but a performer from the beginning. After moving to California in 1929, his popularity increased as he starred in such radio programs as "King Cowboy and His Woolly West Review," "Covered Wagon Jubilee," and "Stuart Hamblen and His Lucky Stars"

In 1933, Stuart married Veeva Ellen Daniels, whom he affectionately nicknamed "My Suzy." From their ranch in Canyon Country, California, where the Hamblens also raised Peruvian Paso horses, Stuart produced the Nationally syndicated radio program, "Cowboy Church of the Air." Simultaneous with his long career in radio, he appeared in several motion pictures with notable stars including John Wayne, Gene Autry, and Roy Rogers.

Stuart Hamblen composed several popular western songs like "Ridin' Old Paint" and "Texas Plains," but I believe his most memorable and lasting songs are those which reflect a gospel message. He wrote such enduring songs as *It Is No Secret, This Ole House* and *Teach Me Lord to Wait* just to name three. In 1954, his song *This Ole House,* was awarded Song of the Year. It was the number one song in seven countries at the same time. Stuart Hamblen was introduced into the Country/Western Hall of Fame in 1970.

Mr. Hamblen was a great storyteller. He relates the events that prompted the writing of this song. Listen as he recounts the birth of the song, *Teach Me, Lord, To Wait.*

"I heard a story about a very rich man who went on an African safari. He hired a lot of natives as porters, and on the first day they covered many, many miles. The next day it was the same, moving rapidly all day long. The third and fourth days were the just like the first two, covering many miles. On the fifth day, the man arose early, walked out of his tent and found the porters just sitting around. They hadn't packed a thing, and what's more, refused to continue. 'What on earth is the matter here' asked the enraged hunter. 'They no travel today,' replied the guide. 'They say they come too far too fast. They say they come so fast they left their souls behind. They say they must wait until their souls catch up before they march again.'"

Mr. Hamblen continues, "Perhaps these innocent, unlearned laborers 'hit the nail on the head.' This generation we live in has traveled faster and further than any other generation. We have seen the telephone, radio, and television develop; we have seen the jet age come, and the conquering of space. We even watched as a human being walked on the moon and returned to earth. Yet in our haste, we've left something behind. We've conquered everything except ourselves. At times it seems this old world is about to come unraveled. Have we too left our souls behind?"

Patience is a virtue, which is hard to develop, especially since we live in a world that expects instant results. We have been conditioned to expect quick, immediate solutions to our needs and desires. We want instant food, instant success, instant gratification, and, I fear, instant religion. I recently heard of a church that provides drive-in services. You can drive into the parking lot and tune your radio to hear the sermon while watching a large TV screen. An attendant will come by, take the collection, and you drive away having satisfied your need to worship without ever leaving the car. Today we often hear, "it's not the quantity of time we spend in service to God, but the quality." This thought has some merit, but for thousands or even millions, the weekly worship service is the only time set aside in their lives to reflect upon God, His goodness, and His purpose, and we expect even this service to be dispatched in a timely, precision-like order. Perhaps it's time to slow down, to spend more time reflecting on the goodness of God and the needs of others rather than our wants or desires. There are many passages in the Old Testament which teach us to have patience and wait upon the Lord. I especially like Psalm 27:14.

Wait for the Lord; Be strong and take heart and wait for the Lord. [Psalm 27:14]

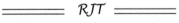

A Song Is Born

I Won't Have To Cross Jordan Alone

He'll be wait-ing for me, I won't have to cross Jor-dan a-lone.

I no longer call you servants, because a servant does not know his master's business. Instead, I called you friends. [John 15:15]

I WON'T HAVE TO CROSS JORDAN ALONE

Thomas Ramsey was born in Guymon, Oklahoma, where his parents lived in a dugout, a shelter dug in the ground and roofed with sod. His father was a talented musician, an old time country singer who taught singing schools and played the piano. Like his father, Thomas loved to sing. He left high school in his junior year to sing with one of the early Stamps Quartets, then based in Jacksonville, Texas. For the next six years, he managed the office for Stamps Music Company and sang with their quartets.

Near the end of 1929, Thomas Ramsey, along with his young wife and infant son, moved to Dallas, Texas, where he took a job with the Dallas Railway and Terminal, then a streetcar company. V. O. Stamps, the founder of the legendary Stamps Baxter Music Company, had recommended this job because they sponsored a quartet in which Mr. Ramsey could sing.

To fully understand the setting for this song, one must remember what life was like in 1929. When Thomas moved to Dallas, the infamous stock market crash of October 1929, had just occurred. Fear gripped the nation. Millions were losing their jobs, often left penniless and without food. Add to this the prospect of moving from a small community where he knew everyone, to a large city not knowing anyone. To make matters worse, his small child became very ill. In this moment of despair

A Song Is Born

and loneliness, Thomas Ramsey wrote one of his finest songs.

"I call this my depression song," Mr. Ramsey said to me. "It was just about the lowest point of my life. We were in the Great Depression, having just moved to Dallas, and my son of only one month was very sick, suffering from a severe case of bronchial pneumonia. There we were all alone in a large city. No friends to call for help or to provide advice. Where were the doctors? In Jacksonville, the doctors made house calls but here it was different! The thought came to me, how great it will be when I make my final move to Heaven, I will have a friend waiting for me to show me the way. This song was one of the easiest I have ever written, requiring only about two hours work."

Not long after Mr. Ramsey wrote this text, he left the Dallas Railway and Terminal Company and joined the US Postal Service, spending the next thirty-three years as a mail carrier and clerk, retiring in 1969. Charles Durham, who wrote the music for this hymn, was a friend and fellow employee of the Postal Service. After several years of poor health, Thomas H. Ramsey made his trip across the River Jordan, June 7, 1997.

We often take for granted the network of friends around us, never realizing how much we need or depend upon them until we move away. For those who have come to know Christ, it is comforting to know that when we make our final move;

> *"There'll be somebody waiting to show me the way,*
> *I won't have to cross Jordan alone."*

Jesus is your friend now and forever! In this high-tech electronic world we live in, you may be a number computers can trace, but Christ knows your need, your name, your heart, and your face.

> *In all things we are more than conquerors through him who loved us. For I am convinced that neither death nor life, neither angels nor demons, neither the present nor the future, nor any powers, neither height nor depth, nor anything else in all creation, will be able to separate us from the love of God that is in Christ Jesus our Lord.* [Romans 8:37-39]

SCRIPTURES

Reference	Page
Genesis 1:31	11
Deuteronomy 33:27	194
2 Samuel 22:31, 33	137
1 Chronicles 29:11	257
2 Chronicles 15:15	305
Ecclesiastes 12:1	4
Job 35:9-10	251
Psalm 9:11	240
Psalm 16:11	107
Psalm 16:2	173
Psalm 17:5	30
Psalm 17:15	89
Psalm 23:6	45
Psalm 25:4-5	149
Psalm 27:14	313
Psalm 29:1-2	206
Psalm 33:12	56
Psalm 33:12; 20-22	57
Psalm 34:17-19	102, 229
Psalm 36:9	69
Psalm 37:23-24	48
Psalm 40:3	18
Psalm 42:1-2	20
Psalm 51:10-12	262
Psalm 57:9-10	222
Psalm 59:16	134
Psalm 73:23-24	252
Psalm 86:1-4	86
Psalm 100:1-4	9
Psalm 115:1	205
Psalm 119:103	307
Psalm 122:1	164
Psalm 126:6	118
Psalm 138:7	52
Psalm 139:11-12	37
Psalm 139:17-18	132
Psalm 147:5-7	68
Proverbs 3:13-15	174
Proverbs 29:25	195
Isaiah 1:18	76
Isaiah 9:6	152
Isaiah 25:4	270
Isaiah 40:31	311
Isaiah 53:3-5	63
Isaiah 55:9	103
Isaiah 63:7	11, 39
Isaiah 63:9	40
Jeremiah 31:3	294
Lamentations 3:22-24	223
Nehemiah 1:5	66
Matthew 2:1-2	111, 112
Matthew 8:23-27	107, 271
Matthew 11:28	75
Matthew 13:37-39	120
Matthew 15:8	260
Matthew 21:28	114
Matthew 28:5-6	97
Matthew 28:19-20	116, 198
Mark 16:15-16	82, 105
Luke 14:23	197
Luke 22:41	156
Luke 24:29	36
John 10:11	46
John 12:32	228
John 13:35	144
John 13:7	104
John 14:1-2	78, 88, 123, 254
John 14:18-19	95
John 14:26-27	185
John 14:27	276
John 14:6	264
John 15:12	125
John 15:15	208, 315
John 16:33	16, 226
John 20:27	302
John 4:13-14	21
Acts 4:11-12	200
Acts 21:5	158
Acts 22:16	304
Acts 26:28-29	53
Romans 3:23-24	141
Romans 8:37-39	316
Romans 8:17	143
Romans 8:28	278
Romans 8:35-37	296
Romans 12:10	127, 287, 298
Romans 13:11-12	98, 99
Romans 14:12	211
1 Corinthians 1:18	63
1 Corinthians 10:1,4	199
1 Corinthians 10:13	74, 176
1 Corinthians 12:14;26	286
1 Corinthians 15:57	225
1 Corinthians 15:57-58	129
2 Corinthians 5:20	106
2 Corinthians 9:15	290
Galatians 2:20	267
Galatians 5:6	23
Galatians 6:1-2	179
Galatians 6:14	213, 236
Ephesians 1:3	273
Ephesians 1:7	284
Ephesians 1:22-23	166
Ephesians 2:8	22, 23, 220
Ephesians 3:17-19	309
Ephesians 4:1-3	58, 191
Ephesians 5:18-20	232, 234
Ephesians 6:10-14	131
Philippians 1:9	167
Philippians 2:9-10	154
Philippians 3:14	172, 249
Philippians 3:20-21	13, 160
Philippians 3:7-9	214
Philippians 4:8	7
Philippians 4:11-12	255
Philippians 4:12-13	93
Colossians 1:10	181
1 Thessalonians 2:4	84
1 Thessalonians 4:16-17	80
1 Thessalonians 5:18	274
1 Timothy 1:12-17	292
2 Timothy 4:7-8	248
2 Timothy 4:17-18	150
Titus 3:5	91
Titus 3:7	139
Hebrews 1:3	258
Hebrews 4:16	85
Hebrews 5:8-9	220
Hebrews 6:17-18	218
Hebrews 6:19	299
Hebrews 10:22	100
Hebrews 10:24	187
Hebrews 11:14-16	162, 202
Hebrews 13:5	148
Hebrews 13:6	70
Hebrews 13:14	122
Hebrews 13:15-16	241
James 1:10	25
James 1:17	216
James 2:14	220
James 2:17	23
1 Peter 1:3-4	246
1 Peter 1:8-9	60
1 Peter 1:23-24	28
1 Peter 2:21-24	32, 237
1 Peter 2:25	46
1 Peter 3:8	178
1 Peter 4:12-13	177
1 Peter 4:16	54
1 Peter 5:7	246, 280
1 John 2:9-10	179
1 John 3:16	244, 282
1 John 4:7-8	61, 167
1 John 4:16-17	69
1 John 4:19	59
1 John 5:14-15	210
Revelation 7:16-17	42, 43
Revelation 20:12,15	212
Revelation 21:23-27	203
Revelation 21:10; 25	35
Revelation 21:25	34
Revelation 21:3-4	14

A Song Is Born

Index of Authors or Composers

Author	Page(s)
Alexander, Cecil Francis	11
Arnold, Robert S.	42
Bacon, Wilkin B.	191
Baker, Mary A.	270
Bartlett, E. M.	78, 225
Bates, Katharine Lee	56
Baxter, J. R.	248
Beddome, Benjamin	69
Bennard, George	187, 236
Bennett, Sanford Bennett	122
Bessire, Amy	222
Blackwood, James	139
Bland, A. P.	202
Bliss, Philip	45, 53, 278
Boring, Holland Sr.	101
Boyce, Robert Fisher	111
Bradbury, William B.	74
Bridgers, Luther B.	16
Bridgewater, Cordie (Mrs. A. S.)	203
Brock, Blanche Kerr	98
Brock, Virgil P.	98
Brumley, Albert E.	42, 78, 225
Carruth, Ruth (Mrs. Roy)	82
Chisholm, Thomas O.	73
Clements, John	34
Converse, Charles	207
Cornelius, Maxwell Newton	176
Cowper, William	103
Crosby, Fanny J.	194, 197, 205
Danks, Hart P.	33
Davis, Jimmie	125
Dean, Emmett S.	248
DeShazo, Barbara Lynn	173
Doane, William H.	166, 195, 197, 205
Doddridge, Philip	304
Dorsey, Thomas	85, 149
Duffield, George Jr.	129
Durham, Charles	316
Eiland, F. L.	115, 146, 157, 248
Elliott, Charlotte	75
Elliott, H. W.	248
Epps, Paul	191
Excell, E. O.	23, 272
Fawcett, John	178
Featherstone, William R.	60
Ferrill, J. W.	115
Franklin, J. B.	115
Furr, Edgar	101
Gabriel, Charles H.	186
Gaines, J. W.	147
Gaither, Gloria	95, 286
Gaither, William J.	95, 286
Giardini, Felice de	104
Gilmour, H. L.	266
Gleason, Jewel M. (Whitey)	139
Gordon, A. J.	60
Gould, John E.	106
Graeff, Frank	280
Green, Keith	260, 282
Green, Melody	282
Hall, J. Lincoln	279
Hamblen, Stuart	91, 311
Hastings, Thomas	198
Hawks, Annie Sherwood	85
Hawthorne, Alice	298
Hayford, Jack	257
Heber, Reginald	36
Hopper, Edward	107
Hudson, Ralph	63
Huntington, DeWitt C.	160
Jernigan, Dennis L.	290
Karnes, Beuna Ora	88
Keble, John	36
Kethe, William	8
Kristofferson, Kris	180
Lehman, Frederick M.	294
Lillenas, Haldor	251
Lowry, Robert	85
Luttrell, Clarence A.	87
Mason, Lowell	68
Mays, Claudia Lehman	292
McGranahan, James	45, 175
Mieir, Audrey	152
Minor, George A.	117
Moen, Don	136
Monk, William H.	35
Moody, Charles E.	156
Morris, Lelia N. (Mrs. C. H.)	228, 264, 307
Mullins, Richard W. (Rich)	30, 66
Negeli, Johann Georg	177
Nehoria, Meir Ben Isaac	295
Newell, Laura	25
Newton, John H.	36
Newton, John	22
Nystrom, Martin J.	20
O'Kane, T. C.	161
Oatman, Johnson, Jr.	273
Ogdon, Ina Duley	187
Pace, Adger M.	110
Palmer, H. R.	270
Peck, Emory S.	232
Peterson, John W.	44
Pitts, William S.	164
Prentiss, Elizabeth	85, 167
Ramsey, Thomas H.	315
Roberts, Warren	39
Rodeheaver, Homer	187
Sammis, J. H.	220

318

A Song Is Born

Index of Authors or Composers

Sanderson, Lloyd O.	10, 70, 215	Towner, D. B.	220
Scriven, Joseph	208	Towner, Daniel	45
Shaw, Knowles	118	Vaughan, James D.	240, 248
Sheppard, John Henry	114	Walker, Cindy	249
Showalter, A. J.	157	Ward, Sam	57
Sides, George W.	244	Watts, Isaac	63, 213
Slater, Will. W.	13	Webb, George J.	128
Smith, Alfred	45	Webster, Joseph	122
Spafford, Horatio G.	275	Weigle, Charles F.	39
Speer, George Thomas	240	Wesley, Charles	36, 58, 192
Stamps, V. O.	7, 248	Wesley, John	36
Stanphill, Ira F.	254	Wihtol, Austris A.	48
Stanton, Melvin	216	Wilkin, Marijohn	181, 302
Stevens, Tex	191	Wilson, Jennie	146
Stowe, Harriet Beecher	26, 132	Winner, Joseph Eastburn	298
Sweatmon, Thomas R.	14	Winner, Septimus	298
Taylor, Austin	100	Wolcott, Samuel	105
Teddlie, Tillit S.	82, 211	Wolfe, Lanny	143
Toplady, Augustus	199	Wright, J. B. F.	4
Torbett, James S.	169	Young, George A.	251

Hymns About Heaven

What will heaven be like? What do you anticipate most about heaven? Perhaps for you, heaven will be a time to renew old friendships, or to meet loved ones gone before. Perhaps this will be a time to have your questions answered. Surely it will be a time to feel the Peace of God and share the presence of Jesus!

Many songs have been written about heaven. Here are a few songs with hymn stories.

An Empty Mansion	87	No Night There	33
Beyond the Sunset	97	No Tears In Heaven	41
How Beautiful Heaven Must Be	201	Mansion Over the Hilltop	253
I Won't Have to Cross Jordan	314	Sweet By and By	121
I'll Fly Away	77		

Hymns Born of Tragedy

If you were required to write down your thoughts and feelings after losing all that you owned, or after losing your wife or husband, or a child, what would you say? When tragedy strikes, we need to know how to react, and the gospel songs help tell us how to respond under fire, how others reacted when crises occured in their lives. Here are a few songs with hymn stories born of tragedy.

From the Cross to the Crown	247	More Love to Thee, O Christ	166
God Leads Us Along	250	Precious Memories	4
He Keeps Me Singing	14	Sometime We'll Understand	175
I Won't Have To Cross Jordan	319	Take My Hand Precious Lord	148
It is Well With My Soul	275		

A Song Is Born

Index of Songs

Song	Page
A Charge To Keep I Have	57
Alas! And Did My Savior Bleed?	62
All People That On Earth Do Dwell	8
All Things Bright and Beautiful	10
Almost Persuaded	53
Alone At Eve	12
Amazing Grace	21
America The Beautiful	55
An Empty Mansion	87
As The Deer	19
As The Life Of A Flower	24
At The Cross	62
Awesome God	64
Be With Me Lord	70
Beautiful Star of Bethlehem	110
Because He lives	94
Beyond The Sunset	97
Blest Be The Tie That Binds	177
Brighten The Corner	186
Bringing In The Sheaves	117
Call For Workers	113
Can He Depend On You	190
Christ For the World We Sing	104
Christ's Love Is All I Need	242
Closer To Thee	99
Count Your Blessings	272
Does Jesus Care	279
From the Cross To the Crown	247
God Is the Fountain	68
God Moves In A Mysterious Way	102
God Leads Us Along	250
God Will Make A Way	135
God's Family	142
He Keeps Me Singing	15
His Grace Reaches Me	138
His Name Is Wonderful	151
Hold To God's Unchanging Hand	145
How Beautiful Heaven Must Be	201
I Need Thee Every Hour	84
I Won't Have To Cross Jordan	314
I'll Fly Away	77
In The Land Of Fadeless Day	33
Into Our Hands	81
It Is No Secret	90
It Is Well With My Soul	275
Jesus, Savior, Pilot Me	106
Just As I Am	74
Kneel At The Cross	155
Let Jesus Come Into Your Heart	263
Majesty	256
Mansion Over the Hilltop	253
Master the Tempest Is Raging	268
More Love To Thee, O Christ	166
More Precious Than Silver	172
My Eyes Are Dry	259
My God and I	47
My Jesus I love Thee	59
Nearer, Still Nearer	227
No Night There	33
No One Ever Cared For Me,	38
No Tears In Heaven	41
Not Now, But In The Coming	175
O Happy Day	303
O Think Of the Home Over There	159
One Day At A Time	180
Precious Memories	4
Rescue the Perishing	196
Rock Of Ages	198
Safe In the Arms Of Jesus	193
Sing and Be Happy	230
Sing Me A Song About Jesus	238
Someone To Care	124
Sometime We'll Understand	175
Stand up, Stand up for Jesus	128
Step By Step	29
Still, Still With Thee	131
Sun Of My Soul	35
Surely Goodness and Mercy	44
Sweet By and By	121
Sweeter As the Years Go By	306
Take My Hand Precious Lord	148
Teach Me Lord To Wait	310
Thank You, Lord	288
The Church In The Wildwood	163
The Family Of God	284
The Glory-land Way	168
The Love Of God	292
The Old Rugged Cross	235
The Scars In the Hands Of Jesus	300
The Steadfast Love Of the Lord	221
There Is A Redeemer	281
To God Be the Glory	204
Trust and Obey	219
Victory In Jesus	224
Walking Alone At Eve	12
We Live In A Changing World	215
What A Friend We Have In Jesus	207
What Will Your Answer Be	210
When I survey the Wondrous	212
Whispering Hope	296

Hymn Story Groups

Hymns about Heaven	319
Hymns born of Tragedy	319
Scriptures	317